W9-CAA-973

Withdrawn

THE SOMALI CHALLENGE

THE SOMALI CHALLENGE

From Catastrophe to Renewal?

edited by
Ahmed I. Samatar

LYNNE
RIENNER
PUBLISHERS

BOULDER
LONDON

Published in the United States of America in 1994 by
Lynne Rienner Publishers, Inc.
1800 30th Street, Boulder, Colorado 80301

and in the United Kingdom by
Lynne Rienner Publishers, Inc.
3 Henrietta Street, Covent Garden, London WC2E 8LU

Library of Congress Cataloging-in-Publication Data
The Somali challenge : from catastrophe to renewal? / edited by Ahmed
   I. Samatar.
     p.   cm.
   Includes bibliographical references and index.
   ISBN 1-55587-363-4 (alk. paper)
   1. Somalia—Politics and government—1960– . 2. Somalia—Social
conditions. I. Samatar, Ahmed I. (Ahmed Ismail)
DT407.S59   1994
967.73—dc20   93-38661
                                          CIP

British Cataloguing in Publication Data
A Cataloguing in Publication record for this book
is available from the British Library.

Printed and bound in the United States of America

   ∞   The paper used in this publication meets the requirements
       of the American National Standard for Permanence of
       Paper for Printed Library Materials Z39.48-1984.

*To the memory of those members of the international community
who lost their lives while serving the Somali people
in their dire moment of need
and to the countless Somalis who, without bravado,
refuse to give up on the return of the spirit of* umma

Contents

Illustrations

Maps

Figures

Tables

Acknowledgments

Most scholars are cognizant of the dependence of their works on the labors of others. This is certainly the case for this collaborative volume. In that spirit, I would like to salute each of the contributors. Together, they brought intellectual maturity and civilized sensibilities to advance the cause of understanding the Somali condition. Their kind of thinking is wonderful grist for the milling that only Somalis would have to undertake. Here, special mention goes to Professor Abdi Samatar, who was the first to articulate the timeliness of the idea and who subsequently coauthored the grant proposal for the conference that was the genesis of this book.

Behind the contributors stand the other sixteen participants in that conference, whose presence and continuous interventions were its energy. From the legendary folklore performers of the likes of Ahmed Ismail Hussein "Hodayde" and Ahmed Naji Saad, to young and rising academics like Professors Ali Jimale Ahmed and Mohamed Abdi Mohamed, to the sagacity of journalist/businessperson Mohamed Yusuf Abshir and attorney/writer Yusuf Jama Ali "Duhul," it was reassuring to note that, despite the collective humiliation of the times, Somali society was not just a cruel cultural desert devoid of intelligent human life. In these souls and minds, one can witness that history was behind and is *ahead* of the Somali people, and that the present need not be so base and so destructive.

The conference would not have been possible without funding and support from four institutions. The Ford Foundation (West and Central Africa Office) was the earliest to endorse the sentiment and became, by far, the most generous benefactor. Special gratitude is due Dr. Michael Chege for his farsightedness, solidarity, and strength. The United States Institute of Peace (USIP) and its senior program officer, Dr. David Smock, were sympathetic from the beginning and made a modest but critical contribution. USIP carried this association further into involved and very valuable postconference activities that became directly relevant to Operation Restore Hope.

When, at the last minute, permission to hold the conference in a coastal city in East Africa was withdrawn, the Centre for the Study of Applied International Negotiations (CASIN) in Geneva, Switzerland, stepped in. Dr. Jean Freymond and his staff offered the best of the Swiss tradition: empathy and stunning efficiency.

There is much to note about St. Lawrence University's involvement with this project. Suffice it to say that without the full generosity of my old institution, this project would have been both more strenuous and costlier. In this context, my colleague Professor Peter Bailey has gone out of his way to go through the entire manuscript to improve syntax and the overall expository quality of the writing. Peter is the embodiment of all that is worthy of academic collegiality. I would like to recognize Ken Alger in University Communications and Laurie Olmstead in the Wordprocessing Office for their assistance. My thanks also to Dr. Greg Chu of the University of Minnesota for cartographical assistance. Particular and profound gratitude is due to Dr. Thomas Labahn and GTZ/Ministry for Economic Cooperation and Development (BMZ) of Germany, who made funds available so this volume could reach the hands of numerous Somalis in the Horn of Africa who could not afford to purchase their own copy.

Finally, a special mention for Marlene Guzman, who has lived with this idea for two years. More than a regular partner, Marlene is an intellectual companion whose fine balance of compassion and no-nonsense thinking are only two of her numerous virtues. She labored hard for this volume, and only I know how much of her time and talent were invested here.

A.I.S.

Note on Somali Orthography

Somali orthography is used in the titles of works in Somali, authors who spell their names in Somali, and in direct quotations. The key to three critical Somali phonetic sounds is as follows: Somali x = h; dh = d; and c = ay.

Part 1

Preliminaries

1

Introduction and Overview

Ahmed I. Samatar

The Condition and the Questions

After years of economic decay[1] and depraved and diabolic politics, capped by more than twenty months of generalized and very bloody chaos, the full range and depth of the Somali predicament finally exploded upon the consciousness of the world.[2] Graphic pictures and descriptions of pathetic Somali children, women, and men reduced to bare skeletons, clinging to the last moments of their lives, became a staple of morning papers, radio programs, and evening television news. But these gut-wrenching glimpses of Somali life were only the tip of the iceberg, for behind the brief reports were the main purveyors of the Somali apocalypse itself: economic and political collapse, cultural withering, famine, and mutual slaughter.[3] Although the total cost in human lives and property can never be fully tallied, by late 1993 these were some of the immediate facts about the devastation in Somalia:[4]

- 350,000 have died since the inception of full-scale civil war in 1988.
- 25 percent of children under the age of five have died, and 80 percent of those alive are suffering from severe malnutrition.
- Almost 4.5 million Somalis (nearly 70 percent of the population)—including more than 1 million refugees in neighboring countries—are being kept alive through emergency assistance.[5]
- Almost 2 million have been displaced internally.

- Diseases such as malaria, tuberculosis, and typhoid are rampant.
- 60 percent of Somalia's basic infrastructure has been destroyed.
- 80 percent of all social services (e.g., schools and hospitals) have been rendered nonoperational.
- 30–40 percent of livestock have been lost.
- Principal urban centers, including Mogadishu and Hargeisa, have been either badly damaged or destroyed.
- Social and political institutions have shattered.
- The death of the Somali state has spawned the privatization of security, widespread banditry, and the proliferation of tens of thousands of loose and lethal weapons.
- The country finds itself a prime site for the dumping of unwanted hazardous waste.[6]
- Northwest Somalia has declared itself as a new state—the Somaliland Republic.
- Charity organizations (aside from the recently deployed and now departed UN/U.S. forces) account for the single most conspicuous international presence and activity.
- Somalia has the unique distinction of being the object of the largest humanitarian military intervention in modern history. The primary purpose of this initiative was to force Somali warring factions to comply with a United Nations resolution mandating the delivery of food and medicine to hundreds of thousands of starving and sick Somalis.[7]

For Africanists, the Somali situation constitutes yet another layer of the continent's worsening social existence and a propulsion toward misery, death, and irrelevance.[8] Disturbing questions raised by the Somali experience include: How is it that one of the very few homogenous societies in Africa can become so bitterly alienated from itself?[9] Is Somalia the ultimate piece of evidence that independence was a seductive farce and that neocolonialism ought to be seen as a positive alternative to failed African bravado? Are African societies like Somalia doomed to perpetual marginalization and receivership? Are they best left to be looked after by international charity organizations? Are African cultures capable of ever picking up the historic gauntlet—that is, the creation of a worthy civilization at home in the beckoning millennium—thrown down by their own abject conditions and the relentless buffeting of the modern world-system? Is there hope for the Somalias of the continent and, if so, when, to paraphrase Zarathustra, will they appear, those great leaders and social forces who make good things happen? What will their paradigm be?

The Project

This volume is a partial result of a conference on the Somali condition held in Geneva during the summer of 1992.[10] That meeting brought together a group of thirty participants, with an equal balance between scholars and notable leaders in the areas of business, civic affairs, and culture. Scholars were asked to bring their academic insights through a series of commissioned papers; other participants' assignment was to respond to these scholarly analyses, findings, and conclusions on the basis of their intimate contact with the condition of quotidian life in Somalia. The formal presentations were preceded by personal statements delivered by two highly respected and experienced Somalis.[11] In the end, the encounter between the scholars and community personages generated five days of intense discussions, which became the basis for revisions of the papers. In addition, David Rawson's superb piece, "Dealing with Disintegration," came to my attention a few days before the conference. Given his essay's thorough analysis of U.S. assistance to Somalia, I asked him if he would permit us to include the piece in this volume. Dr. Rawson was very generous and willing.

There were three objectives of the Geneva conference: First was the rehabilitation of reason. In the belief that Giambattista Vico was right in his conception of reason as the "mind's eye," this effort is part of an extremely slow but growing realization that one of the most critical needs of the Somali people is the return of intelligence, as well as the elevation of that capacity to a new critical level.[12] This particular objective was pursued through (1) an assumption that violence was not only wasteful but demeaning, (2) a strong drive to assimilate part of the important and enormous flux of events that form Somalia's past, and (3) persistent engagement of the turbulence of Somali contemporary life in a way that will make these profound changes intelligible.

Second, participants came to Geneva with no illusions about the difficulties facing Somalia, yet each expressed commitment to analeptic exchange and thinking. Such an orientation was a response to the fact that although there is an unquestionably high degree of existential commonality among the vast majority of Somalis, there is hardly any commensurate cognitive bearing. A dearth, if not absence, of reflective consciousness has created a state of intellectual immobility among Somalis while simultaneously closing out the international community from joining Somalis in a fruitful dialogue on solutions. Consequently, all the papers, formal debates, and informal conversations were guided by a desire to make a contribution to the much needed pursuit for substantive and innovative ideas.

Finally, on a more immediate plane, the conference was conceived as a symbolic event. Given the fact that the media's coverage of Somalis was hardening into the image of a strange people eager to self-destruct yet listless on other accounts, we thought it opportune to demonstrate to the listening and watching world that such a perception, despite its momentary truth, was not totally accurate. An interesting episode that pointedly brought this home to me was an encounter with two correspondents from two leading European newspapers. At the end of the first day's deliberations, they requested an interview with me in my capacity as the conference coordinator. With the preliminaries out of the way, they posed what was for them the most puzzling question: How was it possible for the participants, who they were told represented almost all of the kin families, to sit together peacefully and engage in dialogue? After I had assured them of the authenticity of the range of the conference's representation and inclusiveness, they looked more perplexed and asked a second question that, from my angle, related to the principal focus of the conference: if it is not clan animus that ails Somalia, what is it? Needless to say, I gave an alternative hypothesis, one found in these chapters, and suggested that they stay, talk to others, and read the commissioned papers.[13]

Theory and Strategy

All authors were given full freedom to pursue their analyses within whatever intellectual tradition each felt comfortable. From the inception, it was understood that theoretical and methodological ecumenicism was fitting to such a diverse group. However, an unspoken ambition of this enterprise is to set it off from the conventional perspective where possible (without necessarily forgoing its useful contributions). The rationale for this stance is not due to some blind mistrust of the established approach; rather, it is that the hegemony of the master concept of the clan as the only significant explanatory factor has proven to be a source of analytical stagnation, tedious superficiality, and, above all, repetitive and dangerous stereotyping.[14] At a time in which Somali society is subject to an unprecedented and harrowing convergence of numerous pressures, it is instructive to listen to the doyen of Somali studies, I. M. Lewis:

> Nearly 80 years ago, a brave servant of the empire called Richard
> Corfield . . . tried to bring order to the Somalis, when they were in

rebellion under a religious leader dubbed the Mad Mullah by the British. All Corfield got of his pains was a bullet in the head in battle and a place in the epic poetry of Somalia—a bloodthirsty hymn to victory that has lived on in a society steeped in antagonism to outsiders. . . . The first thing to underscore about the Somalis is that they are not as other men. Richard Burton, the famous Arabist and explorer who trekked across their lands in the 1880s called the Islamic Somali nomads a "fierce and turbulent race of republicans." More pungently, a Ugandan sergeant with the British forces fighting the Mad Mullah went on record as telling his officer: "Somalis, Bwana, they no good: each man his own sultan." In other words, they take orders from nobody; and their sense of independence is matched by a supremely uncentralized and fragmented degree of political organization; a kind of ordered anarchy. The basis of political allegiance is blood kinship, or genealogy. Children learn their ancestors' names by heart back to 20 generations and more. A Somali does not ask another *where* he is from but *whom* he is from. Strangers who meet, recite their genealogies until they reach a mutual ancestor—the more closely they are related the more readily they unite, transiently, against others: "myself against my brother; my brother and I against my cousin; my cousin and I against the outsider."[15]

These canonic-sounding but quite misleading pronouncements cannot pass uncontested. Corfield might have been a hero of the Empire, but from the viewpoint of Somalis, he was an ugly colonialist sent to establish British domination in Somaliland. Moreover, Mohamed Abdille Hassan was not a "Mad Mullah" fomenting rebellion but an indefatigable *sayyid* (i.e., saint) engaged in a long and glorious resistance to colonial humiliation; and his capturing, in poetic form, of Corfield's death in battle is not "a bloody hymn" but an unvarnished yet glowing expression of hard-earned victory against conquest and subordination. Somali society of old was not "steeped in antagonism to outsiders" but, on the whole, known to be giving and generous—particularly to strangers who came in peace and good faith—and to have a reverent consciousness of human eschatology.

Finally, the idea that the Somalis are the ultimate individualists, almost man-beasts bereft of social sensibility, is the sort of declarative truth making that easily slips into further axiomatic fallacies and erroneous typecasting. This, in turn, mummifies the Somali as a different creature programmed by a primeval sociobiological gene called "clanism" extrinsic in its potency and durability.

All of this is not to deny that Somalis, given their exacting environment and pastoral mode of livelihood, have historically acquired a somewhat tetchy personal style buttressed by a haughtiness and adversative disposition toward any sign of denigratory treatment. However, it is a major claim of this volume that the stock of tradition that calibrated the complexities of Somali character and behavior is under enormous battering, if it hasn't already been fully undermined.[16] Consequently, the contemporary bloody decomposition of the society is not a recidivistic reminder of an original sin peculiar to Somali culture; on the contrary, these events are witness to the denudation of a moral order, one sustained by kinship *heer* (customary code of conduct) and Islamic divinity and *qanoon* (law).[17] Great historic conjunctures of this kind, then, deserve corresponding theoretical ingenuity and analytical agility.[18] These tools make it possible to reformulate old truisms and establish connections among disparate facts, situations, or ideas. This is one of the aspirations of this work.

Three paramount concepts that gird these contributions are set in the general title: *catastrophe*, *challenge*, and *renewal*. A fourth, *clanism*, is pervasive in any discussion of contemporary Somalia. Each requires a preliminary definition.

1. *Catastrophe*. We argue that the Somali condition of the late 1980s and the 1990s exceeds previous misfortunes of the modern era. This experience is so extraordinarily disastrous that popular Somali culture has coined a term for it—*burbur*—that literally means "complete pulverization." Although Somalis have had to contend with many a hard time before, the present is exceptional in both intensity and pervasiveness. Catastrophe, or *burbur*, then, captures a state of affairs—one characterized by a constellation of crises, the full impact of which is a severe depletion of the material, moral, and intellectual resources of Somalia.

2. *Challenge*. If Somali society finds itself in the midst of very debilitating circumstances, the onset of such a reality need not turn into a condition of irrevocable defeat. Rather, we think that all human communities, at one time or another, enter periods of appalling, sometimes monumental difficulties. That is part of the vulnerability of human life; and it is why St. Augustine, long ago underscoring the inevitable demands of history, likened life to an oil press continuously under tremendous pressures. What is most critical during testing moments is how members of a society respond—either, in Augustinian terms, as groaning dregs to be flushed out quickly through the sewer or as genuine oil that stays unbroken. The former are the losers; the latter are victors ready for the next round. Which it will be is the choice that faces Somalis, and so far the evidence of their response is discouraging. Challenge, then, is an individual and collective positioning grounded in new spiritual

and intellectual resolve that involves specific operational principles: a stand *against* the prostration and negation of the present, resolve *for* a revival of buried options, and an *invention* of new possibilities.

3. *Renewal.* This is the reaction to a challenge by a return to sanity and the creation of a new equilibrium. Work in this direction implies the institutionalization of hope, even in the doldrums of painful decomposition. We suggest, therefore, that any success with the challenge will ultimately be measured in terms of how well the Somali people turn an envisioned alternative (i.e., the merging of old strengths with thinking ahead) into concrete structures. Here, as is to be expected, ideality meets practical effort, and the march toward freed consciousness and renewal subsequently begins. This echoes Vico's concept of *ricorso*, that is, a retrieval of sources of traditional vigor to construct institutions and habits congenial to the creative dialectic between human beings and history.[19]

4. *Clanism.* This is the perversion of kinship through a decoupling of blood ties (particularly male lineage) from the great civilizing or universalizing factors of Somali culture: customary law and Islamic precepts. Without these companion moral directives, Somali male behavior becomes unrestrained and is likely to turn into egotistic criminality. Although contributors might differ in their interpretations of the causes of clanism, there is enough agreement to establish that the phenomenon is not only quite different from the kinship of old (as demonstrated by, among other things, the evaporation of the authority of elders and veneration of *shaikhs*) but, in fact, is a manifestation of other things that have gone awfully wrong in Somalia. In time, clanism acquires a life of its own that transforms it into an active agent for a narrow common identity among some at the deadly exclusion of others—including members of the maternal side of the extended household. But even in such a situation, the new "brotherhood" is beset with suspicion and antipathies liable to foster violent degeneration against itself.

A main drawback of the existent scholarship on Somali society is its fragmented and unrelational treatment of the various components of what is the ensemble of Somali life. For instance, economists tend to focus on market distortions induced by state intervention; political scientists concentrate on individual rulers or regimes, with little reference to connected issues of culture and conflict over resources; historians tend to be oblivious to social dynamics and change; anthropologists reinvent Somali tradition over and over again, as though Somali time and "world time" have stood still; and hardly anyone pays attention to the ecological base or the lot of women.

This project dares to be different by moving toward a more integrative and inclusive tack. We have identified the following four areas as essential to a further apprehension of Somali reality: ecology, economy, politics and governance, and culture. These categories are to be aligned by an underlining of the multidimensional and self-reinforcing nature of the infrastructure of everyday Somali life. In appearance and substance, each chapter can stand on its own; however, the volume is an attempt in transdisciplinary collaboration to capture the traits of each category, as well as their coexistence and interpenetration. This type of scholarly strategy, ambitious and burdensome though it is, seems to hold promise for future studies, in addition to facilitating the detection of the nature and complex texture of this confounding juncture.

Organizationally, this book consists of four parts, followed by an appendix and a bibliography. Part 1 is composed of this introduction and overview, as well as one shortened keynote presentation by an eminent Somali. Part 2 deals with ecology and economy, and Part 3 contains three chapters that focus on the state and international relations. Part 4 contains two chapters that are written from a cultural perspective.

Synopsis of the Arguments

Hassan A. Mirreh's highly abridged argument in Chapter 2 testifies to his role as an elder (in terms of both experience and sagacity). His admonitions reflect a profoundly felt pain for the Somali people and an urgency with which he would like the catastrophe to be treated. Mirreh proposes that the single most disabling failure has been and continues to be the poor quality of leadership. It is here, he stresses, that Somalia's ills congeal. The perfidy of Siyaad Barre's rule and the murderous doltishness demonstrated by the opposition are testimony to a scarcity of political leadership that parallels the indigence of the society. Mirreh's emphasis on leadership, an issue touched upon by some of the other chapters, carries with it a hopeful note regarding the current catastrophe. For him, "clanist politics is a temporary aberration" and trans-kin solidarity (i.e., nationalism) is more resilient than its present purchase suggests. In an intimation similar to Ibn Khaldun's stipulations for a *wazi* (leader), Mirreh sketches out criteria for good leaders, of which critical intelligence, political arête, and practical competence are paramount.[20] A return to communal amity and respect, a worthwhile search for alternatives, and commencement of the pressing work of new political and socioeconomic institutions will, in no small way, depend on a flourishing of wise political leadership.

Part 2 begins with Ben Wisner's chapter, an attempt to introduce the often neglected issue of the relationship between society and nature. Bringing his extensive knowledge of Africa's ecology to the Somali situation, Wisner looks ahead to the time when peace will return to the country and Somalis will begin to engage the fundamental issue of environment and development. Four assumptions underlie the direction of the chapter: (1) peace is a prerequisite for any planning, let alone implementation, of sound environmental policy; (2) ecological issues transcend political boundaries; (3) collaboration between the new state and the private sector is unavoidable; and (4) genuine democratic life is contingent on citizen participation.

The paramount concept in Wisner's theoretical arsenal is "sustainable development," which, in this context, is conceived as "livelihood security." What this concept implies, according to Wisner, is a tight association between the imperatives of securing the basic needs of those who are here now and the livelihood of coming generations. This is the issue of ecological continuity that is so much at the core of generational responsibility and obligation to posterity. The critical particulars in this discussion are water (of which it is said that Somalia will experience even more severe shortages around 2025), land (including the grazing range and forested areas), livestock, energy, marine environments, and urban environments. A startling discovery here that undermines the old perception of Somalia as the quintessential land of pastoralists is the extent of urbanization in the country by the late 1980s—nearly 34 percent of the population were living in towns and cities. This will certainly have major ramifications for future research and will raise important questions concerning Somali development.

In a time of pervasive bleakness, Wisner ends with an optimistic note: that the legendary exiguity of Somali territory notwithstanding, Somalia has more resources than is generally believed (e.g., cultivable land, woodlands, and fisheries). However, these assets can be fully and gainfully summoned for "sustainable development" only if traditional knowledge is retrieved and made the basis of rebuilding livelihoods.

Abdi Samatar, one of the keenest scholars on Somali rural life, focuses on the "disarticulated" nature of the agrarian economy and the fatal consequences of "underaccumulation" in Chapter 4. He deals with both the pastoral/livestock and farming sectors. Samatar commences his arguments by suggesting that the calamity could have been avoided had Siyaad Barre's regime paid any heed to numerous warnings against the colossal costs that always accompany irregular privatization of public resources and "underinvestment in productive sectors." Among this chapter's secondary but important concerns is the issue of varying conditions within the agrarian economy. Samatar concludes by looking into the future, posing the questions of what is to be done, and by whom. He proffers two elements to be requisite for Somalia's revival: a new and positive relationship between a competent state and economic progress, and specific actions capable of reinvigorating production and accumulation. For Samatar and many of the conference participants, acute scarcity and reckless economic policies are the cause of Somalia's condition of mendacity—a powerful corrosive on human relations and social institutions. A dedication to the reversal of these habits is necessary for Somali resurrection.

Part 3 opens with my own contribution. This chapter is based on two assumptions and driven by a thesis. The first premise reclaims Cicero's wisdom by postulating that to have no viable political center of gravity is to have no worthwhile collective existence, particularly in this late hour of the century. The second premise holds that Somali society cannot return to the acephalous arrangements of old in place of designing democratic public institutions. My thesis is that foremost among the problems that face Somalis is the issue of conceiving a new reciprocative ethos and workable governance.

The chapter asks four questions: (1) Why did Somali communitarian identity—embodied in tradition, flag, and state—turn into a violent nightmare? (2) What is a state? (3) Is a Somali state worth resurrecting? (4) If so, why and in what guise? One of the main arguments of the chapter is that the Somali state has died three times—as a regime, as an apparatus, and as an idea of group consciousness, or what Ibn Khaldun calls *asabiyah*.[21] Consequently, I argue that the remaking of each element of the state will demand tremendous effort. The most elusive yet crucial tasks involve the reemergence or initiation of individual and communal atonement, and an ethic whose lodestar is *fides* (a mixture of civility and rationality). Only when such work has been accomplished can retrospective acrimony come to an end and the practical lineaments of human rights–based democratic order and able governance be debated and constructed.

The chapter concludes by suggesting three possible sources for the generation of a new asabiyah: Somali kinship values, Islamic principles, and secular thinking and experimentation. In my estimation, although these are only the raw materials available, their synthesis and a consequent successful transition are the supreme tests to be faced by this generation of Somalis and those to follow.

David Rawson is both a learned Africanist and an astute diplomatic observer of the Somali scene. In a tone very different from current discussions on Somali politics and the fate of the state, Rawson reminds us in Chapter 6 of Somalia's glory days, when the country was "once a leader in the nonaligned world." With that background, he fixes his optic on the last decade of Siyaad Barre's regime, the causes of disintegration, and more saliently, the Somali state's relationships with the "donor community."

This analysis is extremely instructive given the paucity of any examination of this crucial area, particularly at a time when the regime was fully alienated from the society and the machinery of governance and the idea of state were atrophying fast. In this context, Rawson keeps his gaze on one of the most important of the Somali state's external links, that with the United States. He challenges the thesis that a U.S./Soviet strategic tug-of-war was primarily responsible for the eventual fate of the Somali state. Rather, he suggests that the "controlling" factors for the decay were essentially internal: the nature of elite competition, the militarization of state apparatus, and Siyaad Barre's style of leadership. The latter is seen as particularly lethal, given how an inflated personal rule folded into an exaggerated conception of Somali self-importance in regional and global politics. This, according to Rawson, encouraged gross miscalculations in the making of Somali foreign policy.

But Rawson does not fully absolve donors from contributing to the catastrophe. For instance, he establishes how the troubles of the economy in the 1980s were partly a result of ill-conceived large-scale projects funded by outsiders. In the end, a number of lessons for both the "donor community" and Somalis are registered. Perhaps the most interesting of all is the idea of learning from "disaster as well as success," including the question of when it is time for external actors to give up on a hopeless cause.

The last piece on the Somali state and international affairs, Chapter 7, is by Terrence Lyons, a perceptive student of the Horn of Africa. Lyons regionalizes the Somali crises by emphasizing the "porous" nature of all kinds of boundaries; he therefore demonstrates why events that happen in one country (e.g., conflagrations, democracy, famine, secession) are bound to have an immediate impact on the others. The chapter starts with a compressed history of the role of the Somali state in the region. Lyons stresses the overwhelming pressures for unification of Somali-inhabited areas of the Horn and its concomitant ideology of Pan-Somalism as the supreme spirit, or mana, that has shaped and conditioned Somalia's relations with the rest of the region. For Lyons, this ideology is based on kinship ties and ecological affinity.

Now that the bottom has dropped out of Somali nationalism, there is an opportunity to start creating new regional institutions based on a novel conception of identities. This could be a redemptive feature of an otherwise grievous period. But Lyons is quick to remind us that new dreams of regionality and transnational solidarity can materialize only when "a more just order is constructed" that, in turn, "will depend on the quality of the Somali participation in rethinking the crucial issues of sovereignty, citizenship, borders, and survival."

It is Lyon's concluding point and warning that this process will be neither easy nor quick. Rather, capitalizing on the opportunity side of the Somali catastrophe and other difficulties in the area will require persistent intelligence, generous giving toward healing, casting out of bigotry, and years of practical and conscientious effort toward the building of new regional institutions.

Part 4 concerns culture and the catastrophe. Chapter 8 is by Lidwien Kapteijns. Although a number of issues are raised here, the two that stand out are communal identity and the making of gender. Kapteijns is a pioneer in this area. One of the very few non-native Somalists fluent in the Somali language, she has already embarked on long-term research intent upon retrieving the identity of Somali women by pouring light into the dark alleys of Somali historical studies. Pursuing a powerful intuition (one increasingly being verified by data trickling out of Somalia) that Somali women have suffered most under the old patriarchal order and are now paying the heaviest price for the further rancidity of those very social relations, Kapteijns poses this fundamental question: Why do many present-day Somalis practice clan hatred and mobilize accordingly? Among her answers and insights, unconventional as well as multiple, two are primary: (1) that communal identity is not "natural" or "innate," and (2) that contemporary and dominant guises of communal identity (i.e., clanism) are anything but a pure bequest from precolonial times. Rather, the phenomenon has been "forged by Somalis in their interaction with each other and the colonial and postindependence states in the context of patriarchy and the capitalist world-economy." In the end, this chapter generates much needed intellection at the crossroads of clan, class, and gender. Kapteijns does not bring forward specific recommendations, but there is a constant intimation in her essay that any alternative to the prevailing debacle requires the full engagement of Somali women.

We close the volume with Maxamed D. Afrax's interesting take on the relationship between Somali culture and the making of the catastrophe. Like Kapteijns, Afrax embraces Cabral's gnomic wisdom that "culture, the fruit of history, reflects at every moment the material and spiritual reality of society."[22] His first premise, then, is that some "understanding of Somali culture" is a precondition for any worthy action toward reconciliation and reconstruction.

Afrax poses a number of specific questions that include (1) what does Somali culture tell us about these times? and (2) is precolonial custom responsible for the burbur? To address these questions, he utilizes Somali literature and oral tradition. This is a fearsome assignment that, heretofore, has not been attempted. The chapter is organized into four sections. First is an effort to discuss the salient cultural mores of early society, followed by an interpretation of the 1940s through the 1960s as a time of great flourishing for Somali culture. The third section treats 1969–1990 as a time of calculated moral and social defoliation that culminates in the collapse of the 1990s. The last section puts responsibility for the current violent disorder primarily on Siyaad Barre's deranged insistence on retaining power and the warring factions' consuming violence and vulgar struggle for state power that no longer existed.

The major conclusion of the chapter is this: Any endeavor toward renewal cannot come to full fruition until culture is revived and given refuge and "Somali mentality" is rehabilitated. Key to an effectual strategy are poets, composers, and performers (i.e., the artistic community), whose own shattered lives must first be rebuilt.

A Note on External Intervention

By December 1992, the rest of the world, and most significantly the United States, decided that they had had enough of the cruelty and horror of unnecessary starvation that was Somalia.[23] Soon, the Secretary-General of the United Nations reported that the small multinational force already in Mogadishu was ineffective and that events in Somalia had become "intolerable."[24] After one of the speediest consultations seen inside the august halls of the United Nations in some time, on the night of 3 December 1992, the Security Council unanimously approved a resolution authorizing military intervention.

Characterizing the Somali situation as unique, Resolution 733 was predicated on the principle that the Somali people, in the final analysis, were responsible for national reconciliation as well as the rebuilding of their country. In the meantime, there were three major objectives of the resolution: (1) immediate establishment of logistics conducive to humanitarian relief wherever there was need in the country; (2) creation of a secure climate for the delivery of assistance to the hungry and sick; and (3) restoration of "peace, stability, and law and order with a view to facilitating the process of a political settlement."[25]

Viewed in global terms, the Somali condition brings to the foreground two new questions, the consequences of which are portentous for contemporary international relations. First, what is to be the role of the United Nations in the post–Cold War era?[26] Second, can humanitarian need legitimate the use of external military intervention to literally force, perhaps in a Rousseauian sense, an ostensibly sovereign state and people to observe minimum standards of civilized conduct within their territory?[27] The answer (or answers) to the first question is (or are) bound to be explored and hotly debated by theorists of multilateralism and practitioners of statecraft; the latter, the peculiarity of the Somali circumstances notwithstanding, has a precedent in the Somali case. At the time of this writing, many are arguing that the United Nations be given wider powers and an extended mandate, including a serious military high command and substantial and immediately deployable forces to intervene in situations such as that in Somalia.

Notes

1. The dismal material existence and quality of life predates the collapse. In fact, there is wide agreement that a compounding and generalized destitution was a key determinant in the collapse of Siyaad Barre's regime and the country's further descent into total ruin. Note how badly Somalia compared, by 1990, with the rest of an impoverished Africa in these critical measures: gross national product (GNP) per capita—U.S. $120: U.S. $340; debt as a percentage of GNP—284 percent: 89. 8 percent; overseas development aid—U.S. $65: U.S. $41; average daily caloric supply—1,932:2,360; life expectancy—47 years:54 years; adult literacy—24 percent: 50 percent; rate for children under 5 per 1,000 mortality—215:167; access to safe water—37 percent: 44 percent; and access to health care—27 percent: 52 percent (Harsch, "Somalia: Restoring Hope," p. 18).

2. As far back as 1979 and certainly by the early 1980s, some keen observers and scholars were underscoring and warning of the grim as well as destructive times that were closing in on the Somali people. Somalia's world-class novelist, Nuruddin Farah, was one such observer. His trilogy, *Sweet and Sour Milk* (1979), *Sardines* (1981), and *Close Sesame* (1983), depicts vivid and rich evocations of a degenerative and dictatorial political order. Farah's fiction was exceptionally prescient in the way it captured the poi-

soning of intersubjectivity and collective humiliation that became the trademark of Siyaad Barre's regime. Also, see Mohamoud, "Somalia: Crisis and Decay"; Laitin, "The Political Crisis in Somalia"; and A. I. Samatar, "Somalia: Crisis of State and Society."

3. An unreported but serious contributor to the current devastation of Somalia was the daylight theft of public property (Mitchell, "Fifth Horseman of Somalia: Stealing").

4. Harsch, "Strengthened Somalia Relief Effort Threatened by Continued Fighting"; and Dagne, *Somalia: War and Famine.*

5. On the miserable fate of some of the fleeing Somalis, particularly women, see "Seeking Refuge, Finding Terror," *Africa Watch.*

6. Tolba, "Disposal of Hazardous Wastes in Somalia."

7. At the height of the deployment, the multinational force (more than 20 countries represented) was just over 36,000 troops, of which 24,225 were Americans. Other nations that provided significant numbers of troops included France, Italy, Canada, Turkey, Belgium, and Pakistan. The biggest financial contributor to the operation, besides the United States, was Japan, which pledged $100 million of the initial cost of U.S. $450 million. By early March 1993, the initial goal of delivering immediate humanitarian assistance to the most needy areas was reported to have been largely accomplished. Consequently, to deal with the more tenacious problem of general scarcity, reconciliation, and rebuilding, a new agenda was put forth by the UN Secretary-General, Dr. Boutros Boutros-Ghali. On 26 March 1993, the UN Security Council approved Resolution 814, which stipulated the transfer of the operations of the United Nations task force (UNITAF), headed and dominated by the USA, to full UN control and supervision. United Nations Operations in Somalia (UNOSOM II) formally took over on 1 May 1993 and was approved for an initial period of six months. UNOSOM II started with 20,000 troops and 8,000 support personnel from 30 countries. The United States reduced its military presence to under 5,000 troops to be deployed for emergency situations, only to strengthen them again when, in October, 18 of its troops were killed and 70 wounded. UNOSOM II has a number of specific objectives, of which the most critical are (1) to disarm and demobilize all the armed groups, using force if necessary; (2) to establish a Somali police force; (3) to help in the creation of a constitution and institutions of governance; and (4) to facilitate the return of refugees and assist the displaced. The cost of UN military operations for one year is estimated at about U.S. $1.5 billion. No one knows yet where this money will come from. UNOSOM II forces have run into problems. At least 60 of its troops have already been killed and many more wounded in attacks by armed groups mostly linked to General Aideed's followers ("UN Demands Arrest in Ambush," *The Globe and Mail,* p. 1). All of these factors affected American withdrawals. See Cushman, "5 GI's Are Killed," and Apple, "Clinton Sending Reinforcement."

8. Morrow, "Africa: The Scramble for Existence."

9. Homogeneity in this context does not mean that everyone is exactly the same on all accounts. Rather, I acknowledge that there are areas of Somali society that diverge from the mainstream in the forms in which certain social practices and rituals are administered. Moreover, even in the category of Somali language, it is important to note that some of the Somali people of the riverine area (Juba and Shabelle) speak *Maai*—a regional and

distinctive dialect—whereas those of some of the old urban centers of Mogadishu, Merca, and Brava speak a dialect called *Banaadri*. In view of this, critics of the homogeneity thesis, such as Professor Mohamed H. Mukhtar, have a point. Consequently, an analyst ought to be mindful of regional and subcultural variations. In the final analysis, however, I insist that Somali homogeneity, construed in the Wittgensteinian sense of "family resemblance," is more than defensible, for beyond these differences in dialect and ritual administration, Somalis hold on to a common ancestral origin, a broad tradition of rights and obligations (*heer*), and the principles of Islam.

10. Other results of the conference are available in a two-hour video program, in Somali, in which interesting debates are recorded. These tapes are now circulating among Somalis.

11. One of the related addresses, in highly compressed form, is included here. The main substance of the other is covered by chapters on the state and governance.

12. Testimony to this assertion, among others, is the recent appearance of *Hal-Abuur* (quarterly journal of Somali literature and culture), edited by Maxamed Daahir Afrax and published in London.

13. It is amazing how simplistic readings of Somali society have turned into a fixed truism. It is also alarming how eager most analysts are to shoehorn everything Somali into "clan" loyalty, identity, and thinking! This mysterious fixity of analysis awaits explanation.

14. For a further and more interesting deconstruction of this tradition, we look forward to the provocative work of Ahmed, ed., *The Invention of Somalia*.

15. Lewis, "In the Land of the Living Dead," 9. I thank Ahmed Q. Ali for bringing this article to my attention. Note the affinity between these pronouncements and the following statement made in another part of Africa during the height of settler colonialism: "Tribal fights are inevitable. In fact, I think the natives rather enjoy these incidents." Cited in Van Onselen and Phimister, "The Political Economy," p. 43.

16. We hold with Hannah Arendt that, "without tradition—which selects and names, which hands down and preserves, which indicates where the treasures are and what their worth is—there seems to be no willed continuity in time and hence, humanly speaking, neither past nor future, only sempiternal change of the world and the biological cycle of living creatures in it. " *Between Past and Future*, p. 5.

17. For specific arguments on this, see Chapter 5 in this volume.

18. This is in line with Furedi's important point that "a critique of history is essential for the restoration of the consciousness of *reason*, the *human potential*, and the possibility of *change*" (*Mythical Past, Elusive Future*, p. 268).

19. Renewal as an active and virtuous insertion into the world is nicely captured by Mumford. He writes, "Even destructive processes have a positive value when they are the prelude to a new period of constructive activity: at that moment, the wrecking crew becomes an essential arm of building. " *The Condition of Man*, p. 231. Vico, *The New Science*, Books Four and Five. Also, Caponigri, *Time and Idea*, pp. 130–143.

20. Keen on explaining how a state and civilization come to be, Ibn Khaldun emphasizes two ingredients: (1) the political nature of human beings and social relations, and (2) the indispensability of justice and restraint administered by a wazi. Ibn Khaldun also propounds certain attributes as

prerequisites for a leader: knowledge, probity, competence, and health (*The Muqaddimah*, pp. x and 158).

21. Ibn Khaldun makes a direct linkage between asabiyah and the state and civilization. He writes that "civilization is necessary to human beings and that care for the (public) interest connected with it is likewise (necessary), if mankind is not to perish of neglect" (ibid., p. 171).

22. Cabral, *Return to the Source*.

23. Gelb, "Shoot to Feed Somalis. "

24. The gravity of the situation and a diminishing expectation of the efficacy of the United Nations' involvement were underscored earlier by (1) the failed naivete of Deputy Secretary-General James Jonas, who thought that an African form of shuttle diplomacy (from Nairobi to Mogadishu to New York) would bring quick and positive results; and (2) the sudden resignation of Ambassador M. Sahnoun, who, once appointed by the Secretary-General, had moved to Mogadishu with a strategy of establishing a careful and delicate dialogue with the leaders of warring factions. After some time in Somalia, Sahnoun began to criticize the UN approach to Somalia, which in turn brought hard admonitions from New York. Ambassador Sahnoun then submitted his resignation, bringing more suspicion on UN commitment and competence to deal with Somalia's difficulties. Needless to say, many Somalis were waiting, with some apprehension, to see if UNOSOM II could salvage the reputation of the United Nations among the people of Somalia. It is important to note that as of summer 1993, critical voices had already appeared. For the most scathing report, see Rakiya Omaar and Alex de Waal, *Somalia, Operation Restore Hope*.

25. "Excerpts from UN Resolution. "

26. On these issues, see the early but relevant statements by Boutros Boutros-Ghali, *An Agenda for Peace*, and Gerlach, "A U.N. Army?"

27. See Damrosch, *Enforcing Restraint*, and Gottlieb, *States Against Nations*.

2

On Providing for the Future

Hassan A. Mirreh

The philosopher Socrates handed down to posterity a priceless insight through his maxim "An unexamined life is not worth living." As rational creatures, women and men think about the purpose of their existence and are capable of looking critically at the conditions of their lives, environment, and destiny. Stripped of this partly learned and partly inborn trait, women and men cease to be human beings.

In an attempt to affirm this humanity, I invite Somali readers to join me in focusing our collective thinking on the events that have engulfed the country. A close reflection on these times raises many questions that are crying out for answers. Chief among them are the following: Why did Somali society descend to such a perdition, one in which butchery and plunder have become acceptable everyday behavior? Why has there been such an abrupt disintegration of all forms of authority—religious, traditional, and secular—and moral values? Why has there been such a glaring loss of direction?

The search for comprehension of what happened to Somalia requires thoughtfulness and a bit of daring. I hope this book takes us in this direction. In this spirit, I will open with a few general remarks.

Where Are We?

The end of the military dictatorship has not led to the birth of a democratic political order. What followed has thus far proven to be worse than the despotism that ended in January 1991. Anarchy, massacre, and the willful destruction of both public and private property are common. Indeed, all the pent-up frustrations of three decades of postcolonial independence exploded into the ugly rise of fratricide, which has made the barbaric killing of innocent members of other kin communities a worthy goal. This immediate situation is due primarily to the failure of the armed dissidents to reach an agreement to keep public order, establish a provisional authority, and undertake rebuilding. From the beginning, opposition groups never planned for more than the overthrow of the dictatorship and were therefore unable to deal successfully with the vagaries of the vacuum created by the bloody demise of Siyaad Barre's order.

The prevailing Somali condition basically emanates from a fundamental conflict between two cultures: the essentially pastoral-cum-peasant way of life of the majority of Somali people and that of modernism. One of the chief consequences of this historic clash is the appearance of a new conjuncture in which neither the traditional nor a bona fide modernist approach are in place. Rather, this is a strange moment of transition—one replete with ugly contradictions and severe challenges to all. These very uncertain times and the deep stress that accompanies them generate a horrific climate that turns regular tensions into deadly confrontations. This is the context in which the current communal conflagration must be situated. But this is not the end of history.

Notwithstanding the complete dissolution of the Somali state and social institutions, we must not despair. There are some factors on our side. First, Somalis share many basic characteristics, such as a convincing degree of common identity (despite variations in kin relationships), language, culture, and religion. Despite the failures of early regimes, the cruel politics of Siyaad Barre, and the current relapse into primitive communal warfare, communication and dialogue still continue across kin lines, sometimes with fruitful results. Indeed, a modicum of sanity is slowly beginning to reassert itself through these modest contacts. Consequently, the existence of the Somali nation is neither a fabrication nor an illusion. Rather, it is a reality embedded in the collective heritage of the Somali people. Rickety and badly damaged in its present state, Somali identity stubbornly refuses to disappear from the consciousnesses of many. Although there is no denying that the impact of the civil war has been very costly, it seems that the emergence of clanist politics is a temporary aberration that will inevitably give way to a new nationalist thinking.

If Somalis are to face the challenges of the long transition and the changing world order, they will need to adapt to today's complex global environment. Obviously, fragmentation into isolated kin and subkin groups provides no practical solution to the great problems at hand. How, then, can the Somali people move beyond this dehumanizing present and provide for a mutuality conducive to a new pattern of life?

What Do We Need Most?

From my vantage point, the single most immediate factor responsible for the Somali catastrophe is the nature of political leadership. In a modern society, it is not just a constitution that matters but the caliber of those generations of leaders who frame such documents, interpret them, and put them into execution or adjust them to changing circumstances. But who is a good leader—the one who makes the historical difference? At the danger of being too arbitrary, I suggest that the following traits are indispensable: critical intelligence; a commitment to development, education, and efficiency; and vision.

There are other important qualities that public officials must possess and practice, such as a sense of fairness, tolerance, and a belief in a democratic approach to power. For Somalia and its people to close the door on the legacy of the past and reverse the current bloody disorder, the nature of leadership ought to be taken very seriously. Somalia and the rest of Africa cannot afford anymore to be ruled by the forces of ineptitude and ignobility.

I hope this volume and the videotapes of our conference's plenary sessions now in circulation highlight the Somali plight in new ways, offer novel and lasting insights for mature discussion, and move many to act constructively.

Part 2

Livelihood and the Catastrophe

3

Jilaal, Gu, Hagaa, and *Der:* Living with the Somali Land, and Living Well

Ben Wisner

The Somali people, their development institutions, and their land have suffered a series of weakening shocks over the last twenty years. The catastrophe in Somalia is one in which institutional collapse, economic failure, decreasing feasibility of traditional livelihood options, and environmental degradation are inseparable. This chapter has two main purposes: to analyze the interplay of these elements of the Somali predicament, particularly the nexus of environment and development, and to look ahead to the relationship between society and nature in a future peaceful Somalia.

In order to do this, I must make several assumptions. The first has already been mentioned: peace is a prerequisite for a normalization of life and for any kind of stabilization of the society/nature relationship. Second, without taking any position on recent geopolitical events such as the declaration of an independent Republic of Somaliland in the North, I treat the question of environment and development on both sides of the boundary at present separating Somalia and the Republic of Somaliland. Third, I assume the existence of a mixed economy with a certain degree of state planning. Fourth, I assume widespread and deeply rooted democracy. This will be seen to be very significant when one asks how highly localized environmental potentials and problems are to be addressed. Throughout this chapter, the perspective of citizen participation in planning is adopted. Citizens have a right to know of the existence of environmental risks that may be created by proposed large-scale resource development projects (e.g., hydropower, mining, irrigation) and industrial investments.

The Backdrop

Somalia has suffered great human and environmental devastation over the last twenty years. A new approach to society/nature relations and a new way of thinking about such things as "natural resources" and "environment" are necessary for a peaceful and viable future.

One might arbitrarily begin by considering the destructive drought of 1974–1975. The "command" planning approach to this challenge led to the resettlement of northern nomadic people in large-scale agricultural projects and new fishing schemes, as well as investments in expanded irrigation, hydropower, commercial livestock infrastructure, and marketing. This approach to economic development failed (although it is possible to identify some positive and promising programs at the field level—for instance, certain initiatives in women's education, pastoral cooperatives, dryland farming technology, and health care).[1]

The development policy of the military government reinforced the top-down export/plantation model inherited from colonialism and further encouraged by international donors. It also resulted in a spiral of commercial food importation and eventual dependence on international food aid. Furthermore, the question of long-term sustainability of society/environment relations was neglected. Forest and wildlife conservation received very little attention. Foreign export of charcoal made from the important tree species *Acacia nilotica* was allowed. No integrated coastal zone management was practiced, although Somalia has 3,000 kilometers of coast and highly productive fisheries. Mangroves were allowed to be destroyed. No protected marine areas were established.

War in the Ogaden was a further stress that followed quickly in the late 1970s. Long-established seasonal patterns of livestock movement back and forth across the Somalia/Ethiopia border were disrupted. Such events eroded traditional herd management strategies that had reduced the risk of drought and animal disease.[2] Coupled with the drive to sell more meat and animals in the Gulf States and elsewhere in the Middle East and the overstocking that resulted from this policy, this meant that the pastoral economy was made much more vulnerable to extreme cycles in nature and extreme price shifts in the marketplace.

By the early 1980s, at least one million refugees from the Ogaden War lived in dozens of camps at many locations in Somalia. Others lived in the towns unsupported by relief agencies. These circumstances imposed an added economic burden on the country and also put great strain on local camp environments because vegetation was stripped for fuelwood.[3]

During this period, urban growth in Somalia accelerated dramatically, overtaking neighboring Kenya and Ethiopia in terms of the percentage of urban population. This situation was driven by deteriorating conditions in rural areas. Town and city water, sanitation, and health services and housing stock could not keep up. Further serious environmental problems were therefore created in urban habitats.

The 1980s saw increased resistance to the regime of Siyaad Barre and worsening subsistence difficulties that were part of greater African economic decline. Rural living was disrupted by armed conflict between opposition and government forces. Meanwhile, prices of all major export crops went down, whereas the prices of imported energy products and technology increased.

With the final overthrow of Siyaad Barre's regime and the civil war that has followed, there has been a complete collapse of the infrastructure for meeting human welfare and for mediating society/nature relations.

Peace will bring with it a series of immediate needs for rehabilitation, starting with a reestablishment of the basic infrastructure of environmental health: water supplies, sewage treatment, refuse disposal, and vector and vermin control. Urban areas and other zones of conflict need to be cleared of land mines and undetonated explosives. Chemical and oil spills that have occurred during the fighting near industrial areas will need to be cleaned up. Other urgent recovery needs will be reclamation of the integrity of forest and wildlife reserves, reinitiation of sand dune stabilization programs, pasture improvement, and veterinary programs. It is likely that the breakdown of services has meant that without dipping and other preventive actions, there is a danger of epizootic diseases.

Restarting the formal sector of the economy will carry with it environmental risks and opportunities. One such danger is that the perception of urgency will lead to shortcuts that could further threaten human health or environmental quality. A major opportunity is that a people-based planning process can reveal new investment options—large, small, and microentrepreneurial. At a minimum, as Abdi Samatar argues elsewhere in this volume, economic rehabilitation will require seeds, implements, credit, and marketing facilities. The large-scale irrigation facilities serving plantations have become clogged with silt and will need attention in the short term.

In the long run, the entire complex of cause and effect connecting the management or mismanagement of pasture, arable and forested land, the two rivers, and coastal and marine resources will need to be rethought. The following review of the relationship between development and the environment in Somalia suggests that there are considerably more options than the limited ones that have historically been the focus of investment and encouragement.

Critical Concepts

Sustainable Development

The Brundtland Commission defines a "sustainable livelihood security" as follows (emphasis added):

> Livelihood is defined as adequate stocks and flows of food and cash to meet basic needs. Security refers to secure ownership of, or access to, resources and income-earning activities, including *reserves and assets to offset risk, ease shocks and meet contingencies.* Sustainable refers to the maintenance or enhancement of resource productivity on a long-term basis.[4]

I have emphasized risk reduction as an aspect integral to the notion of sustainable development because of the importance of risks in the lives of peasants, pastoralists, and people who depend on fishing in Somalia, especially such risks as drought, epizootic diseases, flash flooding, and storms.

This definition of sustainability concerns more than local livelihood systems; it has necessary regional, international, and intersectoral aspects. For instance, how can the livelihood of a community dependent on small-scale fishing be secure if effluent from a nearby factory pollutes the breeding ground of fish or if commercial development of salt flats or a tourist complex destroys the wetlands that provide that breeding ground? Likewise, the best-conceived local and regional plans can be rendered unsustainable if powerful international agents intervene, for example, by locating a depository for toxic waste from overseas (see below). Once again, upstream river management for large-scale irrigation or hydroelectricity can adversely affect such downstream activities as flood-retreat irrigation, dry-season grazing on riverbanks, and fishing.

There are, in short, both an epistemological challenge and a political challenge wrapped up in the easy-sounding rhetoric of "sustainable development."[5] First, one has to comprehend the complex interactions of various livelihood activities over space and time. For

instance, in Somalia there is little understanding of farmer/pas-
toralist relations, although they have interacted intensely for centuries. Second, one has to have social institutions that adjudicate
among the various interests involved and distribute the costs and
benefits across social groups, regions, and—an essential dimension
that is often forgotten—future generations. What is the point of saving the lives of children suffering from famine and disease if these
children will inherit a wasted, degraded land?

Environment

Many Africans are demanding a new epistemological starting point
for thinking through and acting out their own future. In common
with native peoples in many parts of the world, they have struggled
for decades to decolonize their minds. They are reasserting the significance and richness of their own philosophical and scientific traditions.[6] Nowhere is the contrast between Eurocentric rationalism
and African philosophy greater than where the environment is
concerned.

The Western-trained technocrat (WTT) thinks of the environment as a geometrical container, a box, with "things" in it. Some of
these things are useful to "man" and are called *resources*. The very
notion of *carrying capacity*, at the heart of arguments about population growth in Africa, is a derivative of such geometrical thinking.
Land becomes a geometrical surface that "carries" people: the statistical expression is "persons per square kilometer" (or square
mile).[7]

These simplified, highly pervasive mental images bear no relation to vernacular thought and action. Far from living out their lives
on stages with such linear dimensions, Africans create *livelihood systems* that depend as much on other people as on the flow of energy
through natural systems.[8] The shape of the life space can change
from season to season. There are likely to be both urban and rural
lifelines.[9] Mobility across space is common not only among the pastoral people of Africa, but also among so-called sedentary cultiva-
tors. Many diverse pockets of soil, water, wild and cultivated annual plants, perennial grasses, and trees support livelihoods.

If humanized places, rather than "environments," are the spaces
within which Africans arrange their livelihood strategies, how are
we to conceptualize the physical and biological characteristics of
those many diverse pockets where people work? Nature becomes
resource only when two things are added: human labor and a
human project.

The human labor involved is neither brute force nor individual genius. Knowledge of an indefinite number of physical and biological characteristics of the life space is socially constructed and passed along to children. In Somalia, people have a highly developed body of knowledge concerning water, vegetation, soil, and animal health. These properties of the environment are not known simply technically or functionally, but as part of a shared cultural heritage. Witness how the aesthetic, social, and ecological characteristics of place are fused in Somali poetry:

> I hate the Maaro mountain because of the early morning heavy rains, I hate having camels in a windy place, and I hate cattle when it comes to "jilaal," the dry season . . . *Gumar [Acacia oerfota]* tree, can you tell me where our herds are grazing? . . . Your beauty is reminiscent of grazing land on which it rained recently and on which a bright sun shone.[10]

Ecology

The word *ecological* as an adjective describing development projects also needs to be redefined critically. Development agencies, nongovernmental organizations (NGOs), and government ministries have tried to take an "ecological" approach to Africa during the 1980s. However, livelihood systems have not been protected by these attempts to reverse so-called ecological crises (e.g., desertification, deforestation, erosion).

In particular, there has been very little attention to the fact that women are often the primary managers of that complex of places that make up the life space.[11] Well-meant ecological approaches to ecological crises have demanded too much of women's time (e.g., hand terracing of hillsides), interfered with their ability to use certain places (e.g., woodlots excluding small livestock), and shifted control over "resources" from women to men (e.g., cooperatives led by men are formed to market forest or wetland products, or factories are set up to dry ocean fish previously processed by women).[12] Indeed, the role of women in pastoral production is an area that has been even more neglected than others.[13]

The word *crisis* also has to be considered carefully. There is much evidence for hard times in the continent and Somalia: villages abandoned on the edge of once fertile land that has turned into desert; charcoal and fuelwood coming into growing cities of the working poor from more than a hundred kilometers away, leaving rural people even poorer as the trees come down; surface- and groundwater reserves in many countries reaching their limits; sleeping sickness, malaria, guinea worm, and other environmentally linked diseases increasing in prevalence; and the breakdown of ordered life in Somalia.

Yet *crisis* is an ambiguous word. To be sure, the times are grim, but history has not come to a halt. Rather, this moment can be seen as a turning point for opportunities. For instance, by building on the basis of the people's knowledge of the environment and local social institutions, the Somalis themselves are capable of disproving the stereotypes of chaos and dependency generally associated with the continent and now more specifically with the Horn.

Arid and Semiarid
Development Policy in Sub-Saharan Africa

Ever since the United Nations Conference on Desertification (UNCOD) in 1977, there has been a great deal of attention paid—at least in word if not in deed—to Africa's arid and semiarid lands (ASAL). Numerous soil, pasture, water, and forest conservation and rehabilitation projects have sprung up.[14] Work against desertification has been seriously underfunded. Although a UN study recommended investing U.S. $4.5 billion for twenty years in the problem, the UNCOD program of action had received only U.S. $26 million by 1984.[15] Furthermore, most action to combat desertification has treated symptoms rather than causes, has been poorly coordinated, and has involved very little citizen participation.[16]

Aside from such conservation and rehabilitation efforts, irrigation, dry-farming improvement, and ranching have been the three major interventions by the postcolonial African states in semiarid and arid zones. In many ways these programs differed little from colonial antecedents. Several generalizations are possible:

• Projects have generally been undertaken on a large scale. Irrigation has been based on capital-intensive hydroengineering and managed in a "top down" mode—for example, the Gezira scheme in Sudan; colonial Office Niger and contemporary Manankali schemes in the West African Sahel; irrigated wheat fields south of Kano in Nigeria; Mwea Tebere and Bura rice schemes in Kenya; and irrigation schemes on the lower Shabelle and Juba rivers in Somalia. There has been little concern for the people displaced by such schemes, who often suffer a serious disruption of their livelihood and are definitely the losers in these circumstances.[17]

• Less money and attention have been devoted to dryland farming. There was a colonial obsession, which seems to have persisted, with finding the "ideal" cash crop for low-rainfall areas. Other programs have focused on breeding seeds that are more drought resistant: sorghums, millets, pigeon peas, cow peas, and maize. There has been considerable technical success with some of these seeds, but often the management and other social and economic aspects of production have been overlooked, leading to only a partial adoption of the successful aspects.

• Pastoral development schemes have focused on destocking (linked with commercialization and marketing); provision of services such as water points, dips, and other veterinary services; and various organizational initiatives aimed at producing associations, group ranches, or cooperatives that allow for more control of grazing (hence pasture improvement). Such programs have very weak records.[18]

• Little attention has been given to the traditional relationships between dry-farming and pastoral populations or to the fact that workers, tenants, and other participants in irrigation schemes often also retain livestock off the scheme (or sometimes illegally on-site).

• There has been a lack of awareness of the need to include the management of wildlife into programs for arid and semiarid lands. Where wildlife reserves have been established, the resident farming and pastoral population have tended to become the losers and to be viewed as a problem rather than as potential partners.

• Social infrastructural investment in arid and semiarid zones has tended to be adapted poorly to the needs of nomadic people. "Standard" stationary facilities, such as health clinics or schools, have been built with no provision for seasonal movement of nomads. There have been few experiments with mobile services or nomadic service providers who, in the tradition of earlier itinerant teachers of Islam,[19] move with the people.

• There has been very little respect for local knowledge in arid and semiarid development programs. Nor have planners and administrators recognized the extreme flexibility and adaptability of nomadic people, who can learn to fish (as shown by the experience on the coast of Somalia following the 1974–1975 drought or by freshwater fishing schemes for Turkana drought refugees in Lake Turkana in Kenya)[20] or learn to irrigate (as shown by spontaneous irrigation by Kenyan Somali in Isiolo District during the 1971–1972 drought).[21]

• In particular, indigenous methods of coping with drought have not been valued by outside authorities. One researcher in

Kenya documented more than 75 possible drought crisis adjustments in the semiarid zone of eastern Kenya below Mt. Kenya.[22] Others have found similar patterns in West Africa[23] and in the Horn of Africa.[24]

• Development work in the arid and semiarid zone has very seldom explicitly recognized or attempted to take into consideration ethnic, class, and gender relationships that are responsible for much of the deterioration of traditional systems for coping with drought.[25] For instance, privately financed bore hole wells were responsible for the overextension by rich investors of grazing into drought reserve areas of Botswana, to the ultimate peril of poorer pastoralists.[26]

• Except for extraction (large-scale charcoal production, salt production, sand and gravel quarrying, mining, and hydroelectricity production), the arid and semiarid zones have not been thought of as sites of rural industry. Industrial investment has been made on a piecemeal basis and has not been treated as part of an integrated development program that would accomplish the following: (1) put the local residents in charge, (2) maximize internal connections (i.e., water, energy, forestry, food production, industry) within the zone, (3) maximize complementarities with better-watered zones in neighboring countries or within the same country. Slaughterhouses, leather-tanning and grain-milling operations, and charcoal production account for nearly all the industrial plans in many such zones.

Future Opportunities and Challenges for Somalia

Prior development programs in Somalia have matched the preceding ten generalizations. Somalia tried large-scale irrigation, large mechanized state farms, and settlement schemes in agricultural areas and fishing villages for destitute nomads. It also tried grazing associations and improved veterinary services for the livestock sector. Little attention was given to dryland farming or, more generally, to peasant and pastoralist knowledge and initiative. The usual search for cash crops was carried out, including unsuccessful experiments with cotton. Bananas and livestock remained the leading export food sources, and dependency on imported food increased.

The future Somalia will have to break away from such conventional approaches in order to create wealth and security in arid and semiarid zones. Development will depend on highly detailed knowledge of local environments and active participation by the people. As a Somali saying goes, "If you don't know the country you will get lost; if you don't know the people, you will go hungry."[27] Therefore, the discussion now turns to specific features of the Somali physical environment, ways in which the people have either understood and utilized or avoided them, and the contribution to the reconstruction of Somalia that they might make.

Water

The only two permanent rivers are the Shabelle and Juba, both of which rise on the Ethiopian plateau and flow through southern Somalia to the Indian Ocean. Map 3.1 shows patterns of rainfall drainage, other important physical features, and urban places. Throughout the North there are no permanent streams, only intermittent watercourses. There is plentiful groundwater just below the surface on the northern coastal plain. Deeper wells are necessary in the northern plateau area, but in a normal rainfall year, wells are sufficient for a permanent population of people and animals. The Haud grasslands further to the south can be used only in the wet season because groundwater is too deep to supply year-round needs. During the wet season, depressions in the Haud fill and become temporary lakes and ponds.[28]

Rainfall is scanty and highly variable. Somalia is extremely arid along the northern coast, all the way from the border with Djibouti around the Horn and to the south (nearly halfway to Mogadishu). There are two "islands" of annual rainfall exceeding 500 millimeters. One is in the North, and the other is in the South in the zone between and near the two permanent rivers. These two zones support dry farming.

Rainfall is not only generally meager in Somalia but also highly variable and often spatially distributed in an uneven way. All of this makes dry farming a very demanding and risky enterprise. One survey of farmers found that they expected two good crops, one poor crop, and two years with no crop in an average five-year period. Among practitioners of flood-retreat farming along the Shabelle River, the expectation was for three good crops, one fair one, and one poor crop.[29] Droughts have occurred somewhere in Somali territory in 1910–1912, 1914, 1918, 1921–1922, 1925, 1927–1928, 1931–1934, 1938, 1943–1944, 1950–1952, 1955, 1959, 1963–1965, 1968–1969, 1973–1974, 1978, 1984–1985, and 1990–1991.[30]

Somalis recognize four seasons: *Jilaal* and *Der* are winter seasons, and *Gu* and *Hagaa* are summer ones. Abdi Samatar describes the seasons as follows:

Map 3.1   Annual Rainfall Pattern in Somalia

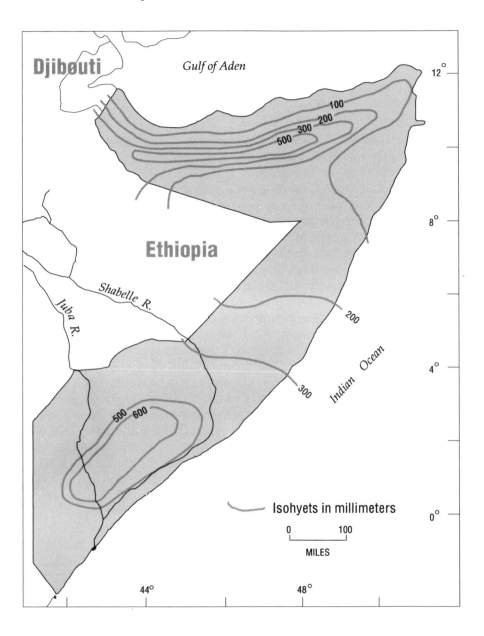

The summer rains fall between April and September. *Gu*, which is the first part of the summer (late March, April, and May), witnesses the heaviest rainfall in the Ogo and the Haud. This is the season of fresh grazing and abundant surface water. It is also the breeding season for livestock. Winter (*Jilaal* and *Der*) is the season of dearth thirst. The onset of the dry season starts in October and lasts until the end of March or early April. The Ogo and the Haud receive virtually no rainfall in winter; the *Der* rains fall in the coastal zone between January and March.[31]

These seasons are determined by northwest and southeast monsoon winds, with transitional periods in between that result in alternating patterns of moist and dry.[32]

Over many years, the Somali population has developed very skillful ways of managing water. These include both traditional techniques and ones introduced through projects. In Somalia, as in other arid and semiarid parts of Africa, rainwater harvesting is widely practiced.[33] In arable farming, many forms of bunding and microcatchments are used to concentrate rainfall and runoff.[34] Subsurface dams in dry riverbeds are used to concentrate subsurface flows in areas where wells can be dug during the dry seasons.

Viewed on a long-term national scale, Somalia could face severe water shortages by the year 2025.[35] Consequently, the highest priority should be given to ensuring that urban, industrial, and irrigation use of water are as efficient as possible, and that water quality is maintained or renewed throughout use so that it can be reused. The prevailing tendency in the past to think in terms of very large dams should be reconsidered. Large-scale dams and irrigation systems can have very high maintenance costs and can exclude or reduce secondary benefits and activities such as river fishing.[36] Forest cover should be protected and, where possible, extended, so that rainfall is intercepted; runoff should be slowed so that natural or human systems can store water. Flash floods are not only potentially destructive, but a sign that water is not being managed optimally (see later sections on forested land and natural hazards).

Because Somalia's only two permanent rivers originate in Ethiopia, it is important to plan their long-term management in cooperation with that country. The means for doing so may already exist in the form of the Inter-Governmental Authority for Drought and Development (IGADD). One important issue urgently needing attention is the sediment load of water in the Juba and Shabelle rivers. High sediment, caused by erosion upstream in Somalia and Ethiopia, shortens the life of dams (by filling up the reservoirs), causes wear on turbines and pumps, and changes the ecology of coral reefs and coastal wetlands. This last consequence can seriously reduce the breeding of ocean species that have economic importance.[37]

Land

Somalia is composed of diverse land systems ranging from the arid northern coastal strip (*guban*), high plateau (*ogo*), and undulating haud grassland to the southern arable zone between the Shabelle and Juba rivers. Table 3.1 gives an overview of land capability.[38]

Table 3.1   Estimated Land Capability

	Area (in thousands of hectares)	Percentage of total
Total area	63,800	100.0
Northern regions	17,800	28.0
Southern regions	46,000	72.0
Land use type		
Total suitable for crops or		
potentially cultivable	8,000	12.5
In crops or fallow	650	1.0
Uncultivated but cultivable	7,350	11.5
Total suitable for grazing	35,000	54.9
Total forest	8,800	13.8
Actual forest	2,500	3.9
Bush and scrub	6,300	9.9
Other land	12,000	18.8

Source: World Bank, *Somalia: Appraisal,* p. 5.

Arable land. In the mid-1970s, only about 8 percent of the 8 million hectares of potentially cultivable land in Somalia was cropped. By the early 1980s, there were still only about 700,000 hectares under cultivation.[39] Of this, the vast majority (650,000 hectares) was worked as small family farms with low input technology (e.g., ox plowing, few chemical inputs or improved seed)[40] and low yields (e.g., sorghum, 400 kilograms per hectare; maize, 800 kilograms per hectare; rice, 2000 kilograms per hectare). These small farmers devoted 55 percent of their land to sorghum and 25 percent to maize.[41]

Four-fifths of this arable land is situated in the valleys of the Juba and Shabelle rivers, the areas immediately east and west of the rivers, and the upland between them (much of it in the Bay and Shabellaha Hoose Regions). Another significant area of arable agriculture is in the ogo uplands in the Northwest, in the belt around the towns of Hargeisa and Borama.[42]

Irrigated land measured about 50,000 hectares in the early 1980s and was scheduled to increase by 1,000–2,000 hectares a year. The large Bardera dam project on the Juba River was designed not only to generate hydropower but, in its fully developed form, to allow irrigation of 220,000 hectares.[43] This project has never been finished. Irrigated land areas and further potential for expansion are given in Table 3.2.

Table 3.2   Present and Potential Cultivated Areas (in thousands of hectares)

	Present	Potential	Present Percent of Potential
Under controlled irrigation			
Shabelle River Valley	35	86	41
Juba River Valley	14	160	9
Northwest region	1	4	25
Subtotal	50	250	20
Under uncontrolled hydrological situations			
Flood irrigation	110	—a	—a
Rainfed farming	540	7,950	7
Total	700	8,200	9

Source: H. Lewis and Wisner, "Refugee Rehabilitation in Somalia," p. 17, adapted from Government of Somalia, Three-Year Development Plan.
Note: a. Full extent not known.

This table is adapted from the Somali government's *Three-Year Development Plan, 1979–1981*, published in 1979.[44] Since that year, the estimate for the area potentially irrigable on the Juba increased from the 160,000 hectares given in Table 3.2 to the figure of 220,000 hectares published in 1983. Whatever the estimated potential, the Bardera dam project was clearly a centerpiece of previous development strategy, in both the energy and agricultural sectors. Planners should review the present status of the project as a high priority and also review the record of very large irrigation schemes worldwide. The International Irrigation Management Institute in Kandy, Sri Lanka, is a good source of such experience. It is likely that a number of smaller irrigation schemes would be cheaper and easier to implement and less costly to maintain, and would spread benefits more evenly.

Table 3.2 also calls attention to the large amount of traditional flood (i.e., flood-retreat, or regression) irrigation practiced in Somalia

(110,000 hectares with unknown, but probably large, potential for expansion). Although the table refers to these technologies collectively beneath the heading "under uncontrolled hydrological situations," there is a good deal of skillful water management involved. Such language is typical of the systematic misunderstanding of peasant technology. These systems usually involve erecting small earthen bunds by hand, by animal traction, or with mechanical aids. The bunds trap runoff, and the residual soil moisture is used to produce a crop. A variation is to follow retreating floodwaters with a sequence of crops that are planted in the soil that has very recently been under water.

Because so little of the irrigated potential nationwide (about 20 percent) and even less of the dry-farming potential (about 8–9 percent) is tapped, it would seem obvious that Somalia could produce more food. Until the 1970s, the country was self-sufficient in grains. Could it not feed itself again?

The question is not a strictly technical one. Since the 1970s, several government policies have converged to produce a great dependence on commercial food imports and an even greater dependence on food aid donations.[45] First, the nomadic population was encouraged to sell more animals for export. With the money earned, they began to buy more grain and other foodstuffs from the small family farmers. Meanwhile, urban growth was taking place. Food that the urban population needed was being consumed in greater proportions by the nomads. This shift in consumption was also due to the fact that pastoralists had become accustomed to the nontraditional foods typically consumed in cities, such as wheat and rice, that had been used for international famine relief in 1974–1975.

Imports filled this emerging urban food gap. Then, in the late 1970s and early 1980s, food aid was needed to support refugees from the Ogaden War. Such aid continued despite good crop years in the 1980s. Public taste for wheat and rice continued to grow as a result, and the producer price for traditional grains was depressed. Thus, a whole series of economic policy issues need to be addressed in answering the simple-seeming question "Can Somalia feed itself?" Clearly, it is not just a matter of totaling up the arable acres, calculating yields, and counting mouths to feed. The notion of *carrying capacity* (for humans or livestock) is never as simple as it looks.

One variable that always intervenes in the population/environment equation is technology. To date, various Somali governments have not applied the same vigor to improving dryland farming as they have to supporting irrigation. Somali farmers have considerable traditional skills in water management, yet government schemes to construct bunds that focus runoff have had serious deficiencies.

Abdi Samatar visited the Gabileh District in the North, where a major government program had been active for some time. This program promoted bunding, introduced marketable crops (e.g., grapefruit trees), and had been praised elsewhere.[46] However, Samatar found participants to have the following grievances:[47]

- Peasants had to bribe government workers to come to their areas to help construct bunds.
- The number of bunds on a farm was not the outcome of a technical calculation, but was instead subject to the discretion of the government team.
- On farms where gully erosion was occurring, the team did not concern itself with the problem.
- Often the cultivation area was not leveled after bunds were constructed, so water accumulated unevenly, forming ponds adjacent to dry areas.
- Animal and human water points, also part of the program for this area, were poorly constructed and frequently in disrepair.

An analysis of the military regime's spending in the agricultural sector in the 1970s shows that the most common dry-farming crop, sorghum, received very little attention. For instance, looking at the *Three-Year Development Plan*, Lewis and Wisner found that only 9 percent of agricultural investment bore any relation to the issue of raising sorghum yields (even when one credits items such as "strengthening agricultural research" and "seed production and certification," as well as the full 55 million Somali shillings for the Bay Region Agricultural Development Project, to the side of sorghum).[48]

A high priority of a new government should be to formulate a national food security plan that takes into account major traditional food crops, the significance of subsistence for camels and small stock, and the shift in food habits that has occurred as a result of prolonged international food aid.

Another high priority related to Somali land is to review the state of soil erosion. Bureaucratic bridges need to be built or departments reorganized so that the circumstances never again arise that a team responsible for bunding has no interest in soil erosion. There is a very strong relationship between erosion, desertification, deforestation, and food security,[49] and there is some very positive evidence from Somalia that integrated programs can work. For example, a seventeen-year retrospective evaluation of soil and water conservation projects supported by the U.S. Agency for International Development (USAID) showed 100 percent increases in yields from bunded farms initially and—what is very encouraging—a 50 percent yield above unbunded holdings that appears to have continued after these many years.[50]

Grazing land and livestock[51]   As shown in Table 3.1, the World Bank estimate of land suitable for grazing is 35 million hectares (about 55 percent of Somalia's land area). The FAO estimate is lower (29 million hectares) but still shows the great potential for livestock production. The nomadic population of Somalia have inherited management systems that have allowed them to reach, and indeed surpass, levels of production supportable by this grass cover. The mid-1970s animal population was estimated to be from 21 million to 34 million. The lower estimate includes 15 million goats, 9.5 million sheep, 5.3 million camels, and 4 million cattle.[52]

Grasses in Somalia are, of course, adapted to low rainfall. However, soil deficiencies (salinity in some places, low organic matter in others) can reduce the usefulness of the grass cover for grazing. The best pastures are found on the red calcareous soils in the semiarid zone known as the Haud in the North. The coarse, gray sands of the northern coastal plain also provide excellent pasture. In the South's coastal sand dune area, there is an extensive stretch of reddish to yellowish sandy soil, containing small amounts of organic matter, where reasonable pasture is found.[53]

Traditional livestock management in Somalia is economically and ecologically rational, as elsewhere in Africa.[54] Mobility and diverse herd composition are two keys to successful livestock management in Somalia's dry, highly seasonal environment. Access to grazing lands has traditionally been allocated by kin.[55] Herd composition is determined by such animal characteristics as their hardiness, reproductive cycle, uses in consumption, and—of increasing importance—demand for them on the market. Sale of Somali sheep and cattle, in particular, has increased dramatically in Middle Eastern markets since the 1960s.[56] This has been one factor contributing to the growth of the number of livestock supported on grazing lands. Other factors include the growth of the human population, the corresponding subsistence and cash needs, and the availability of veterinary services and water points.

Map 3.2 shows the network of livestock marketing. As the figure suggests, livestock for sale are collected over a wide area, even in isolated nomadic camps, by a variety of middlemen (*dilaal*) who finance their activity in different ways. They walk the animals out to collection points, where they sell them to licensed exporters (*ganacsato*).[57]

Overgrazing has become a problem as commercial exploitation of livestock has grown. However, it is important to consider what one might mean by the term *overgrazing*. In the past, the term has been used to imply the existence of some built-in propensity of pastoral people to degrade their environments through an unchecked increase in human or livestock populations. Contrary to this view, there is much evidence that African pastoralists exercise effective checks on human and animal reproduction and are generally in possession of clear management strategies.[58] Where such management strategies are destabilized by such forces as commercialization or climate change (among many other possible forces), "overgrazing" can occur.[59]

This is what happened in Somalia. Wells were dug that allowed year-round occupancy of some zones that had been only seasonal pastures in the past. For instance, the number of such privately financed cement tank reservoirs (*berkado*) in the Burao Region increased from 1 in 1954 to 18,000 in 1970.[60] Allegations have been made that, in the 1960s, parliamentary deputies sold their votes for cement tank permits. The government later banned the construction of such wells and tanks. Further undermining traditional livestock management practices, traders encouraged nomads to sell as many animals as possible, and some of the income from sales was used to purchase immature stock from other parts of the country to raise for sale. Established seasonal movements were disrupted, as were the long-established composition of herds and ratio of cattle to camels to small stock. Among the results were degraded pastures (e.g., brush encroachment), erosion, and, in some cases, sand dune destabilization (resulting in localized desertification).

The term *overgrazing* is a tricky one for another reason. What level of livestock utilization is required to allow such land degradation to be reversed? In the past, *carrying capacity* was considered to be easily definable in terms of animal units per unit of territory. The problem is that recent work on semiarid environments suggests great fluctuations in rainfall and grassland production over time, a fact that undermines one's confidence in the ability to estimate "sustainable" levels of stocking.[61] Hence, in this context, *overgrazing* refers to a physical deterioration of rangelands that may or may not have been caused by an overutilization by livestock and that may or may not be quickly reversed after use by domestic animals is decreased. In other words, climate fluctuations appear to be very

Map 3.2   Livestock Export Routes in Somalia

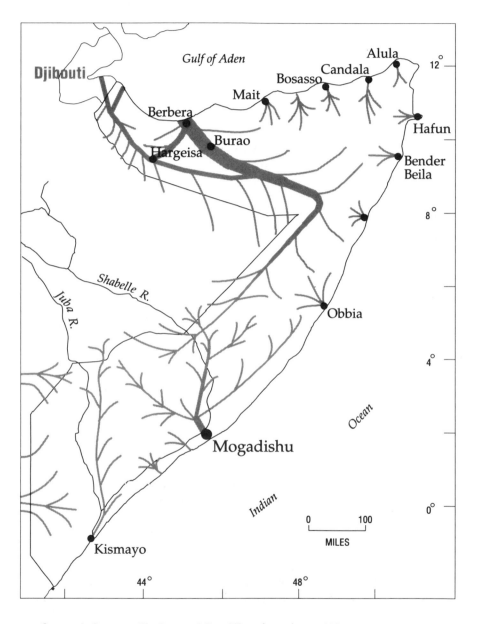

Source: A. Samatar, *The State and Rural Transformation*, p. 104.

important in these processes, and they confound the issue of live-stock pressure. Great care and constant monitoring (by the people themselves) will be required in establishing locally sustainable levels of use.

Increased commercialization in the last few decades not only has had a possibly negative impact on the land, but it has also reduced the ability of nomads to cope with occasional droughts. Commercial pressures have resulted in a change in the composition of herds. A comparison of 1944–1951 with 1973 shows that the ratio of camel to cattle decreased from 5.4:1 in the North and 1.4:1 in the South to only 1.8:1 in the North and 0.5:1 in the South.[62] This change increased the risk of drought because it reduced the effectiveness of time-tested coping strategies such as mobility. Cattle are not only less resilient than camels and more dependent on a constant water supply, they are also less mobile.

The situation is not hopeless. Grass will regenerate, and human systems of coping with drought have the capacity to adapt and change. A number of experimental systems of rangeland management have been tested, and the technical feasibility of pasture rehabilitation is beyond doubt.[63] However, these approaches all require some control of stocking densities and the use of rotational or deferred grazing—which in turn require a level of cooperation and social control that is difficult to attain.

Government and donor-assisted attempts to control grazing in the 1950s and 1960s ran up against social norms mandating widespread sharing of water and pasture resources, a problem that has been reported in many parts of Africa. However, in the 1970s, government-supported village or town grazing areas and pastoral cooperatives found greater success. In all cases, grazing areas were demarcated, with the participation of organized groups, and certain sections were reserved for dry-season pasture or even held back altogether as drought reserves. Beginning in 1976, a National Range Agency (NRA) was established to plan and coordinate the division of land into grazing reserves, to provide water points, and to provide guards to keep nomads from using closed sections.

A thorough review of the experiences of pastoral cooperatives and the NRA would be a high priority for any new political order in Somalia.[64] A related but broader set of questions that ought to be considered a high priority for research concerns the relationship between pastoralists and farmers in the inter-riverine zone. Were there seasonal exchanges? What were the complementarities or conflicts? Is there a basis for developing or reconstructing mutually beneficial relations? It should also not be forgotten that, before the crises, there were some 30,000–40,000 dairy cattle stall-fed near urban centers. How were these animals provisioned? What would it take to revive this dairy industry?[65]

A major issue for the future is the imbalance in favor of cattle as opposed to camels. Not only has the ratio of camels to cattle shifted dramatically in favor of cattle, as discussed earlier, but there has also been less research on the camel and fewer programs to improve camel production.

The potential of the camel for Somalia's future economy and the well-being of the people is very great.[66] The camel is hardier than the cow (although not without health problems of its own).[67] Because they are mainly browsers and are large, they can eat a variety of plants, bushes, and leaves and twigs of trees and their pods that other livestock cannot reach or do not eat.[68] This gives them greater resilience during times of drought, and it also makes them useful in brush clearance to allow room for other livestock and pasture improvement.[69]

Camel milk is still the mainstay of the nomad's diet, with the average herding family requiring around 28 camels to meet their subsistence needs.[70] Surveys of camels in southern Somalia found that herds were generally younger than those in Kenya and that the milk production potential was very large.[71] Somali culture, in its oral tradition, mirrors the importance of the camel in risk reduction and the provision of a sustainable livelihood:

He who does not own camels lives under the protection of others.

At a place where camels did not calve I will not stay.

For a man who doesn't own camels the event of his death will pass unnoticed.[72]

In addition to their milk production capacity, camels are efficient converters of biomass to meat. In the future, they could be used intensively in fattening and dairy farm operations (in addition to their extensive use at present). They excel in transportation and in providing traction power for arable farming, milling, and lifting water from wells. Their skins are the basis of a leather industry. Their hair and fat are prized for many uses.

Coupled with major programs in forestry conservation, reforestation, and research into agroforestry and silvipastoral tree species, use of the camel—a browser adapted to arid conditions—could expand in importance, not just in terms of subsistence, but also as the basis of many industries in Somalia. However, parallel work on forest issues is vital. Genetic improvement of the camel is not, by itself, enough to raise production without adequate attention to its nutrition.

Any attempt by a new Somali government to increase its involvement in camel production should be careful and respectful of the knowledge of the nomads. One major theme of this chapter is that more genuine popular participation in environmental management planning is required. This is nowhere else as essential as in the relationship among camels, people, and the natural environment (e.g., water, grass, browse, and salty plants such as *Atriplex spp.*, all distributed widely and variably in space and time). Despite spending more than half a billion dollars on pastoral livestock schemes in Africa, a former chief economist at the International Livestock Center for Africa (ILCA) finally decided that the pastoral people who were studied managed affairs as well or better than most outside initiatives, such as veterinary services, grazing schemes, creation of ranches, and marketing and animal improvement programs.[73]

One area where outside interventions have been effective is livestock disease control. However, some disagreement remains,[74] and the years of economic crisis and civil disruption can only have made the problem worse for three reasons: disruption of animal prophylaxis (e.g., dipping), deterioration of animal nutrition (hence, a loss of disease resistance), and habitat changes favoring resurgence of disease vectors. For instance, during the worst of the instability in 1992, pastoralists in the South, in the hinterland of Mogadishu, fled with their animals into marginal areas to avoid the depredations of armed gangs. Animals weakened by disease and scarce fodder died in large numbers.[75]

Tsetse fly–vectored animal sleeping sickness (i.e., trypanosomiasis) is one of the diseases that has to be faced.[76] It affects camels as well as cattle in Somalia. In other parts of Africa (the border zone between Zimbabwe and Mozambique, for instance), prolonged civil disruption produced depopulation, which allowed regrowth of tsetse fly habitat. An urgent priority is to restart control programs that have been discontinued in Somalia because of instability. Assistance in this task may be near at hand because the ILCA is headquartered in Addis Ababa and the International Center for Insect Physiology and Ecology (ICIPE) is based in Nairobi.

During the period of rehabilitation and reconstruction, care will be needed in balancing the urgent need to (re)establish disease control and the longer-term imperatives of sustainable development. For instance, it has been suggested that a prior tsetse control program along the middle reaches of the Shabelle River, funded by the European Economic Community (EEC) at a cost of $20 million, actually resulted in pasture degradation; the argument is that, without the fear of tsetse flies to push them off in search of wet-season pasture, pastoralists remained near the river, where their animals trampled and consumed what would normally be reserved for the dry season.[77]

The grazing resources of Somalia are also shared by wild herbivores (antelopes, gazelles, etc.). Somalia has never had a highly developed system of game reserves, and poaching has been a problem in the past in the reserves.[78] Civil disruption has further eroded discipline in these reserves; as in other African territories affected by war (e.g., Uganda, Angola, Mozambique), armed forces have resorted to killing game on a large scale for food. Wild animals are often more effective in converting grass to meat than livestock, and game cropping has become a viable economic venture in Kenya and Zimbabwe. Game viewing is also an important part of tourism in Africa. Thus, another priority should be to review the status of local wildlife.

Forested land. Around 14 percent of Somalia's land area is classified as "forested," a total of 8–9 million hectares.[79] However, this consists of savanna woodlands, of which perhaps 2.5 million hectares have dense tree stands, including various acacias. Above 1,500 meters, some remnant juniper forests were at one time protected by the state. In total, there are around 100,000 hectares of largely degraded high forests in the Northern highlands and the extreme Southwest. The rest has only very scattered tree covering.

This tree covering is important economically as watershed, domestic fuelwood (see below), building material, forage for animals, wild fruits for human consumption (especially in the dry seasons and times of drought), honey production, medicinal herbs used in traditional human and veterinary medicine, and commercial production of frankincense, myrrh, and gums.[80] The function of trees in slowing runoff and thus increasing control of water cannot be overemphasized.

Through the late 1970s and early 1980s, only about 150 hectares of trees had been planted under official reforestation programs. Two main tree nurseries were established by the government, and twelve regional ones were established. Woodfuel plantations were discussed, but as late as the mid-1980s there had been no implementation beyond the pilot phase. Sand dune stabilization along the southern coast through the use of prickly pear was the most successful program, but more detail on the situation by the end of Siyaad Barre's regime is needed. The valuable role of trees in controlling runoff and managing water, and the positive interactions of acacias with crops and animals (well developed by the Dogon of Mali, for instance) are reasons why much more emphasis needs to be given to the forest sector. The increasing demand for woodfuel is another reason (see below). A great deal of experience has been accumulated on semiarid species and on agroforestry interactions.[81] Fortunately for Somalia, a world center of such work, the International Council for Research on Agro-Forestry (ICRAF) is located in neighboring Kenya.

Agroforestry and silvipastoral research are already under way in Somalia, and possibly fruitful avenues include the propagation of certain indigenous and introduced tree species as fodder sources,[82] increased utilization of indigenous trees for nitrogen fixation in agricultural soil,[83] the role of soil fungi, the effectiveness of *Acacia-Commiphora* trees in the revegetation of degraded areas,[84] and traditional, community-based forest management systems.[85]

Another urgent task in peaceful Somalia should be to review the actual status of forested lands by using satellite images and field mapping. The economic crisis of the 1980s, together with the effects of the civil war, may have caused a rapid degradation of forested land.[86]

Energy[87]

Somalia has no known petroleum, natural gas, or coal deposits, although its location and geology suggest that someday oil or gas may eventually be found.[88] It imports all of its petroleum (5.8 petajoules in 1980, as compared with 138 for Kenya, 44 for Tanzania, and 19 for Mozambique) and has only a modest refinery capacity. Aside from imported oil, Somalia's main source of commercial energy in the 1980s was hydropower. Altogether, commercial energy consumption in Somalia amounted to only 11 percent of the total consumption of 54 petajoules. (Again for comparison, the size of the total commercial and noncommercial energy system for the 1980s was 429 petajoules in Tanzania, 331 in Kenya, and 282 in Mozambique). The remaining 89 percent was consumption of biomass energy (e.g., wood, charcoal, crop residues, animal manure) for domestic energy needs (such as cooking) and rural industrial uses.

Because of increasing urbanization, the zone within which fuelwood is gathered and transported has grown enormously. Mogadishu's supply comes from as far as 500 kilometers to the south.[89] Cutting mangroves for fuel, as well as for building material and extractable tannin, has considerably reduced the extent of mangrove swamps, with a possibly negative impact on the breeding of commercially important ocean fish and crustaceans.[90] In the zones around refugee camps in the late 1980s, there was an almost total devegetation as a result of fuel needs. Although it has been estimated that woodfuel resources exceeded demand by a ratio of 4:1 in the early 1980s,[91] there is no reason for complacency. As already noted, severe ecological damage has already been done. With population growth and increasing urbanization, steps need to be taken to grow woodfuel nearer to towns and cities. Especially because the extent of forest protection probably lapsed during the civil war, the remaining forest reserves need to be inventoried and protected.

Other energy options exist. Preliminary studies reveal the existence of extensive geothermal energy resources in the center of the country.[92] Wind farms and solar steam turbines have been used in desert zones in the United States and elsewhere very efficiently. Wind power might be appropriate in parts of coastal Somalia. Biogas (methane) generation could be a possibility in locations where large numbers of livestock congregate (e.g., dairies, marketing collection points). This biogas could certainly satisfy the lighting and cooking needs of the installations themselves and could be sold to surrounding towns.

Marine and Coastal Ecosystems

The ocean fisheries off the coast of Somalia have a very great potential:

> Only the fast-flowing Somali current during the Southeast Monsoon (April–October)—which transports 40–60 million cubic meters per second of water—causes a significant enough up-swelling to result in a seasonally high fisheries potential off the Somali coast. Comparatively, the rather low-nutrient, mainly surface flowing East African current that washes the shores of Kenya and Tanzania, offers much smaller yields.[93]

However, the Somali do not traditionally eat fish, and fisheries never contributed more than a few percent of GNP during the 1970s and 1980s. The sustainable yield has been estimated to be 180,000–200,000 tons, but additional studies are required to verify and update these numbers. The possible catch includes a wide variety of fish: pelagic (open sea) species—such as anchovies, sardines, herring, tuna, and mackerel—with a potential estimated to be 108,000 tons annually; demersal (bottom-dwelling) species—such as flounder, groupers, porgies, and snappers—with an estimated potential of 40,000 tons annually; 30,000 tons of sharks and rays; 2,000 tons of spiny lobsters; and 400 tons of shrimp. These are all estimates of sustainable yields, but further research and monitoring would be necessary to achieve a sustainable management plan, especially if foreign mechanized fishing fleets are involved.

In the 1970s, the catches registered by licensed Soviet and Italian fleets were only a few thousand tons and a few hundred tons, respectively, each year. The total catch in the early 1970s was 4,000–5,000 tons annually. After some 15,000 destitute nomads were settled in coastal fishing cooperatives during the 1974–1975 drought and small motorized boats were provided, the annual catch increased to nearly 8,000 tons a year, but still nowhere near the limit of sustainability.[94]

In the late 1970s and early 1980s, Somalia entered into joint fishing ventures with Iraq and Italy and acquired trawlers from Australia, Italy, and Yugoslavia. At this time, Somalia also had about 6,500 small-scale fishermen and 2,500 small boats. The combined total catch under these more developed circumstances rose to 75,000 tons in 1978 and 33,000 tons in 1979.

During 1992, there were alarming reports that in the vacuum created by the fall of the Barre regime—which meant the absence of a central government to enforce rights over territorial waters—fishing ships from as many as two dozen countries were plundering the marine catch offshore. These claims need to be investigated as a very high priority and the practice brought to an end.[95]

Nearly 29 percent of Somalia's 3,000-kilometer coastline has some mangrove ecosystems.[96] These are very important habitats for the young of some ocean-dwelling fish and crustacea. Cutting for woodfuel and other uses has begun to threaten the mangroves.

Somalia has coral reefs that are potentially subject to a series of destructive processes, as in a number of western Indian Ocean countries such as Kenya, Madagascar, the Comoro Islands, Tanzania, Réunion, Seychelles, Mauritius, and Mozambique. These hazards include coral mining, anchor damage, use of explosives for fishing, collection for ornamental trade, sewage pollution, industrial pollution, agricultural runoff, and siltation. Despite these threats and the threats to mangroves mentioned above, Somalia has no officially protected marine areas.

Partly as a result of the lack of such protected areas, many endangered species in Somalia are not afforded refuge: a sea mammal (the dugong), two turtles (the green turtle and the hawkbill), the green snail, the fluted giant clam, the small giant clam, the pearl oyster, the spiny lobster, black coral, and whip coral.[97]

Another challenge of coastal zone management is the shifting of formerly stable sand dunes.[98] In the South, brush and wood cutting for urban fuel,[99] in combination with trampling and grazing pressure by livestock (especially during a drought in 1978), has produced a serious problem because these dunes are encroaching into agricultural land, burying coastal roads, and threatening power lines. About 5,000 square kilometers of shifting dunes were present by the early 1980s, and labqr-intensive stabilization programs using prickly pear cactus had succeeded in dealing with only 50 square kilometers.[100]

Transportation of petroleum also brings environmental risks for coastal ecosystems. The heaviest oil tanker traffic in the world, approximately 475 million metric tons each year, moves off the coast of Somalia. Data on the average number of sightings of oil slicks per 100 nautical miles of ships' tracks in the Indian Ocean show a fairly high level of pollution immediately off Somalia's northern and southern coasts,[101] and the potential for a catastrophic spills is always present. For example, further south on the same coast, a tanker spilled a million gallons of oil off Maputo, Mozambique's capital, in May 1992. As of 1981, Somalia had no oil-pollution-fighting equipment.

Urban and Industrial Health and Safety

No discussion of the relationship between environment and development would be complete without dealing with the urban environments created by our own hands.[102] Sub-Saharan Africa has had very high rates of urbanization over the last few decades. Even before the current crises, Somalia was urbanizing rapidly as livelihood options in rural areas grew more difficult. Now, with so much of the population dependent on a few towns for relief feeding and with the sanitary infrastructure, shelter, and energy supply of these towns in disarray, the potential for health disasters is very high. There are already reports of cholera and widespread tuberculosis among famine victims.

Spatial movement patterns of people are known to put them at risk. Studies in Africa have noted the association of mobility patterns with malaria,[103] measles,[104] cholera,[105] and a number of other waterborne diseases.[106] Somalis under stress live in crowded, poorly ventilated houses, often full of smoke that predisposes women to respiratory disease; when conditions ease, many Somalis will go to work—if they can find employment—in dangerous environments.

The period of economic reconstruction will be fraught with potential health hazards for Somali workers and citizens. Foreign firms have tried for some time to export hazardous waste to Africa's "wasteland."[107] In Somalia, during the confusing months following Siyaad Barre's overthrow, a Swiss broker apparently negotiated a deal on behalf of Italian companies with Ali Madhi's minister of health at the time to allow importation and disposal of hazardous waste.[108]

Africa is not the stereotypical rural continent that some may think it to be. Fifteen African countries, including Somalia, had more than 30 percent of their populations living in urban centers in 1985.[109] Eighteen countries were more than one-fourth urban. This is an urgent problem for Somalia. With 34 percent of its population in towns in 1985, Somalia was already among the top dozen countries in terms of percentage of urban population. Somalia has a higher proportion of urban people than do Ghana or Nigeria and much higher than its neighbors Kenya and Ethiopia. The destruction of rural livelihoods and the presence of relatively secure famine relief and health care in towns have undoubtedly increased the degree of urbanization. A vital question is, how many of these people will remain in towns after the crisis is over and for how long?

A vicious circle must be avoided. As seen elsewhere in this chapter, urban consumption demands (e.g., for construction material, fuelwood, electricity, food) can place severe degrading pressures on the surrounding environment and produce distortions in the rural economy (through the effect on urban markets). Such a cycle of degradation further erodes rural livelihood options, forcing more people to seek refuge in the towns. The towns, in turn, are unable to cope with such an influx, and such infrastructure needs as sanitation, health care, and housing are in short supply. Facing such demands for basic urban needs, the government has few resources for the job training and economic rehabilitation efforts that would allow migrants from the countryside to return and reestablish themselves in rural areas.

A closely related issue is the health and safety of the workplace. One must also not make the mistake of thinking of Africa as nonindustrial. Somalia may lack large-scale manufacturing, but its plantations, mines, ports, construction industry, and fishing fleet all present hazards to the workers.[110] Pesticide exposure in Africa is as bad as or worse than it is anywhere else in the world. Given the economic crisis, machinery is growing older and is not well maintained, which makes it even more dangerous.

Somalia will face important decisions when reviving its plantations, mines, port facilities, and manufacturing industries.[111] Worker health cannot be separated from more general health questions.

Health, in turn, cannot be separated from questions of environmental control. Each development strategy has implications for environmental quality and health.

Natural Hazards

Another factor to be taken into account during the planning for sustainable development in a future Somalia is the occurrence of extreme natural events. Drought has already been mentioned as a hazard. There are areas, including much of the Nugaal Valley and Mudug Plain, where low and highly variable rainfall and the absence of permanent streams put nomadic livelihood at a particular risk. This zone suffered the most during the destructive drought of 1974–1975. During the period 1990–1991, the civil unrest accompanying the last days of Barre's regime was compounded by the additional stress of drought in the central part of Somalia, which is estimated to have killed one-third of the livestock.[112]

In addition to drought, a substantial portion of the northern coast is subject to tropical cyclones that can cause flooding, destruction of fishing boats, and beach erosion. Earthquakes of magnitudes sufficient to destroy buildings are possible in the extreme Northwest. This zone includes the major town of Hargeisa. River flooding can affect the more densely populated hinterland of Mogadishu along the lower Shabelle River.

Human actions can exacerbate or mitigate these hazards. For many centuries, the management of herd composition, size, and movement has proven adequate to avoid the worst impact of fairly frequent droughts. Three fairly recent changes have disrupted these traditional patterns of risk management. First, skilled herdsmen have been migrating to the Gulf States in search of wage income. This deprives the herding group of skilled labor (although in return they receive a certain amount of remitted cash). Second, there has been an increasing commercialization of herding for the Gulf market, as discussed earlier. This has encouraged overstocking and damage to pasture in some areas and has also altered the composition of herds. Third, and probably most important, conflict between Somalia and Ethiopia has reduced the range of seasonal movements of Somali nomads. Clearly, thirty years ago there was much freer movement across international frontiers, especially across the vast Somali Plateau that lies between the northern Somali mountains and the highlands of southeast Ethiopia.[113]

Whereas the livestock economy is very old and in many ways aware of and well adapted to the physical extremes of climate it must face, ocean fishing is relatively new on any scale at all. Especially because it is dominated by many very small boats, the fishing fleet is highly vulnerable to storms. Lacking a long tradition of navigation and risk management, and working from a coast with almost no natural shelter, marine-based livelihoods face many hazards. Improvements could be made through training courses, the establishment of early warning systems, and coastal shelters. Possibly, in the long run, a shift toward larger boats that can be equipped with navigational equipment and radios for receiving storm warnings will be feasible.

Earthquakes are not presently predictable; however, building designs and construction techniques have been developed to greatly reduce the possible loss of life and property. The same applies to damage from the high winds of cyclones. A survey of the buildings of Hargeisa should be conducted to assess the vulnerability to seismic stress. Such lifeline structures as schools, hospitals and health centers, fire stations, water and sewage treatment plants, police stations, and communication centers should be structurally strengthened as a high priority. The locations of these buildings and facilities should also be considered. Steep, unstable slopes can collapse in an earthquake. As a result of such a survey, some buildings may have to be relocated.

Overgrazing and cutting of coastal vegetation (such as mangroves) for building material or charcoal both contribute to conditions favoring the erosion of beaches and inland movement of sand dunes. Such conditions also allow much more severe storm damage. As mentioned above, a major dune stabilization program was carried out in the 1980s, especially in the South between Mogadishu and Kismayu. This will need to be revived and extended.

Conclusions

The preceding section has discussed priority areas of action by a new Somali government. From the earlier discussion, we can surmise that the actions of the previous governments and donors have had mixed results. In the process of sifting out the positive from the negative and charting a new course, the fundamental issue will not be *what* to do (i.e., the technical problems and opportunities), but *how* to do it. A command approach that dictates programs from the top down will not achieve much, no matter how well supported it is by scientific data. The positive experiences in Africa to date—and there are positive experiences, although they are often overlooked—

suggest that a participatory approach is more effective.[114] Further-more, the Somali people have a long tradition of consultation, debate, and consensual decisionmaking, especially during times of stress.

The Imperative for Participatory Planning

The subtitle of this chapter held out the promise that one could live *with* the Somali environment, as well as live *well*. The discussion of the Somali environment has revealed several important facts. First, the natural environment is diverse and not as austere and harsh as stereotypes suggest; there is rich arable land, water for irrigation and hydroelectric power, woodland with valuable products and renewable biomass, productive pastures, and underused fisheries. Second, the Somali and non-Somali citizens of the territory have developed skills and knowledge of their environment over generations. Third, previous approaches to development and the environment in Somalia have not respected the knowledge of the people. They have tended to be top-down, command approaches based on large-scale transfers of population, often into large-scale engineering or occupations and places that were alien to the people.

An alternative strategy must be based on the desires of the people affected, and the goal should be the satisfaction of human needs. Living *well* with the Somali land means satisfying human needs first. The strategy is to reinhabit and rehabilitate places (i.e., homes, life spaces) and eventually to connect them in mutually supporting networks. *Development* takes on the aspect of *nurturance*, of both human potentials and the potentials of microenvironments. This approach stands in stark contrast to the approaches of developing the forces of production or exploiting natural resources. In the conventional practices, human beings are seen as *outside* of nature, as manipulating and working on nature. Instead, they should be seen as *internal* to the process of nuturance and "living with."

The International Context

A participatory approach to Somalia's environmental problems and opportunities will touch on international relations in two ways. First, a strong position will need to be taken with donors, international experts, and the World Bank. There will be pressure to continue with "business as usual" and "comparative advantage." Attempts to readjust emphasis from cattle to camels or to try smaller-scale irrigation and hydropower approaches will be met with objections.

The second international context is relations with regional neighbors. There are several regional groupings: nations of the western Indian Ocean; a preferential tariff association (PTA) that involves a large number of Indian Ocean and East African nations; a regional group sponsored by the World Meteorological Organization for early warning of cyclones; and the Inter-Governmental Agency for Drought and Development (IGADD), which involves Somalia, Ethiopia, Djibouti, Sudan, and Kenya.[115]

IGADD could be a very important vehicle for common efforts on food security—early warning systems for famine and pests (e.g., locusts), coordinated management of international rivers, the sharing of research results on drought-resistant plants, pasture improvement, etc.

Famous in antiquity as the Land of Punt, source of frankincense and myrrh, Somalia could again become famous for its efforts at national reconstruction based on radical participation and commitment to sustainable development focused on human needs. Leafing through a beautiful volume of photos of Somalia[116]—its people at work making pots, fishing, and plowing; its houses; its musical instruments, the old sketch of the bend in the Shabelle at Afgoi juxtaposed with a recent photograph—one is filled with sadness for what has been destroyed and for the suffering that has occurred. Yet, one also becomes aware of the rich cultural heritage and antiquity of these people. Ironically, despite or even because of this terrible period of violence, Somalia may achieve sustainable development before the West does.

Notes

1. Davidson, "Somalia in 1975"; A. I. Samatar, *Socialist Somalia: Rhetoric and Reality*; Swift, "Pastoral Development in Somalia"; Cahill, *Somalia: A Perspective*.

2. For more on well-established Somali ways of coping with drought, see I. M. Lewis, *A Pastoral Democracy*; Swift, "Pastoral Development in Somalia"; and Cassanelli, *The Shaping of Somali Society*, pp. 60–65.

3. Melander, *Refugees in Somalia*; Lewis and Wisner, "Refugee Rehabilitation in Somalia."

4. World Commission on Environment and Development, *Food 2000*, p. 3.

5. There is a rapidly growing literature that questions orthodox development economics from the point of view of sustainability. It is vital that Somalis involved in the reconstruction of their country consider these arguments and not allow themselves to be driven by perceived urgency into the arms of conventional solutions that, in the long run, will simply reproduce

the conditions that led to ecological collapse. See Ekins and Max-Neef, *Real-Life Economics*; Adams, *Green Development*; Pearce and Turner, *Economics of Natural Resources*; Costanza, *Ecological Economics*; Pearce et al., *Sustainable Development*.

6. Mudimbe, *The Invention of Africa*; Gyerye, *An Essay*; Verhelst, *No Life Without Roots*; Wisner, "Teaching African Science."

7. Prothero, *People and Land in Africa*.

8. For more on livelihood systems, see Chambers, *Rural Development*, and also World Commission on Environment and Development, *Food 2000*. For more on the life space, see Richards, "'Alternative' Strategies for the African Environment."

9. The connection between rural and urban in Africa has seldom been given proper weight. See Guyer, *Feeding African Cities*; Southall, *Small Urban Centres*.

10. Rirash, "Camel Herding," pp. 53–66.

11. Sen and Grown, *Development, Crises, and Alternative Visions*; Trenchard, "Rural Women's Work."

12. Rogers, *The Domestication of Woman*.

13. For more on gender relations in Somali society, see Chapter 8 in this volume.

14. Harrison, *The Greening of Africa*; Timberlake, *Africa in Crisis*; Grainger, *The Threatening Desert*; Independent Commission on International Humanitarian Issues, *The Encroaching Desert*.

15. Independent Commission on International Humanitarian Issues, *The Encroaching Desert*.

16. Ibid., pp. 15–17.

17. Horowitz and Little, "African Pastoralism and Poverty"; Sörbö, *Tenants and Nomads in Eastern Sudan*; Horowitz and Salem-Murdock, "The Political Economy of Desertification."

18. Swift, "Why Are Rural People Vulnerable to Famine?"; Awogbade and Hassan, "Settlement Scheme"; Rigby, *Persistent Pastoralists*; Galaty, Aronson, and Salzman, *The Future of Pastoral Peoples*; Parkipuny, "Some Crucial Aspects of the Maasai Predicament"; Hedlund, "Contradictions. "

19. Mustafa, "An Appeal for a Modified Camel Productivity."

20. This is not to imply that such fishing schemes have been problem-free. See Brock-Due, "From Herds to Fish."

21. Wisner, "An Example of Drought-Induced Settlement."

22. Wisner, *The Human Ecology of Drought*; Wisner, "Nutritional Consequences"; Wisner and Mbithi, "Drought in Eastern Kenya."

23. Watts, *Silent Violence*; Mortimore, *Adapting to Drought*.

24. de Waal, *Famine that Kills*.

25. Meillassoux, *Qui se nourrit de la famine en Afrique?*; Copans, "The Sahelian Drought"; Franke and Chasin, *Seeds of Famine*; Bondestam, "People and Capitalism"; Kloos, "Development, Drought, and Famine"; A. Hussein, "The Political Economy of Famine in Ethiopia."

26. Cliffe and Moorsom, "Rural Class Formation."

27. Cassanelli, *The Shaping of Somali Society*, p. 9.

28. I. Kaplan, "The Society and Its Environment," p. 71.

29. Kaplan et al., *Area Handbook for Somalia*, pp. 241–242.

30. Cassanelli, *The Shaping of Somali Society*, p. 52.

31. A. Samatar, *The State and Rural Transformation*, pp. 15–16.

32. I. Kaplan, "The Society and Its Environment," p. 69.

33. Beyer, "Africa"; Pacey with Cullis, *Rainwater Harvesting*; Reij, "Indigenous Soil and Water Conservation in Africa."

34. Reij, "Indigenous Soil and Water Conservation in Africa," pp. 25–27.

35. Falenmark, "New Ecological Approach to the Water Cycle."

36. I am grateful to M. Rashid Hassan for emphasizing the potential importance of river fishing during discussions concerning the background paper for this volume.

37. Finn, "Land Use and Abuse."

38. International Labour Office, *Economic Transformation in a Socialist Framework*, p. 262.

39. Whitaker, "The Economy," p. 148. As Dr. Abdi Samatar pointed out while discussing the background paper for this volume, extreme care should be used when quantitative estimates of land use are used. Such economic processes as the growth and collapse of the Middle Eastern livestock market in the 1970s and 1980s may have changed the percentage of land utilized, and certainly the years of civil disturbance must have had a profound effect. New studies are therefore needed.

40. At one point in the mid-to-late 1970s, possibly half of these small family farmers had access to tractor services. This is likely to be one of the government services that would have to be rebuilt. See International Labour Office, *Economic Transformation in a Socialist Framework*, p. 55.

41. Lewis and Wisner, "Refugee Rehabilitation in Somalia," p. 17.

42. Whitaker, "The Economy," p. 148; A. Samatar, *The State and Rural Transformation*, p. 14.

43. Finn, "Land Use and Abuse in the East African Region," pp. 296–301.

44. Lewis and Wisner, "Refugee Rehabilitation in Somalia," p. 18.

45. Farzin, "Food Aid."

46. International Labour Office, *Economic Transformation in a Socialist Framework*, p. 55.

47. A. Samatar, *The State and Rural Transformation*, p. 135.

48. Lewis and Wisner, "Refugee Rehabilitation."

49. National Research Council, *Food Production Systems*.

50. McCarthy, "A Soil and Water Conservation Project."

51. Whitaker, "The Economy," pp. 141–148.

52. Ibid., p. 144.

53. Ibid., pp. 141–142.

54. Simpson and Evangelon, *Livestock Development in Sub-Saharan Africa*; Toulmin, "Economic Behaviour Among Livestock-Keeping Peoples"; Dahl and Hjort, *Having Herds*; Monod, *Pastoralism in Tropical Africa*.

55. A. Samatar, *The State and Rural Transformation*; I. M. Lewis, *A Pastoral Democracy*.

56. Reusse, "Somalia's Nomadic Livestock Economy."

57. International Labour Office, *Economic Transformation in a Socialist Framework*, pp. 291–293.

58. Monod, *Pastoralism in Tropical Africa*; Little and Horowitz, *Lands at Risk in the Third World*.

59. Blaikie and Brookfield, "The Degradation of Common Property Resources," pp. 186–196.

60. I. Kaplan et al., *Area Handbook for Somalia*, p. 247.

61. International Institute for Environment and Development/Overseas Development Institute, "Rethinking Range Ecology."

62. International Labour Office, *Economic Transformation in a Socialist Framework*, p. 79.

63. For example, see Yasin and Holt, "Increasing Fodder Production"; Thurow and Hussein, "Observations on Vegetation Responses" deGroot, Field-Juma, and Hall, *Taking Root*.

64. Swift, "Pastoral Development in Somalia."

65. I am grateful to Dr. Mohamed A. H. Ibrahim, president of the Ecological Association of Somalia, for drawing my attention to these two last points in discussion of my conference paper. For more on relations among pastoralists and farmers, see Cassanelli, *The Shaping of Somali Society*; Unruh, "Integration of Transhumant Pastoralism and "Nomadic Pastoralism."

66. Hjort af Ornäs, *Camels in Development*; Wilson, *The Camel*.

67. "Although the camel is a hard and tough beast . . . there are a few important known diseases affecting camels in particular, e.g., Surra or Camel trypanosomiasis, Camel pox, Sarcoptic mange, gastrointestinal diseases caused by helminths like the gutworm Haemomchus spp. or bacteria like Salmonella spp., Clostridium spp. There are also respiratory diseases caused by viruses and bacteria like haemorrhagic sepoticaemia" (Bornstein, "The Case of African Drylands and Balanced Camel Production," p. 101).

68. Mariam, writing of the southern Bale province of Ethiopia, where Somalis also live, lists 29 dry-season species of shrubs and bushes that are eaten by camels as forage, 19 species eaten during the main wet season, and 19 eaten as emergency fodder during droughts ("Pastoral Systems at Loggerheads," p. 44).

69. Bornstein, "The Case of African Drylands and Balanced Camel Production," p. 100; Evans and Powys, "Camel Husbandry in Kenya."

70. Hussein and Hjort af Ornäs, "Camel Herd Dynamics"; Dahl and Hjort af Ornäs, *Having Herds*. For subsistence calculations, a "reference family" was used: a father around 30 years old, a pregnant mother of 25, two children of 3 and 8, and one girl of 15 and one boy of 18 attached to the household. They would need a total of 318 grams of protein and 13,800 kilogram calories of energy per day.

71. Hussein and Hjort af Ornäs, "Camel Herd Dynamics," p. 110.

72. Rirash, "Camel Herding," pp. 64–65.

73. Storäs, "Does 'Development' Always Imply Progress?" p. 70.

74. Rutagwenda, "The State of Knowledge on Camel Diseases"; Dirie, Wallbanks, Molyneux, Bornstein, and Omer, "Haemorrhagic syndrome associated with T. vivax infections of cattle in Somalia."

75. Personal communication from Dr. Mohamed A. H. Ibrahim during the conference.

76. United Nations, Food and Agriculture Organization, *Joint Meeting of the FAO Panels*; Jerve, "Livestock Trypanosomiasis and the Pastoral Crisis in Semi-arid Africa"; Dirie, Wallbanks, Aden, Bornstein, and Ibrahim, "Camel Trypanosomiasis and Its Vectors in Somalia"; Dirie, Wardhere, and Farah, "Sheep Trypanosomiasis in Somalia."

77. Personal communication from Dr. Mohamed A. H. Ibrahim during discussion of my conference paper.

78. According to Dr. Mohamed A. H. Ibrahim, in discussions at the conference, the government had identified in the 1980s a dozen areas to be developed as wildlife conservation areas, but had not actually conducted the development. He fears that all but two or three of these areas have now been depleted by the hunting activities of armed gangs.

79. Much of this subsection is based on Whitaker, "The Economy," pp. 156–157; I. Kaplan, "The Society and Its Environment," p. 74.

80. Thanks to Mohamed Abdillahi Rirash for emphasizing the importance of wild human foods during discussion of my conference paper. A high priority should be given to identifying these foods before their use is forgotten by the present generation, especially given the great geographical and social disruption suffered during these years of crisis.

81. For instance, see International Fund for Science, *Trees for Development in Sub-Saharan Africa*; Rocheleau, Weber, and A. Field-Juma, *Agroforestry in Dryland Africa*.

82. Drechsel and Zech, "Site Conditions"; Drechsel, Zech, Kaupenjohann, Nurr, and Klein, "About the Ecology"; Zohar and Lovenstein, "Food, Fodder and Firewood."

83. Wieland, "Native Legumes."

84. Michelsen and Rosendahl, "Mycorrhizal Symbiosis."

85. Niamir, "Traditional Woodland Management Techniques"; Shepherd, "The Communal Management."

86. Dhanani, "Forestry and Range."

87. The major source for this section is Munslow, O'Keefe, Pankhurst, and Philips, "Energy and Development."

88. I. Kaplan et al., *Area Handbook for Somalia*, p. 51.

89. Finn, "Land Use and Abuse," p. 296.

90. Kundaeli, "Making Conservation and Development Compatible."

91. Munslow, O'Keefe, Pankhurst, and Philips, "Energy and Development," p. 336.

92. Mohamed, "Etude Géologique."

93. Kundaeli, "Making Conservation and Development Compatible," p. 328.

94. Whitaker, "The Economy," p. 156.

95. This point was raised at the conference by M. Y. Abshir, who stated that the lights of the large fishing boats could be seen nightly from Djibouti and northern Somalia. Others at the meeting believed that illegal fishing was taking place and agreed to include a denunciation of the practice in the conference recommendations.

96. Bliss-Guest, "Environmental Stress."

97. Kundaeli, "Making Conservation and Development Compatible," p. 327.

98. As with the issue of "overgrazing," it is an unanswered question just how "stable" these sand dunes were and for how long. Climate changes may also have had a role in reactivating the dunes. There may also have been several prior cycles of movement and stability.

99. Many *Acacia nilotica* trees were cut during the mid-1970s, when the government relaxed a ban on the international export of charcoal that had been in place since 1969. This pressure on vegetation was added to increasing urban fuel demands. (These comments were made by Mohamed A. H. Ibrahim in a discussion of my conference paper.)

100. Finn, "Land Use and Abuse," p. 297.

101. Ferrari, "Oil on Troubled Waters."

102. For more on the lives of the poor in Third World cities, see Hardoy and Satterthwaite, *Squatter Citizen*; Hardoy, Cairncross, and Satterthwaite, *The Poor Die Young*.

103. Prothero, *Migrants and Malaria*.

104. Ferguson and Leeuwenburg, "Local Mobility."

105. Stock, *Cholera in Africa*.

106. Roundy, "Altitudinal Mobility."

107. O'Keefe, "Toxic Terrorism"; Center for Investigative Reporting and Moyers, *Global Dumping Ground*.

108. Tolba, "Disposal of Hazardous Wastes in Somalia."

109. World Bank, *World Development Report*, pp. 284–285.

110. Packard, "Industrial Production."

111. For example, slaughterhouses located on the coast at Merca and Mogadishu discharge their waste directly into the sea. This is typical of the situations that the new government will have to face. What are the ecological and health consequences of this disposal? What should it cost to change it? Who should decide? (Bliss-Guest, "Environmental Stress").

112. Personal communication with Mohamed A. H. Ibrahim, president of the Somali Ecological Association, in discussion of my conference paper.

113. Prothero, *Migrants and Malaria*, p. 69; I. Kaplan, "The Society and Its Environment," p. 71. Colonial records show that a British officer remained in the nominally Italian portion of the haud to look after the interests of "British" Somali who moved in and out seasonally. See Rinehart, "Historical Setting."

114. Harrison, *The Greening of Africa*; Wisner, *Power and Need in Africa*; Pradervand, *Listening to Africa*; Cheru, *The Silent Revolution in Africa*; Rau, *From Feast to Famine*.

115. One assumes that newly independent Eritrea will soon join.

116. Loughran, et al., *Somalia in Word and Image*.

4

Empty Bowl: Agrarian Political Economy in Transition and the Crises of Accumulation

Abdi I. Samatar

The desolation of Somalia has ushered in a new form of crisis. By *crisis*, I refer to a condition in which existing structures cannot sustain themselves along established norms. Thus, such systems either move toward stasis, involution, and possibly extinction, or they go through profound metamorphoses that imbue them with a novel and greater vibrancy to sustain development.[1] In times of this kind, scholars can make a contribution by going beyond conventional assumptions to envision deep structural change and long-range reconstruction. The Somali case suggests that momentary victories (e.g., the defeat of the Barre regime) do not ensure real amelioration of great social predicaments.

The unnecessary death of hundreds of thousands of Somalis since the end of Barre's dictatorship and the famine that afflicted many parts of the country indicate the passing of a particular period in Somali history. Transition from one era to another is neither smooth nor automatic and can lead to a dangerous dead end. Events of the last two and a half years represent sharp warnings that the Somali people are indeed racing toward such a blind alley; and the common and fatalistic Somali utterance *"Wuxuun ba dici- doona"* (Something positive will somehow happen), which was the byword of both the elite and the commoners in the final days of the old regime, now sounds inane and meaningless.

Contrary to the popular interpretation of the calamity as the will of Allah, this situation was not inevitable and could have been staved off had the leaders of the dominant strata heeded the warnings of critics about the consequences of privatizing public resources and underinvesting in productive sectors.[2] The astounding slide toward destruction was made partly unavoidable by the pursuit of individualized self-interest on the part of the elite, without much regard for the reproduction of conditions necessary for the preservation of the social system. In the face of such circumstances, systematic accumulation is just not possible.

The collapse of political institutions in Somalia marks the close of a historical period and acts as a warning against attempts to resuscitate the past.[3] If Somalis are to avoid further protraction of prevailing debilities and greater loss of life and property, they must clearly understand where they have come from and the dynamics of the present. A fundamental part of this history is the disarticulated structure of the economy.[4] The Somali economy had four principal attributes. First, its organization perpetuated a mismatch between the basic needs of the people and an external orientation of the productive structure. Second, it relied on conditioned foreign loans and grants as the sole source for investment and development, which reinforced the economic status quo. Third, very few public resources were directed to improving and expanding agricultural production. Fourth, the state, unsteadily controlled by factions of the elite, dominated the distribution of foreign aid. The centralization of investment in the hands of the governing clique led to misappropriation and misuse of resources and political instability. These features of the old social system must not be a part of any program of resurrection.

The disintegration of sociopolitical order and the depressing plight of millions of ordinary people in Somalia were preceded by a long period in which socioeconomic conditions markedly and progressively became worse. A pivotal element in the evolution of the present situation was the conflict between competing factions of the elite over the control and use of the meager resources of the country.[5] This struggle starved the productive sector of the economy, which in turn intensified social cleavages and communal strife. The crisis of the Somali economy, then, resulted from a process of underaccumulation of capital, which led to the dire situation faced by most Somalis. It is generally assumed that all sectors of the economy suffer from the same maladies and, therefore, that the country is in *a* crisis. Such a monolithic conception of the problem often leads to a simplistic and generalized prescription for what is, in actuality, a multitude of crises.[6] There can be many types of crises (e.g, specific to an industry, a sector, or a region) that coexist.

As the overview of this book and subsequent chapters elucidate, Somalia faced many difficulties long before the fall of the old regime. The first two major sections of this chapter investigate different manifestations of the issue of capital underaccumulation in two components of the Somali agrarian economy: the pastoral/livestock sector and the farming sector (i.e., export agriculture and grain/domestic production). This focus is warranted because of the absence of a vibrant industrial economy and the fact that agriculture is the only productive area that holds a promise of growth and development in the immediate future—that is, in terms of contributing to accumulation while providing for the basic needs of a significant portion of the population. Moreover, nearly half of the Somali population make their living in agriculture and therefore constitute a viable base on which to build.

Although this chapter examines crop and livestock production, it does not negate the value of other sectors.[7] It is important to note here that reports are coming in that underscore excessive and illegal fishing along the Somali coast by ships from Taiwan, Russia, Japan, Italy, etc. This is certain to endanger the health of marine life as well as accelerate Somali impoverishment.[8] Furthermore, any long-term development strategy must include a program of industrialization, without which sustained improvements in the standard of living are impossible. The third section of this chapter comments on the diversity of the predicament of the agrarian economy, and the conclusion is a brief personal statement on some of the challenges ahead.

The Crisis of Pastoralism and the Livestock Economy[9]

Livestock production has been the dominant part of the Somali economy in terms of employment and foreign exchange earnings since the early 1960s. The health and vitality of the national economy was always contingent on the performance of this sector and will continue to be so in the near future, albeit at a reduced level. Consequently, a coherent understanding of the problems faced by the pastoral/livestock sector is essential for any attempt at reconstruction. To fully appreciate the dire condition of this crucial element, we need to broaden our conceptual horizon in assessing the dynamics and the nature of the pastoral system.

Background

The term *pastoralism* is employed by most contemporary social analysts to characterize those individuals and communities who make a living by raising livestock in semiarid regions. *Nomadism* is also

used in similar fashion.[10] This is historically and analytically impre-
cise, and most of the scanty literature on the subject is either ill-
informed, outdated, or both. Pastoralism is a means of livestock
production employed under a variety of social and historical conditions. The method or the tools of production do not define the nature of a social system; e.g., capitalism is not defined by the instruments or the method used by producers, but rather by the social
relations into which various groups enter in order to produce values and reproduce the existing social order. Consequently, pastoralism can exist under several different social and economic systems. For example, the communitarian pastoralism in precolonial
Somalia was a social order in which the production of use values
predominated. In contrast, contemporary Somali pastoralism is
dominated by a commercial system and the production of exchange
values. The commercial system that prevails in the country can be
thought of as peripheral capitalism. Thus, pastoral production has
become central to the reproduction of a larger social constellation,
dominated by the state and merchants, of which the producers are
a part.

Precolonial Somali society was stateless in character. In this society, all adult members were engaged in production. Somali pastoralism was fundamentally communitarian in that it lacked an institutionalized social and economic hierarchy. This interpretation of
Somali social history does not deny the existence of some communities (e.g., the riverine areas of the South) whose local social relations were at variance with the dominant system. Nevertheless, the
principal mode of production, communitarian pastoralism, lacked
the institutionalized forms of oppression associated with class societies. However, as Somali society became an integral part of the
global capitalist system, the forces of the world-system had a conditioning effect upon it.

The transition from one social system to another entails the
transformation of previous social and property relations. The emerging social system bears the imprint of the new age, although it re-
tains aspects of the old regime. Contemporary Somali social structure displays the emblem of capitalist transition, clearly heralding
the passing of a way of life. Communitarian pastoralism, through
production and consumption of use values, sustained the producers,
whereas contemporary pastoral production supports two additional
and dominant social groups: merchants and the state.

Precolonial pastoral Somalia was not isolated from the mercan-
tile world.[11] However, the external world and the logic of mercan-
tilism had only a marginal influence over the reproduction of every-

day life. It was only after livestock became the chief object of trade that the present social relations emerged. The constitution of pastoralist/merchant/state relations over the last century entailed the emergence of social classes and the gradual eclipse of communitarian pastoralism. I will use this broad conceptual framework to outline the genesis and nature of the pastoral crisis.

The slow but steady decomposition of communitarian Somali tradition began in the nineteenth century with the imposition of colonial rule and the gradual "commodification" of livestock (i.e., the shift toward viewing livestock as a commodity). The development of livestock trade since the last decade of the nineteenth century laid the foundation for the colonial and postcolonial economy. Among the earliest and most visible changes was the emergence of pastoralist/merchant relationships based on livestock trade. The general history and organization of this trade have been dealt with elsewhere.[12] Merchants have not been the only group that siphoned resources from pastoralists. The (colonial) state did so as well. Somali pastoralists have produced surpluses that have been captured by the state since the society first became a colony in the 1880s. In more recent years, livestock exports have been the single most important hard-currency earner, accounting for nearly 80–90 percent of the total annual foreign exchange earnings (until this trade was disrupted by the civil war in the North in 1988).

The development of merchant/pastoralist/state relationships in Somali society over the last century marks a sharp break with precolonial tradition and indicates the passing of a distinct period in Somali social and economic history. The relationships sketched above constitute the domestic matrix that shapes the configuration of changes taking place in the pastoral areas. Moreover, the existence of such a relationship between merchants and the state, on one hand, and producers, on the other, has had deleterious effects on pastoral development. Consequently, a key element in the contemporary trauma of Somali pastoralism is its declining capacity to sustain the intensifying reproduction requirements of the producers, the merchants and the state class.

In the highly commercialized context of Somali pastoralism, little is known about the degree of internal differentiation among pastoralists. However, property relations in the rangeland have not been formally restructured, and the process of privatizing community resources is not as advanced as in Botswana.[13] In the absence of direct appropriation of Somali rangeland by nonpastoral producers, most students of Somali society continue to assume the vitality of a precapitalist social system. In view of this, the pastoral/merchant/

state relationship first established during the colonial era seems stable and often problem-free to most Somalists.[14] Their argument is that pastoralists, by selling their livestock, earn a return sufficient to enable them to purchase basic foods and other goods, while merchants make profits sufficient to sustain themselves, and the state collects taxes and gains precious foreign exchange.[15]

The production of an indigenous food commodity by pastoralists and its subsequent export appeared to satisfy three often contradictory objectives of development in Africa: the need to earn foreign exchange, the need to increase or maintain domestic food production, and the desire for a wider distribution of income. This view of Somali society, premised on pastoral democratic notions as originally enunciated by I. M. Lewis in 1962, and subsequently perpetuated by Somalist scholarship, conceals the qualitative transformation of social relations described earlier. More significantly, such a conception fails to grasp the problem of reproduction in the emergent social formation, to which I now turn.

Transformation and Conjuncture

Most of the scholarly literature on Somali development seldom addresses directly the reproduction of the pastoral/merchant/state relationship. The only exceptions are certain works by Jeremy Swift and Dan Aronson.[16] Swift was the first researcher to point to the deterioration of pastoral barter terms of trade since the turn of the century. He noted that the commercialization of pastoral life brought about the decomposition of traditional Somali social relations. The disintegration of the precapitalist Somali pastoral system under the tutelage of commercial capital led to ecological degradation and increased pastoral vulnerability to the fluctuations of the semiarid climatic regime. Aronson extended this analysis by indicating that Somali pastoralists are caught in an exploitative trap engineered by the state elite and the merchants.

Swift and Aronson's studies are significant contributions because they call for a new direction for Somali (pastoral) development research. These studies, however, suffer from one major weakness: written at a time when livestock prices were very high and the merchants and state elite were enjoying tremendous windfalls, they overlooked the structural weakness of the system. In other words, although both were sympathetic to the position of the pastoralists and their future, neither author saw the structure of exploitation and the struggle over its reproduction as problematic.

In the 1950s and 1960s, Somali livestock export earnings were enhanced by the simultaneous development of oil resources in Saudi Arabia and the significant increase in the number of livestock-sacrificing pilgrims to the Islamic holy land.[17] The oil price shocks of the early 1970s and the resultant phenomenal growth of petrodollars in Saudi Arabia led to a construction boom. Consequently, shortages of both skilled and unskilled labor in Saudi Arabia necessitated the importation of thousands of workers from the Middle East and Northeast Africa, which in turn led to increased demand for food imports, particularly meat. The growth in the demand for meat and the global inflationary pressures of the period drove up livestock prices enormously. Somalia, which accounted for nearly 90 percent of Saudi livestock imports, reaped fantastic windfalls for the whole decade.[18] For example, the prices of sheep/goats, cattle, and camels increased between 1960 and 1978 from about $8, $30, and $40 to $44, $195, and $278 per head, respectively. Such increases in livestock prices far outstripped the domestic inflation rates of the period.

The 1980s were not as kind to Somali livestock export trade as the 1970s. Subsequently, the internationalization of the Saudi market in the 1980s triggered a tremendous increase in the supply of livestock with the consequent downward pressure on prices. The sudden decline in oil prices in the mid-1980s and the resultant financial difficulties in Saudi Arabia generated domestic economic pressures. In the end, the globalization of the livestock trade in the Middle East and a growing competition in the industry, as well as the ambivalence of the Somali government about losing its share of the reduced market in the oil kingdom, led to a substantial reduction of Somali livestock prices in January 1985 (see Table 4.1).

The decline in livestock prices, coupled with the long-term stagnation in the quantity of animals exported (livestock exports peaked in 1972), presented a grave threat to the continuation of the established social relations between pastoralists, merchants, and the state. This threat came in the form of declining terms of trade for producers, declining profits for the merchants, and reduced foreign exchange earnings for the state. For the pastoralists, the threat induced by the price squeeze might have meant a reduction in their basic level of subsistence. In the past, they were able to mitigate such pressures by increasing their livestock holdings and exploiting more marginal areas. However, this time-tested strategy is no longer effective because virtually all the marginal land exploitable under current methods of production has been put to use.

Table 4.1   Official Livestock Prices (in $/head)[a]

	Before January 1984	After January 1985	Percent change in price
Sheep	53	42	-20.76
Cattle	280	213	-23.93
Camels[b]	450	390	-13.13

Source: A. Samatar, "Social Classes," p. 112.
Notes: a. Export prices fluctuated but were consistently higher in years prior to 1985.
b. Although there has not been an increase in the downward pressure on camel export prices, camel prices declined because of the generalized price reduction policy of the regime. Such losses were unnecessary.

A common but unexamined belief among many Somalists is that pastoralists, whose superior skills have been honed by centuries of experience, are the most appropriate custodians of the pastoral range.[19] This contention notwithstanding, the lore and appropriate skills of the pastoralist, which made the semiarid region productive and profitable, have progressively been undermined by the scarcity of accessible rangeland and an ecological deterioration induced by the commodification of pastoralism under a peripheral capitalist regime.[20] The ecological ruin of the Somali range is rendering precapitalist pastoral knowledge and management systems defunct or incapable of sustaining this form of commercial pastoral production. In this sense, the prevailing situation of the Somali social formation echoes the condition of the rural economy in Botswana in the early 1970s:

> By the early 1970s the situation in the rural areas was nearly chaotic, yielding the possibility of a long-term damage to the environment and apparently providing absolute limits to the further development of capitalist cattle production. The conditions for the expansion of that production in the 1960s became its fetters in the 1970s.[21]

The stagnation of livestock exports, a diminishing capacity of the rangelands, downward pressures on livestock prices, and skyrocketing domestic inflation finally exposed the exploitative and unproductive relations between the claimant classes and rural producers. The pressure of price and the profit squeeze on the system can possibly be treated in the short run by simply redistributing the losses. However, in the long run, reproduction of these relations will require a significant restructuring of the system.

How did the price squeeze affect livestock exporters? Although merchants constitute a class as defined by their relations to the producers, they are by no means a monolithic group. For example, the 923 livestock exporters based in the hinterland of Berbera from 1981–1986 can be differentiated into three strata on the basis of the number of animals they exported and the profits they obtained during that period. The distribution of livestock exports among the merchants over this period indicates a process of social differentiation wherein this class is segmented into poor, middle, and rich merchants. The three groups are those who exported from 0–9,999, 10,000–49,000, and 50,000–149,000 animals, respectively. The first category consists mainly of those whose operations were barely sufficient to satisfy their requirements for basic subsistence. The median sale of these merchants was about 580 animals annually, with a corresponding profit of $1,740 (the minimum net profit per sheep or goat was $3). The median export for the middle group was 4,500 animals annually, with a profit of $12,600. By contrast, the median sale of the rich strata was 12,500 animals annually, with a profit of $37,500. About 85 percent of the merchant population fell into the indigent camp, and 12 percent and 3 percent belong to the middle and rich strata, respectively. This means that the top 15 percent of the merchant class accounted for about 70 percent of the sales and, hence, for the industry's profits.

It seems that, based on the above distribution of sales and profits, the three strata of merchants have contrasting reproduction requirements in spite of their common class base. In other words, the priority of the poor group in the current circumstances is simply to survive as merchants; they have little prospect of enhancing their location in the hierarchy. It is important to note here a common assumption in Somalia: that most livestock merchants are in the profitable import trade and consequently have large real estate investments. Such a perception is contradicted by the results of field research. Of the seventy indigent merchants interviewed, only two had real estate properties, and none were involved in the import trade. In contrast, the decline in export prices has reduced the profit margins of the middle and rich merchants, but it has in no way endangered their immediate status as one of the wealthiest groups in the country. Most of the members of these two groups are heavily involved in the import trade and have relatively extensive real estate properties in major towns and cities. However, over the long haul, a continuing decline in export prices and the long-term stagnation of the number of animals exported boded ill, even prior to the dissolution of social order, for the future of middle and rich merchants. This is because their capacity to import commodities (in the lucrative import trade) has always been contingent on the availability of foreign exchange.

Finally, the Somali state, strapped for foreign exchange, is further impoverished by the combined effect of the drop in export prices and the stagnation of livestock exports. In the absence of other domestic sources of foreign exchange, its reliance on external assistance has been further intensified, deepening the disconnection and alienation between the state and society.

The Crisis in the Farm Sector

The farming economy is the other main productive area of Somalia's national economy. The farm sector consists of the grain-producing and largely peasant-dominated economy and the export-oriented banana plantation enterprises. As with the pastoral sector, which produces livestock for both export and domestic consumption, grain and banana production contribute to the external and internal accounts as well. Unlike livestock, however, national grain production has usually fallen far short of satisfying domestic needs, although the potential for growth, particularly in irrigated areas, holds great promise. Given the potential for growth and contributions to national food self-reliance and possibly exports, any strategy for renewal and development must account for the constraints imposed on the sector by previous programs.

The Grain Sector

Somalia was a grain-deficient country long before the military rule and the disaster of the 1990s. Unlike the civilian regimes that preceded it, the junta proclaimed its commitment to a policy of food sufficiency.[22] Although this new strategy increasingly relied on state farms and agricultural crash programs to produce the bulk of the country's food needs, such projects never yielded more than a fraction of their planned targets. Consequently, the country never produced enough food for itself, and, state neglect notwithstanding, the peasantry remained the principal producers of food grains. State/peasant relations during the 1970s were characterized by (1) an extraction of resources through both price controls and forced produce deliveries (through marketing boards) and (2) absolute neglect in the provision of credit and other necessary agricultural inputs.[23] The net results of this strategy were a decline in crop production and stagnation (see Table 4.2).

Table 4.2   Production of Food and Nonfood Crops, 1970–1986 (in thousands of metric tons)

	Grains, beans, and oil seeds	Sugar, vegetables, and fruits	Total food output	Nonfood crops	Total output	Output index (relative to 1970)
1970	342.2	376.6	718.8	1.3	720.1	100
1971	278.6	375.7	654.3	1.0	655.3	91
1972	323.4	377.3	700.7	1.2	701.9	97
1973	229.3	390.2	619.5	1.1	620.6	86
1974	274.2	379.2	653.4	1.0	654.4	91
1975	294.3	333.4	627.7	1.1	628.8	87
1976	350.7	333.2	683.9	1.2	685.1	95
1977	319.0	320.1	639.1	1.2	640.3	89
1978	313.1	327.8	640.9	1.2	642.1	89
1979	312.3	312.0	624.3	1.5	625.8	87
1980	315.9	316.8	632.7	1.5	634.2	88
1981	449.3	338.0	787.3	1.1	788.4	109
1982	478.1	349.4	827.5	1.8	829.3	115
1983	444.8	364.0	808.8	1.5	810.3	112
1984	563.7	394.4	958.1	1.5	959.6	133
1985	634.0	398.0	1,032.0	.5	1,032.5	143
1986	713.0	365.6	1,078.6	1.5	1,080.1	150

Source: World Bank, Somalia: Agricultural Sector Survey.

Although the sharp declines in grain production from 1970–1980 were in some years certainly due to unfavorable climatic conditions (e.g., the 1973–1974 drought), the principal cause for the decade-long failure to make progress toward national food self-sufficiency was inappropriate agricultural policy. The state-inspired approach during this period reflected the opportunistic and quasi-nationalist predispositions of the governing elite. Without much understanding of the needs of peasant producers and the technical requirements of food production in the peasant environment, the regime imposed a rigid policy that undermined its own objective of food self-reliance. The regime's leaders had two reasons for adopting such a strategy. First, under the tutelage of the Soviets, they believed that controlling the marketing of agricultural produce was "proof" of their socialist orientation.[24] Second, the strategy brought an important sector of the economy under the ambit of the regime and therefore provided an avenue to employ more bureaucrats to make good on the inflated promises made on the morrow of the coup. The consequence of this was an expanding but unproductive bureaucratic class at the cost of robust and thriving rural production.

The introduction of liberal economic reform, a result of the 1981 structural adjustment agreement between the International Monetary Fund (IMF) and the Somali government, eliminated both price controls and mandatory grain deliveries to the state. These reforms, coinciding with favorable rains, reversed the stagnation of the 1970s. However, a critical factor in the resulting increase in grain production was extensive horizontal expansion, rather than an improvement in the productivity (or intensive use) of land.[25] Sorghum and maize cultivation increased from a low 109,000 and 460,000 hectares, respectively, at the end of the 1970s to 259,500 hectares and 516,200 hectares in 1987 (see Table 4.3). Sesame and other beans also showed similar trends. All of the grains in Table 4.3 (except rice), particularly maize and sorghum, are rainfed crops produced by peasants.

Table 4.3   Cropped Areas in Somalia, 1970–1987 (in thousands of hectares)

	Total crop land[a]	Maize	Sorghum	Rice	Wheat	Beans	Groundnuts	Sesame
1970	571	133	290	1.3	0.9	21.9	3.3	73
1971	500.4	102	280	1.4	0.6	17.8	2.6	44
1972	638	117	390	1.2	0.8	20.8	3.3	57
1973	591.8	101	345	1.2	3.5	17.9	2.9	77
1974	580.7	99	330	1.4	3.5	17.6	2.8	84
1975	641.1	106	400	1.6	3.5	18.8	3.3	57
1976	733.5	119	490	1.8	3.5	19.7	3.5	45
1977	764.5	150.6	458.3	4.4	3.5	18.8	2.5	75
1978	730.8	148.7	420.1	9.8	3.5	21.8	1.9	75
1979	765	147.5	460.8	4.8	3.5	16.6	2.4	80
1980	730.8	109	456.8	5.9	3.5	18.5	2.5	83
1981	896	197	517	5.7	3.5	25.9	2.6	90
1982	931.9	209	540	6.0	3.5	27.0	3.0	90
1983	745.5	218.6	335.5	1.0	3.6	27.0	3.0	98.4
1984	964.7	220	544.7	1.3	3.6	38.1	4.7	92
1985	909.1	234.3	447	2.6	3.6	46.8	5.2	109.2
1986	802.7	245.1	385	3.2	0.3	28.9	2.9	81
1987	984.8	259.5	516.2	3.6	0.0	48.3	4.2	104.7

Source: Somali Democratic Republic, Ministry of Agriculture, *Food Early Warning.*
Note: a. Total crop land is greater than the sum of crops listed because not all of the land that could be cultivated is.

Rice production was stable for the first half of the 1970s but grew significantly in the latter half of the decade. However, the area under rice cultivation fell from 6,000 hectares in 1982 to 1,000 hectares in 1983. Its recovery was slow but steady. Before 1983, rice, unlike other grains, was primarily grown on large estates. Located near the towns of Jowhar and Jilib, these estates were managed as parastatals by the Ministry of Agriculture. Although the producer prices for other grains were significantly below the global market price during the periods of price controls, that of rice was almost identical to the world market price.[26] Regardless, farmers were unable to take advantage of the high price for rice because they had to sell their produce to the state marketing board.

The 1980s was a decade of growth in the grain-producing areas of the country (see Table 4.2). There was significant improvement in grain production in both rainfed farming regions and the irrigated areas of the Shabelle and Juba rivers. As noted earlier, this growth was largely a product of horizontal expansion of cultivation and reclamation of farmland abandoned during the era of price controls. In spite of these promising circumstances, these gains were not sustainable because they entailed either (1) bringing more marginal or fragile land into cultivation in rainfed areas or (2) neglecting institutional support for the relatively high-potential irrigated river valleys. As an illustration of the problems of the grain sector, consider irrigated rice production in the Jowhar Valley along the Shabelle as a case in point. The Shabelle River valley around the town of Jowhar is a flat, fertile, alluvial plain. It is less than 500 feet above sea level and about 60 miles northeast in the capital. Average annual rainfall in the valley is about 600 millimeters. The Shabelle River, which meanders through the valley, dries up in most years between the months of January and March. Historically, the valley was home to peasants and pastoralists. However, after the Italian colonization of southern Somalia, it had attracted many investment projects.

The first and the largest investment was a sugar plantation and an associated sugar mill. This plantation/mill complex was established in 1920. Initially owned by Italian colonial interests and later taken over by the Somali government, the enterprise dominated the town of Jowhar and the surrounding area. At the height of its operations in the early 1970s, the complex produced enough refined sugar to meet the country's domestic needs. But it has since declined, from production valued at $50 million in 1970 to $15 million in 1981[27] and to complete collapse in 1988–1989. The demise of the sugar complex devastated the local economy. Mismanagement, the hallmark of the military regime, and the apparent siphoning of enterprise resources for the private use of senior national and regional public officials killed the enterprise, though the demand for sugar was growing. The experience of the sugar industry is a telling example of the ills of public enterprises and the negative consequences for communities all over the country.

Rice production was introduced to the valley in the 1960s. This economic program began in an experiment station five kilometers northeast of Jowhar through a project sponsored by the People's

Republic of China. The purpose was to explore whether Somalia could grow enough rice to meet a significant part of its own increasing demand. At the end of the decade, the experimental phase was completed, and the staff at the station began to encourage its field laborers, most of whom were peasants from the nearest villages, to plant rice on small plots on their land.[28] By the mid-1970s, a small but increasing number were growing rice. The station supported the efforts of these peasants by providing advice on improved cultivation methods and seeds. Before this effort had a chance to blossom, however, the newly established Agricultural Development Corporation, a marketing parastatal, imposed price controls and mandatory deliveries on rice and other crops. This policy effectively stopped the expansion of rice cultivation. Peasants who were already cultivating the crop abandoned it altogether within two years. Between 1974–1975 and 1983, rice was grown only in the experiment station and in state farms elsewhere. The promise of improving food self-sufficiency (particularly in terms of rice) disappeared.

The town of Jowhar and the surrounding villages in the Shabelle Valley were economically devastated from 1974–1984 by the disintegration of the sugar complex and the involution of the rice project. Relaxation of price controls in the early 1980s was a necessary but insufficient condition to rekindle peasant enthusiasm. An initiative of a German private voluntary organization (PVO), Agro-Action, and its offer of material support to two peasant communities were the catalyst that helped rejuvenate rice production in the Jowhar Valley. The experiment station, which was transformed into a moderately successful state-run rice farm, was there to provide the necessary seed, advice, and some other services.[29] The new initiative took off within two years. The growing economic crisis of the country, the increasing prices of food staples, and the liberalization of land tenure laws made rice production the most attractive productive investment for anyone who could muster enough resources to get access to irrigated land. It was not long before many non-peasants (e.g., merchants, bureaucrats) started producing rice. By the winter/spring growing season of 1990, peasant rice producers were outnumbered by urban-based growers.

Initially, most of these new farmers rented or borrowed land from peasants and other owners who had extra acreage. As more people realized the gains to be made, land prices skyrocketed (from about the equivalent of U.S. $25 per hectare per growing season to over U.S. $125 per hectare per season in the fall of 1989). With rent and the price of irrigable land escalating and economic conditions in the country further sliding, a land rush ensued. Much riverine land previously utilized by peasants and pastoralists for grazing and other purposes was carved up by urbanites, many of whom were well connected to the state. For instance, most of the irrigable land along the Shabelle in the Jowhar Valley was expropriated through administrative fiat without attention being paid to those who traditionally used it. Titles to some of this land were then given to the favorite sons and daughters of the regime. By the spring of 1990, urban-based farmers dominated the industry and accounted for most of the rice produced in the area. Of the estimated 1,500 rice growers in the valley, nearly three-fourths were urban. Although no one knew the exact area under rice cultivation in the valley, estimates range from 5,000–6,000 hectares. This growth is substantial, particularly because nonstate rice farming did not exist before 1983.

The preceding discussion of rice production in the Jowhar Valley indicates that the liberal reform program had induced growth in the region. Such growth reflects only one side, albeit the positive one, of the impact that the program had on the agrarian economy. The other area in which the impact of the reform program was felt was agriculture-related public institutions. Here, forces were set in motion that went beyond production and affected the capacity of public institutions. Among the principal aims of the IMF/World Bank–sponsored liberalization program were a contraction of the state as a source of employment and a deregulation of the economy in order to reduce bureaucratic red tape, economic mismanagement, and resource misuse.

The greatest changes in the public sector induced by the reform program were not the employment reductions in that sector or the degree of state intervention in the economy, but rather a subversion of the ethic of public service and an elevation of greed to new heights. Moreover, a loss of income brought about by new levels of inflation, combined with the liberalization of prices, severely eroded public employees' incomes and ultimately led to the decay of public service. As the reform program unfolded and the monetarist strategy took hold, inflation rose dramatically. This drove the private sector to adjust its operations by increasing prices and wages at a comparable rate. In contrast, the state failed to do the same, thereby allowing public employees' wages to decline precipitously. Thus, the new "prosperity" in the private sector made the incomes of public employees, including senior ones, seem paltry. In essence, public employees were expected to facilitate the accumulation of private wealth without directly and immediately benefiting from it. As a result, public servants ruthlessly began to exploit their offices for their own gain. Such ethics brought ruin to the state's capacity to manage public property and undermined agricultural development, as the following case demonstrates.

The Agricultural Extension and Farm Management Training project (AEFMET) was planned and designed to overcome the managerial and technical inadequacy of the Ministry of Agriculture.[30] The project was funded by World Bank loans from its inception in the late 1970s until the disintegration of the regime in January 1991. Despite the initial intentions of its designers, AEFMET was appropriated by the rentier structure.

The project's principal mission was to improve agricultural productivity, particularly for small farms. It was expected to popularize new and improved methods of cultivation and husbandry. One of AEFMET's important regional offices was in the Middle Shabelle, outside the regional capital of Jowhar. The significance of this office lay in the fact that the office itself is in one of the two most important agricultural regions in the country. Moreover, it is in this location that the new crop, rice, had taken root and was beginning to flourish. Rice producers who were eager to expand and intensify production were in desperate need of technical support and guidance, in the form of timely tractor service, fertilizers, herbicides, and properly operated irrigation systems. However, getting access to these necessary inputs at a reasonable price proved virtually impossible for the majority, and the dogged few had to spend inordinate amounts of time and resources to procure these necessary inputs.

Why did AEFMET's provisional and national staff pay so little attention to the need of rice farmers in the Middle Shabelle? Both the regional officers and the general manager were engaged in rentier activity.[31] First, the general manager owned a large farm of over 100 hectares along the banks of the river. He took proprietorship of this land in the early 1980s, when laws were relaxed and liberalized. The farm was not bought but was simply a "grant" from the Ministry of Agriculture; and the equipment that went into leveling it and preparing it for cultivation was publicly owned. Moreover, project vehicles were consistently used for personal and farm-related purposes. In addition, the regional director of AEFMET would often lend resources and personal assistance to the general manager's farm operations; he also spent some of his energy securing project-sponsored scholarships for students to do graduate work in the United States. In the course of doing these things, the regional director had to serve the interests of his superior. In a nutshell, the resources of the project were captured by rentiers who were not accountable to anyone. But this practice did not dissuade the World

Bank from continuing to fund the project, thereby burdening the Somali public with more debt but without much improvement in agricultural services.

Export Sector

When the military regime proclaimed its "scientific socialist" credentials in 1970, the banana economy of the two river valleys was the most developed capitalist production process in the entire country. Both labor and agricultural land in the region, particularly on plantations, were highly commodified. Furthermore, the working conditions of both bonded and temporary labor, particularly the former, were characteristically colonial.

The plantation system in southern Somalia clearly presented the regime with an opportunity to implement the "received idea" of socialism, given the regime's commitment to that doctrine.[32] Abiding by the tenets of the doctrine and conscious of the constraints imposed on it by the underdeveloped structure of its economy, the regime had several options in dealing with the plantation question. First, it could take the standard doctrinaire approach by simply appropriating the plantations and turning them into state farms. Second, given its proclaimed commitment to self-reliance and food self-sufficiency,[33] it could gradually transform these estates into food-producing farms run by quasipublic agencies. Third, the regime could put forth farm labor legislation to enhance the bargaining power and well-being of farm workers. This method could have enabled the regime to avoid some of the pitfalls associated with state farms and the supposed loss of foreign exchange. The fourth policy option was to enact and implement land reform. Had this alternative been selected, it may have necessitated a shift away from banana production, unless some kind of a small, farmer-based contract system had also been introduced.

Surprisingly, the military regime did not adopt any of the now familiar radical agrarian reform strategies. Its first legislative act concerning the plantation economy was to take over the banana-marketing apparatus previously run by a settler organization. This step gave birth to the National Banana Board, assigned to "manage" the industry. Whatever its function was supposed to be, the board had little positive impact on the plantation economy. Banana output increased from 145,500 tons in 1970 to 168,300 tons in 1973. The area under cultivation grew from 6,500 cultivated hectares to 9,500 hectares. Such growth was the result of investments and improvements made before 1969 or immediately after the regime came to power. The regime also retained the power of supreme landlord; and the state's general ban on the formation of independent labor unions and industrial action, coupled with the severity of military justice, foreclosed any possibility for progressive social action in the plantation economy. Labor worked under conditions no different from those prevailing during the colonial order or civilian regimes. In addition, property and social relations inherited largely from the Italian fascist rule remained the basis of the plantation system.

In spite of the growth and expansion of the banana economy in the early 1970s, production began its downward spiral in 1974. The area under cultivation fell by more than 50 percent from its peak in 1973 to 3,600 hectares in 1981. Fruit production hit rock bottom in 1981 at 59,000 tons, less than a third of the 1973 output. The downturn in production has been attributed to various maladies: (1) the erosion of technical know-how as a result of the departure of many of the Italian planters; (2) increased soil salinity as a result of poor drainage systems; (3) lack of good field supervision; (4) extremely low fertilizer application (approximately 100 kilograms per hectare, as opposed to the standard 800 kilograms per hectare); and (5) low export prices and increased domestic costs of production, i.e., packaging and transport.[34]

The banana economy was stagnant and in dire straits in the early 1980s, as were the rest of the country's productive sectors. The diplomatic rift between the regime and the Soviets in the late 1970s, the realignment of the country's foreign relations toward the West, and, finally, the adoption of structural adjustment as a development strategy changed the fortunes of the plantation economy. The confluence of these conditions spelled the inauguration of a liberal economic policy, prompting Italian interests to initiate new negotiations with the government regarding private investment in the banana sector. These discussions were successful, and an agreement was signed that established Somalfruit in 1983. Somalfruit, a joint venture, was dominated by the Italian group De Nadai.[35]

De Nadai, through Somalfruit, made credit and agricultural inputs available to producers and invested in irrigation and marketing. Consequently, a slow but steady progress was made in revitalizing the industry. Except during 1984 and 1985, when the river valleys were flooded and the crops damaged, banana exports steadily increased until the demolition of the country in 1991 (see Table 4.4). Somalfruit, which was responsible for mending the industry, deserves the credit for expanding production and restoring export quality. Moreover, these achievements and other incentive systems increased returns to the planter, as will be shown later.

Table 4.4   Banana Production and Value of Exports, 1983–1989

	Area (in hectares)	Tons	Dollars/ton	Total value (in millions of dollars)	Percent value change[a]
1983	—	62,448	235	14.7	—
1984	4,592.7	47,860	278	14.3	-2.7
1985	5,121.8	45,321	287	13.0	-9.1
1986	6,150.8	57,943	295	17.0	30.8
1987	6,128.9	64,004	320	20.5	20.6
1988	6,509.9	73,368	320	32.5	58.5
1989	6,434.6	74,652	332	24.9	-23.4

Source: Somalfruit, Statistical Reports.
Note: a. Calculated by author.

The steady transformation and recovery of the banana economy were held up as a model that the rest of the economy could do well to emulate. The growth of the industry was said to be symbolic of the viability and developmental consequences of collaboration between international capital, the state, and local entrepreneurs. Such a contention is partially valid; however, it overlooks some important drawbacks of the banana economy. Although De Nadai's investments in the sector did remarkably transform the plantation system and improve its profitability, the benefits from the growth and expansion of the industry added little to the well-being of those who labored in the fields, or to that of the region and the country as a whole. Unlike the livestock sector, the problem in the banana economy was one in which some of the most productive agricultural land was used to benefit senior members of the old regime, the Italian firm, and fewer than 200 Somali owners.

Banana production is highly labor intensive, and there are over fifteen essential tasks that need to be performed regularly from planting to harvest.[36] The overwhelming majority of these tasks were done by female children whose ages ranged from 8 to 15. Female children who harvested bananas typified the poverty of those who worked in this more lucrative sector. Their average daily wages amounted to less than U.S. $0.10 (see Table 4.5), although the working day began at about 8:30 in the morning and usually ended around 7:00 in the evening, with a lunch break around 1:00 in the afternoon. Those engaged in harvest activity were given a midday meal consisting of cooked bananas with a touch of cooking oil and a sprinkling of sugar. Their wages were supplemented by some bananas to take home. Such low rates of remuneration were not enough to buy more than a loaf of bread or five cups of tea or a kilogram of rice. These were horribly low wages, but the children continued to work under such conditions because unemployment was so high in the region and the country. Most adult males were unwilling to work for such wages, so plantation managers hired hungry children. It is as if the growth and renewed vitality of the industry entailed the "modernization of poverty."[37]

Table 4.5   Earnings of Banana Harvesters

| Person | Age | Number of fruit loads/girl | | | | Average load | Average Daily Income[a] |
		Day 1	Day 2	Day 3	Day 4		
1	15	75	65	75	65	70.0	140
2	9	55	30	55	30	42.5	83
3	8	35	65	35	40	42.8	87
4	13	55	40	55	60	52.5	106
5	11	45	60	45	50	50.0	100
6	10	55	55	50	65	56.3	112
7	8	35	65	35	25	40.0	80
8	10	60	25	60	65	52.5	106
9	11	75	45	75	45	60.0	120
10	12	60	60	55	60	58.8	118
11	11	55	55	60	55	56.3	112
						Overall average daily income	106

Source: Author's fieldwork.
Note: a. Income in Somali shillings, based on 2 shillings per load.

Contrary to the claims of some plantation owners and Somalfruit, the banana commodity was a profitable one.[38] The large amounts of investment that were directed into it and the willingness with which planters were envisioning expansions indicate that the industry was healthy. A rational investor would not sink more resources into enterprises whose profits are marginal if there is no prospect of better returns in the future. This assessment is supported further by a 1977 International Labor Organization (ILO) study that discovered that the problem was not the absence of profits, but the *distribution* of profits among those involved in the industry, from the producer to the retailer (see Table 4.6). The return to a planter who owned a processing center (most planters do not own such centers), including the cost of production, was 11.4 percent of the retail price of the fruit at the export market—a net profit of 1.9 percent of that price. Table 4.6 also shows that the free-on-board (FOB) price was 25.2 percent of the retail price. This means that nearly three-fourths of the value of the crop left the country.

More recent data produced by Somalfruit show that the producer's relative financial position did improve, in terms of the FOB price (see Table 4.7). Using the data from the ILO as a baseline, it can be surmised that the producer's share of the FOB price increased from 50.16 percent to 54.25 percent if the planter owned a packing station. Despite these positive changes, the cost of production accounted for a high proportion of the producer's price, and the profit rates were very high downstream (all Somali banana exports were sold to De Nadai's parent company). Because plantation owners had little control over either the cost of necessary inputs purchased from Somalfruit or the final retail price, the only way they could advance their profit margins was to control other costs of production, particularly labor. Containing the cost of labor and enhancing its quality was the heart of the labor problem in the plantation economy.

The Diversity of Conditions
Within the Agrarian Economy

The crisis in the Somali agrarian economy was not monolithic in nature, and the way in which it was manifested in the pastoral/livestock sector was different from that in the farm economy. For example, although stagnation and decline occurred in the former, growth was a characteristic feature of the farm economy, a result of the liberal reform program that was instituted in the early 1980s.

The condition of the pastoral/livestock sector had two intricately intertwined dimensions, namely the ecological and social aspects. Growth in livestock trade in the last hundred years as a result of the increasing demands by pastoralists to obtain manufactured commodities, as well as the added claims of nonpastoral social groups such as merchants and the state, led to horizontal expansion of livestock production into more marginal areas. Such a growth strategy, combined with the increase in livestock prices in the 1970s induced by petrodollars in the Middle East, kept the pastoralist/merchant/state relationship complementary and unproblematic. The sharp decline in livestock prices in the Middle East reduced the profitability of Somali livestock exports, and the downward pressure on prices and profits meant, in the long run, that old ways of resolving such a squeeze (e.g., herd expansion into marginal areas) were not feasible. Thus, the pastoral/livestock economy came to a crossroads.

The recovery of the plantation economy in the 1980s meant that this sector was not suffering from the maladies that plagued the pastoral economy. Prospects for further growth of plantations were very good

Table 4.6   Estimate of the Main Cost Elements in Banana Exports

	Percent Contribution to retail unit price	Value
Reported production cost before harvest	8.6	
Harvesting and transport to packing plant	0.9	
Producer's gross margin	1.9	
Estimated gross return to growers at packing plant		11.4
Packing	10.0	
Transport to port	0.6	
Loading and stevedoring	1.1	
Export tax	0.3	
Other charges	0.8	
Exporter's gross margin	1.0	
Free-on-board (FOB) price		25.2
Freight and insurance	14.3	
C.I.F. price		39.5
Unloading and handling at port of discharge	2.0	
Import duties	18.5	
Importer's gross margin	5.5	
Free-on-rail (FOR) selling price		66.0
Ripener's gross margin	15.1	
Ripener's selling price		81.1
Retailer's gross margin	18.9	
Retail price	100.0	

Source: International Labour Office, *Economic Transformation in a Socialist Framework*, p. 104.

Table 4.7   Banana Free-on-Board Cost Breakdown

Cost item	Dollars/quintal	Percent of FOB[a]
Producer price	15.7	45.42
Packing station	1.64	4.74
Plastic covers	0.11	0.32
Packing (cartons and plastic)	8.11	23.46
Transport to port	1.35	3.91
Quality control	0.68	1.96
Loading and sundries	0.23	0.67
Export tax	1.47	4.25
Overhead expenses	1.83	5.29
Depreciation	1.35	3.91
Asset revaluation reserve	2.10	6.07
Total costs to FOB	34.57	100

Source: Woodward and Stockton, *A Study of the Profitability.*
Note: a. Calculated by author.

prior to the collapse of the regime in 1991. As such, the problems in the banana economy were not ones of stagnation. Rather, they originated from the use of scarce and precious irrigated land for the production of exports, three-fourths of the value of which was realized outside the country. Theoretically, banana exports contributed to the country's foreign exchange. However, because most of these earnings remained in foreign hands overseas, the net economic impact of the industry on the country's capital accumulation fund was marginal. Moreover, in spite of the growth in banana exports, those who labored in the fields saw no improvement in their wages and working conditions.

The grain sector (irrigated and rainfed) suffered from several difficulties. First, the increase in the quantity of grains from dryland farming in the 1980s was due to an expansion of the area under cultivation. In the absence of new farming techniques suitable to dryland areas and modern inputs to intensify production, rainfed agriculture was unlikely to experience further significant growth because most land suitable for rainfed farming was already utilized. Second, although irrigated grain farming, i.e., rice, had been a growth industry in the 1980s, it began to stagnate because of poor husbandry and a lack of necessary supporting infrastructure. In the future, expansion and intensification of irrigated grain production will be essential in order to rehabilitate the rest of the economy.

Future Prospects:
What Needs to Be Done and Who Can Do It

Neither the call for a new, yet ill-defined, system of governance by some of the militarist "warlords" nor the economic policies that guided the neoliberal agenda of the now-defunct state during the last decade of its life are, in my judgment, a sound recipe for the reestablishment of peaceful coexistence and economic renewal.[39] Rather, the destruction of the Somali state is an unprecedented circumstance that can be turned into a precious opportunity if a capable and *effective* institution takes the place of the old. This is because social resuscitation and economic rejuvenation will require a strong state, not a repressive and authoritarian one.[40] The mandate of such a state should begin with a strategy to help reorganize the productive sectors of the economy in such a way that production for local need is of utmost priority. More specifically, this new state should not engage in production, particularly in agriculture, but should act as an efficient facilitator and coordinator. The ultimate measure of the state's effectiveness in revitalizing the economy should be the rate of growth in production and the fairness in the distribution of productive assets among the population. In short, the new polity's ambition should be the difficult tasks of growth and equity.

How will such an agenda be realized, and what form will it take in the agricultural sector? The first major effort will be the coordination of agrarian reform in the three sectors analyzed here. The purpose of such a program will be to remove any fetters on production, ensure sustainability, and enhance national capital accumulation. Reform in the pastoral/livestock sector will affect three aspects: marketing, veterinary and water services, and, ultimately, range management. Marketing reform will entail significant changes by eliminating export merchants and replacing them with co-ops controlled by the producers. Such co-ops will gradually move into livestock shipping and transportation. This reorganization will reduce the vast number of those unproductively employed who currently draw resources from the sector. In addition, making livestock shipment an integral part of the local economy will ensure that a significant amount of the revenue generated—currently captured by foreign interests—stays in the local economy, enhancing the overall profitability of the sector. These marketing arrangements should not be controlled by the state, but should be monitored frequently and regularly by public agencies; and the results of inquiries of these agencies should be made public.

Veterinary service will be jointly provided and supervised by a ministry of agrarian affairs and the marketing cooperatives of livestock producers. The cooperatives will invest a portion of their revenues in drugs and health facilities, in close consultation with the ministry. The purpose of such an arrangement is to make the service delivery system more responsive to the needs of the producers, but also to keep a close eye on public safety and interest. The development of water resources for the pastoral economy can be managed by a national water resources board, in close consultation with regional associations of producers. Control and use of water resources in the pastoral range is pivotal in undertaking sustainable pastoral development because of the absence of other sound and appropriate methods of range management. The fundamental objectives of pastoral/livestock reform are to (1) increase the returns to producers by incorporating more economic activities into their sphere, (2) secure responsiveness of public agencies who serve producers, (3) enhance producer control over national conditions that affect their well-being, and (4) use foreign exchange earnings for productive purposes in the sector and other complementary sectors.

Agrarian reform in the farm sector will entail land (re)distribution, reorientation of resource use to aim for national food self-reliance, environmental conservation, and the establishment and development of effective and accountable institutions to serve a growing economy. The purpose of land (re)distribution is to ensure equitable access to this increasingly scarce but precious asset in the country. Although farm size distribution will depend on the ecological conditions of particular areas (e.g., irrigated/riverine versus rainfed), a basic farm size of three hectares per household could be envisaged in the riverine environments. A resurrection program should also guarantee access to riverine irrigation to farmers, as well as grazing and watering rights to pastoralists. However, such a program should *not* allow for absentee ownership.

The institution of these changes should be designed and implemented by a joint group of farmers (i.e., local people) and a national agency. This group would constitute the core of a democratically elected body whose purpose is to promote equity of resource distribution and represent farmers' interests in regional and national forums. An organization of this kind can also function as a marketing structure whose books are open to public scrutiny. The rationale for such an organization and its relations to the state is to guard the interests of the farming population and secure a national agenda in the farm sector. The functions of a farmers' association would be similar to those of pastoral producers described earlier.

A land reform program will directly and thoroughly affect the plantation economy in several ways. First, land resources will be redistributed, based on the three-hectare farm size, to those who have worked in plantations and to others in the surrounding areas. The idea here is to get away from a plantation system. Second, these small farmers will become part of a household-based, food-export-producing agricultural system. The emphasis of the farm sector, particularly in high-potential areas, will be food production for local markets. However, a portion of household land (e.g., a third) can be devoted to export crop production. Marketing and transportation of export crops will be in the purview of farmers' cooperatives, as in the case of livestock producers. Again, the purpose is to increase returns to farmers and encourage productive use of resources. Thus, public policy in the agrarian economy must ensure that the foreign exchange saved by the growth of domestic food production and also that earned by livestock/meat and crop exports is used to further enhance the productive capacities in these and other emerging areas. Such a program, and the subsequent growth in the sector, will begin to provide a stable basis for national economic recovery.

The basic function of agricultural agencies will be to conduct field-based research, in concert with a rehabilitated college of agriculture; deliver farm inputs to farmers' associations; watch over the development, management, and maintenance of irrigation systems; and pursue environmental conservation. Agricultural inputs delivered to farmers' organizations will be traded with grain. The barter terms of trade between inputs and grain will be pegged to their real prices. These agencies will be overseen by an expert and a citizen committee that reports directly to an appropriate authority in the executive branch.

Finally, the enormous but necessary task of transforming the country's agrarian economy is an issue still outside the ambit of current discussions among Somalis. A program as sketched here will require an unprecedented degree of foresight, coupled with disciplined intellect, and must be carried forward by a collaboration between a steady public force and civil society. The kind of coordination and market guidance that this will demand will come not through the guise of local Bantustans, but through a responsive and strong state determined to engage the exacting balance between growth and equity. The likelihood of undertaking a sustainable economy in a peaceful united Somalia is quite remote without such a state. An essential companion to this state is an autonomous and democratically organized agrarian population that can hold the state accountable. This is the basis for a viable civil society, and it has the potential of creating broad-based cross-regional alliances of agricultural producers that will supersede the animosity engendered by the polarization of clanism.

In the end, a social arrangement of this kind calls for household ownership of productive resources and for cooperative organizations of producers geared to the provision of necessary services. The strengthening of civil society and the state on their respective terms necessitates a different kind of democracy than anything Somalis have created thus far. If the political history of the first nine years of the country taught us anything, it is that the numerous parties that competed in the last election had the identical interest of raiding the public purse for individual gains. Siyaad Barre and clanistic militarism turned that looting of the commons into a crude and poisonous art. A reintroduction of either form of state/civil society relations will not only be a farce, but will precipitate further descent into the pit of pauperism and sectarian savagery.

Notes

1. For a general discussion of what *crisis* means in a capitalist economy, see O'Connor, *The Meaning of Crisis*; Harvey, *The Limits to Capital* and *The*

Urbanization of Capital, Chapter 1. For a more Africentric elucidation, see Watts, "The Agrarian Crisis in Africa."

2. The implication of underinvestment in the Somali economy is specifically addressed by A. Samatar, *The State and Rural Transformation*; see also Samatar and A. I. Samatar, "The Material Roots of the Suspended African State."

3. Traditional Somalists claim that it is evil men and Somali clanist tradition that is to blame for the current conditions. For an alternative explanation, see A. Samatar, "Destruction of State and Society."

4. Amin, "Accumulation and Development"; de Janvry, *The Agrarian Question*, particularly Chapter 1.

5. For a general discussion of the use and control of resources, see Berry, "The Food Crisis." For the impact of the privatization of public resources on the economy, see A. Samatar, *The State and Rural Transformation*; MacGaffey, *Entrepreneurs and Parasites*.

6. A crisis is often thought to be a single process. For a clear elucidation of the process and its multidimensional nature, see Harvey, *The Urbanization of Capital*; Watts, "The Agrarian Crisis in Africa."

7. I want to thank M. Y. Abshir, a valuable participant of the conference, for reminding me of the potential importance of fisheries in Somalia.

8. The United Nations environmental staff in Nairobi has recently reported that Italian firms were dumping toxic waste in southern Somalia.

9. Much of this part of the chapter, particularly the segment on the social differentiation of livestock merchants, comes from my "Social Classes and Economic Restructuring."

10. Agricultural development requires industrial development, as shown in Kitching, *Development and Underdevelopment*.

11. The principal support for this view is found in I. M. Lewis, *A Pastoral Democracy*; Jamal, "Somalia" and "Nomads and Farmers"; Cassanelli, *The Shaping of Somali Society*.

12. Pankhurst, "The Trade."

13. Parson, "Class, Cattle and the State in Botswana."

14. Jamal, "Somalia."

15. Reusse, "Somalia's Nomadic Livestock Economy."

16. Swift, "Pastoral Development in Somalia," and "The Development of Livestock Trading"; Aronson, "Kinsmen and Comrades."

17. The importance of pilgrimage market for the Somali trade was first documented in A. Samatar et al. , "The Political Economy."

18. A. Samatar, "Merchant Capital."

19. For an articulate defense of the appropriateness of indigenous knowledge systems, see Richards, *Indigenous Agricultural Revolution*.

20. There is a growing body of literature that deals with the relationship between social relations and environmental degradation. See Swift, "Pastoral Development in Somalia"; Helland, "Some Issues"; Blaikie, *The Political Economy*; Hitchcock and Hussein, "Agricultural and Non-Agricultural Settlements"; Starr, "Risk"; Watts, "Drought, Environment and Food Security"; A. Samatar, *The State and Rural Transformation*.

21. Parson, "Class, Cattle and the State in Botswana."

22. Somali Democratic Republic, Ministry of Agriculture, *Agriculture in the Service of the Nation*.

23. A. Samatar, *The State and Rural Transformation*.

24. The Agricultural Development Corporation (ADC), the agricultural marketing board, affected different parts of the country to varying degrees. It devastated the southern region more than the northwestern region.

25. Somali Democratic Republic, Ministry of Agriculture, *Food Early Warning*.

26. World Bank, *Somalia: Agricultural Sector Survey*.

27. Vahcic, "Jowhar Sugar Factory."

28. Conversation with Haji Issa, Jowhar, Somalia, 29 November 1989.

29. Conversation with Ali, Jowhar, Somalia, 19 February 1990.

30. World Bank, *Somalia: Agricultural Extension*.

31. For a discussion of rent-seeking, see Watts, *State, Oil and Agriculture*; Bates, *Markets and States in Tropical Africa*.

32. Post and Wright, *Socialism and Underdevelopment*.

33. A. I. Samatar, *Socialist Somalia: Rhetoric and Reality*.

34. International Labour Office, *Economic Transformation in Socialist Framework*; Dastane, *Salinity*.

35. Although Somalfruit was supposed to be a joint venture, it was overwhelmingly dominated by the Italian group.

36. A. Samatar, "Structural Adjustment."

37. Raikes, *Modernizing Hunger*.

38. Woodward and Stockton, *A Study of the Profitability*.

39. A weak and fragmented system will be in the interest of the warlords and will virtually amount to miniature dictatorships that will not solve the great socioeconomic problems the Somali people face.

40. For the importance of a strong state in launching a dynamic development program, see Wade, *Governing the Market*; Amsden, *Asia's Next Giant*.

Part 3

Governance, International Relations, and the Catastrophe

5

The Curse of Allah: Civic Disembowelment and the Collapse of the State in Somalia

Ahmed I. Samatar

Only barbarians are not curious about where they come from, how they come to be, where they are, where they appear to be going, whether they wish to go there, and if so, why, and if not, why not.
—*Isaiah Berlin,* The Crooked Timber of Humanity

Nothing of all that is done on earth is more pleasing to that supreme God who rules the whole universe than the assemblies and gatherings of men [and women] associated in justice, which are called states.

—*Cicero,* De republica

The demise of Siyaad Barre's rule in January 1991 was a major event in contemporary Somali history. Its significance emanates from specific points: (1) a final closure on a highly detested but durable dictatorship, and (2) a fleeting possibility for Somalis to stand back from the odiousness of their recent past and rethink the nature of power and governance in Somalia. This opportunity evaporated immediately, and in its place arose a nightmare more punishing and costlier than all the years of Barre's malignant rule.[1]

But it was not always like this. A little over thirty years ago, when Somalis, like many Africans, were enthusiastically agitating for decolonization and independence, the intensity of nationalism as a focus of a redeemed identity was unmistakable. Intertwined with the demand for the return of the Ogaden, Djibouti (French Somaliland), and the Northern Frontier District—the final reuniting of Greater Somalia—was an effusive feeling of accomplishment, solidarity, and certainty about better things to come. The following

95

three excerpts from the dozens of celebratory songs of the early 1960s capture the exuberance, sense of history, and marked supreme confidence in the future:

> The sky, oh flag
> Oh flag, oh flag
> You fly majestically on that pole
> You are like an afternoon rain at the beginning of the season
> Bringing relief and life, oh flag
> May you be one of blessings, oh flag
> All your time and through eternity
> In the soil, oh flag, you are everywhere in this land
> You gleam and glisten like sapphire
> May you be one with blessings, oh flag
> All your time and through eternity
> A nemesis, oh flag, or enemy cannot order you
> You are like fresh grass and abundant vegetation
> May you be one with blessings, oh flag
> All your time and through eternity
> Oh flag, oh flag.[2]

> By Allah's mercy, today we are members of the world
> Our head and feet are emancipated
> We have a name and dignity
> Gentlemen and ladies, you are today
> Our head and feet are free
> By Allah's mercy all the honey and sweetness in the land
> It will be soon when we will enjoy
> By Allah's mercy all these chosen and brave
> Today they are at the helm of our affairs
> By Allah's mercy that damned one who came from the damned
>   place
> Today we have kicked him out
> By Allah's mercy grabbers of the poor's meager possessions
> Today they are under our protection
> By Allah's mercy our head is free
> By Allah's mercy our head is free.[3]

> It is the day we pitched the flag
> It is the day we threw out the foreigners
> To grow stronger, cross to the Other with succor
> It is the day of destiny and victory over the enemy
> It is the day we rose up and on our strength
> To grow stronger, cross to the Other with succor
> It is the day we brought together the righteous two
> It is the day we planned for our union
> To grow stronger, cross to the Other with succor
> It is the day of destiny and victory over the enemy
> It is the day of counting ourselves and missing three
> It is the day we prostrated before Allah and repented

To grow stronger, cross to the Other with succor
It is the day of destiny and victory over the enemy.[4]

The times are surely different today. Note the temper of these doleful lamentations recently recorded by a celebrated balladeer-cum-musician:

What necessity has compelled me to do, oh country
When the soil was speared, oh country
When peace was denied to all, oh country
When kin disemboweled each other, oh country
When elders were not spared, oh country
When it growled and then belched poison,
I had to escape with self, oh country.[5]

The flag that belonged to me
The earth that belonged to me
The defense forces that belonged to me
The strength that belonged to me
These protected me from adversity
Oh, Allah, they are all gone and I am miserably alone.[6]

In the last decade alone, the country has fallen into a venomous and obscene form of politics—a civil war of incalculable proportions, resulting in tens of thousands of deaths, a flood tide of exiles, international aspersion, and the dissolution of Somalia itself. Given the astounding distance between the early élan and the utter disconsolation of the present, this chapter asks, why were Somalis so gleeful? How could that ebullient spirit of communitarian identity embodied in the flag (i.e., the state) turn into self-inflicted and generalized degradation? Is it worth resurrecting the Somali state? If so, in what guise?

In an attempt to explore these questions, this chapter presupposes two assumptions and proffers a thesis. First, without a workable state and its concomitant system of spatial and bureaucratic structures, no modern society can exist, let alone move forward. Although individual competition and inter- and intragroup jostling over the composition of regimes, definition of policy, and delegation of authority are to be expected in any normal and, certainly, any democratic society, this complete collapse of governance and order is tantamount to collective and incalculable loss.

Second, much like their contemporaries, Somalis can neither go back to the acephalous arrangements of old nor afford to hack the central public institutions into sectarian pieces—one of the deleterious consequences of a fatal schism. This is *not* an a priori argument for a unitary state, although there is no natural affinity between a central authority and dictatorship. What does inform the position taken here is the undeniable fact that hardly any society has achieved modernity and development without a strong national state.[7] This is true for both the few pioneering and contemporaneously dominant societies and, more positively, successful late developers.[8]

My thesis, in the spirit of a recent volume on the nature and source of conflict in Africa, attributes the causes of the Somali predicament, in large measure, to a failure to construct a viable national governance.[9] But to engage the Somali terrain is also to confront the whole phenomenon of the state. In addition to the unavoidable intellectual relevance of such a discussion, a procedure of this kind compels us to avoid that old habit of treating the Somali experience as a special activity so different from any other, thus occluding an encounter with its deeper complexities. Consequently, a secondary, but nonetheless important, set of questions are raised here: What is the state? What is the interplay between state and society? What does and should a viable state do and in whose interest? To get to the current Somali situation, we must first broach these larger questions.

There are four sections to this chapter. The first surveys the main intellectual traditions on the concept of the state. The second addresses the Somali context and the state. The third focuses on the demise of governance and propounds a theory of the state to allow understanding of what went wrong in Somalia. The fourth, a brief exploration of options toward renewal, concludes with a meditation upon the meaning of the Somali present. Here, I consider the lessons from the doldrums of dissolution and desolation, while keeping an eye on the twin inevitabilities of reconstruction and development—inescapable burdens if Somalis are to avoid the real likelihood of being condemned to an eternal journey through a netherworld of despondency.

Intellectual Traditions and the State

To many who are either caught up in the whirlpool of the Somali catastrophe or who have taken an interest in doing something about it, working through abstract concepts such as the meaning of the term *state* and thereafter theorizing represent an unnecessary delay, if not a downright waste of time and effort. Though I am cognizant of the existential urgency and moved by it, I have for some time now taken exception to such a line of reasoning.[10] To begin with, I am not convinced that a thorough understanding of a given situation is necessarily coterminous with the immediate and experiential. Rather, visible elements of a particular reality may signal that other, more discrete factors could be at work. A cruel but graphic contemporary medical problem—AIDS—makes the point. The visible ailment (e.g., tuberculosis, pneumonia) that finally subdues the AIDS victim is only capitalizing on a preexisting destruction of the whole immune system. By analogy, the collapse of a social system cannot easily be reducible to symptoms or even immediate causes alone; rather, one may have to posit deeper conceptions to fully understand the situation.[11] Second, conceptual work helps in linking with others who have engaged or are wrestling with parallel circumstances.[12] Because it would be the height of ethnographic absurdity to claim that Somalis are altogether a distinct species, historical wisdom, gained through both thinking and feeling into how others have seen and dealt with similar preoccupation, is too precious, particularly for stranded people, to neglect or discount. Third, the act of good conceptualization in relation to practice is done not necessarily to give quick and direct answers to practical issues, but, more importantly, to crush out woolliness and confusion that undermine the construction of real solutions.[13]

In the end, the important issue is not only the amount of information we gather, but, in the words of A. R. Radcliffe-Brown, "the apparatus of concepts and hypotheses which guide our investigation. . . . The difficulty in science is not in finding answers to questions once they have been propounded, but in finding out what questions to ask."[14] In short, as Hegel described, human beings make claims about their reality through the intellect in the form of cognitive knowledge (the transformation of more tender intuition); such a process, of course, is dialectically linked to social circumstances.

Defining the State

A concept as pivotal for modern life as the state is bound to attract attention and a multiplicity of versions. But any survey of thinking about the state first has to come to grips with the question of politics, the larger context in which the state is found. *Politics* can be construed as that broad and practical work that deals with the organization and management of human associations. This includes both the private sphere and the public arena.[15] Private life, in a more precise form, captures those regions of human existence (e.g., households, religious fellowships, women's associations, kin associations, and trade organizations) that are directly and intimately acted upon by individuals. The public sphere is under the domain of the state. According to David Held, "Politics is about the capacity of social agents, agencies, and institutions to maintain or transform their environment, social or physical. . . . It is expressed in all the relations, institutions, and structures that are implicated in the production and reproduction of the life of societies."[16]

To be so prevalent in human life, however, does not tell us much about the nature of that essentiality, for politics is present in both conflictual and collaborative times. In the case of the former, human relations in the context of any social system are fraught with struggles that grow from incompatibilities, structural misalignments, and subjective contradictions (e.g., unevenness of location, status, or choices made). In other words, because human civilization has yet to invent a time of total harmony (never mind its desirability), an eristic attitude and a degree of divisiveness are unavoidable elements of social existence.[17] Political life, then, defines and deals with these clashes, instabilities, and tugs-of-war. But if disorder is not to sunder the fabric of a given society, politics should also include the act of cooperation—minimally, the management of conflict and, optimally, the creation of fellowship or what earlier societies called *communal affinity*.

Balancing the tensions and energy built into the dual tendencies of centripetality and centrifugence that accompany organized human life is the critical edge of politics. Although politics permeates human life, this chapter's purlieu is the more public dimension of that existence, i.e., the state. What, then, is the state? Obviously, the state, like all other institutions of political life, is a social construction made by human beings for human beings—with a historical identity. Rousseau saw the state as synonymous with the "General Will," whereas Hegel, in a similar fashion, construed the state as "the unity of the universal, essential will and the will of the subject."[18] For Charles Tilly, following in the tracks of Max Weber, the state is to be seen as a "coercion-wielding" structure that "controls the population occupying a definite territory in a state insofar as (1) it is differentiated from other organizations operating in the same territory; (2) it is autonomous; (3) it is centralized; and (4) its divisions are formally coordinated with one another."[19] Those thinkers who, like Otto Hintze and Carl Schmitt,[20] accent the militaristic dimensions of international relations in the making of a state, construe the state as the incarnation of physical force. Marxists see it as a cluster of institutions managed by state-appointed personnel.

In African Studies, Crawford Young has offered an intriguing and imaginative conception of the state. In a seminal discussion of the forms of social contention in the continent, Young argues that fundamental forms of social contestation congregate around "principles" of class and ethnicity, and each of them is "defined in important ways by the state, which serves as the primary arena for social encounter and collective conflict."[21] For Young, this crucial phenomenon is defined on two levels, the *concrete* and *theoretical*. The first, according to Young, points to "the matrix of institutions through which rule is exercised . . . the organized public sector of society"; the second is an "expression found in the realm of ideology . . . public doctrine of rule and authority."[22]

Interpreting the Nature of the State

Scholarly discussions of the nature of the state come in many forms. Philip Resnick, for instance, gleaning from earlier thinking, posits five kinds of state: aristocratic, republican, order-based, liberal, and democratic.[23] Aristocratic conceptions underscore a situation of dominance and rule by a small segment of the society through descent or monopoly of specialized knowledge. This rule by tradition, or meritocracy, has been approved of by thinkers as early as Plato.[24] But it is Edmund Burke whose celebration of custom has echoed through the modern ages. As part of his invective against revolutionary politics, Burke writes, "Prescription is the most solid of all title, not only to property but, which is to secure that property, to government."[25] Republicanism, particularly in its earliest guises, denotes a mixture of privilege and populism, the combinations of which, in Machiavelli's words, "make a perfect commonwealth."[26] The order-based category of the state places the state above civil society as a greater and necessary force.[27] The liberal state emphasizes individual liberty, whereas democratic conceptions stress socioeconomic and political equality.

The preceding summary recalls some of the past thinking on the state, which, to some extent, constitutes our intellectual hinterland; contemporary schools or traditions, like their forebears, have taken into account mutations in history. As a result, today there is hardly any discernible interest in either the aristocratic or order-based state; history has rendered them virtually irrelevant. In what follows, I propose three major paradigms[28]—liberal, Marxist, and postcolonial—that, I trust, will help us streamline and negotiate the numerous contemporary interpretations of the life of the state.

Liberalism. Lifting diverse elements from earlier theorizing, the liberal perspective of the state enshrines the centrality of the individual as the bearer of morality and virtue.[29] Such privileging of the individual is not an accident; rather, the energy of the argument comes from the transformation of European society that began with the demise of feudalism and absolutism and the rise of the market. This position is buttressed by the principle that individuals are linked together in a primal fashion by a natural harmony of interests, each individual contributing to the welfare of the other by pursuing his or her interests. As such, exchange networks bring together rational (i.e., utility-maximizing) consumers and producers, the result of which is the appearance of a maze of interactions and relationships that undergird the development of civil society.[30]

The constitution of the liberal state, then, is a combination of Smith's economic vision and John Locke's conception of the rationality and reasoning of individuals—part of the natural gift of human beings. For Locke, the right of being a master of one's own affairs and interests is endemic to the very creation of society. Consequently, each one of us has the right to pursue "life, liberty, and estate." Though having a benign sense of the world of nature—that is, the prepolitical universe—Locke nonetheless suggests that such a highly fragile condition cannot be left without a guardianship of laws, i.e., a state. Assigned to guard the three cardinal pursuits of individualism, this structure of authority, although empowered to set and enforce legislation, would be subject to the supreme sovereignty of civil society itself. Locke here attends to the precarious balance that has to be achieved between freedom for human ego to pursue "natural" interest and the imperatives of order that must exist if that very freedom is to flourish. This is articulated in a most renowned passage, commonly referred to as the "separation of powers doctrine."[31]

Liberal conceptions of the state are to be noted for a number of contributions to modern challenges of political life. First, Hobbes's grim depiction of the world of nature notwithstanding, liberalism enshrines the individual's right to pursue personal interest. Second, this privileging of individuality is the key to the development of civil society. Third, civil society, in turn, precedes the construction of political life. Fourth, the state is, in the first and final analyses, a creature of civil society established for the sole function of protecting private pursuits. Fifth, the power of the state is to be limited by (1) a division of authority between different institutions, and (2) ultimate sovereignty given to the members of civil society. Sixth, and perhaps most crucial for our purposes, the state, as well as the creation of public life, is to be seen as a cross to be carried by the individual so as to enjoy the central purpose of social life itself: maximum private interest.

There is no gainsaying that liberalism made lasting and positive contributions to the enduring onerous work of constructing public identity and the state. More than anything else, the combined ideas of Smith and Locke not only highlight the centrality of individual freedom, but also underscore the importance of consent in the making of public power. Coming on the heels of struggles against more arbitrary powers (e.g., the doctrine of divine right), this ideology redefines authority, interpersonal relationships, and the nature of individuality. From there on, the darkness of capricious power is rejected, reclamation of some of the privileges of citizenship in the classical polis is undertaken, and the seeds of the contemporary and intense debate over the private and the public are sown.

But classical liberalism has its own difficulties. If it succeeded in undermining feudal fragmentation and absolutism, it triggered a new set of contradictions. First, neither Smith nor Locke gave much attention to the underside of the enthronement of private interest. Given their emphasis on minimizing public power lest it encumber individual interest, liberalism seems to have overlooked the real danger of unrestrained competition in the private sphere turning into gruesome "cold war." The consequences of such a condition will include a new stratification that favors those who own and accumulate property—a circumstance that could undermine the very order that sustains private initiative and, in the end, bring back a Hobbesian world. In short, both equality and security represent new challenges to this tradition of liberalism.[32]

The utilitarians did not doubt the centrality of individual happiness and the role of the free market as the most successful strategy to achieve that end.[33] What Bentham and James Mill did, however, was point to the significance of democracy by underscoring the importance of accountability. For them, although subsistence and abundance are to be left in the realm of private exchange and accumulation, parity and stability could be harnessed by empowering the administrative organs of the state, as well as by extending the franchise. Empowerment of the state gives it the legal authority to punish those who refuse to comply with its laws; the extension of democratic features speaks to the need for reckoning, lest the rulers themselves abuse that very power.

The utilitarians' ideas certainly nudged thinking on the state toward equivalence with governance as well as its assessment as an estimable site. However, their contributions were vitiated by their exclusion of working groups and women from the political arena. Moreover, such a limited conception of political life, coupled with emphasis on satisfaction of individual desire, was bound to be confronted with the growing historical transformation of industrializing societies. It would be left to John Stuart Mill to finish the work of the utilitarians by tightening the linkages between liberalism and democracy.[34]

For Mill, the conjoining of the liberal, individualist conception of social life and the public elements of that very individuality was indispensable to making a viable society. The state, therefore, is the arena where that conjunction is to be achieved, resulting in both the autonomy of the individual (i.e., pluralism) and the construction of accountable public institutions governed by openness, reason, and intelligence (i.e., representative government). Of course, Mill, in the end, still left the issues of resources and the power associated with them in the realm of the private. This bifurcation, fueled by changing economic relations, generated social contradictions in Mill's liberal democracy, which has since become the Achilles' heel of all brands of liberalism.

Rousseau saw through liberalism. Some of his lasting contributions are worth noting: (1) his conception of the original world of nature as inhabited by humans, born free and equal, only to be destroyed by individual weakness and natural disaster,[35] (2) his view of the dawn of private ownership as one of the damning events in human history,[36] and (3) his notion of the state, particularly one characterized by direct participation, as the embodiment of "General Will."[37] Rousseau certainly discerned the problems that were to accompany the world of civil society. On the other hand, he pointed to the positive trade-offs that such a transformation offered, e.g., laws, order, and social freedom born out of maturity. In brief, Rousseau underlined the corrosive elements of liberalism while at the same time advancing our thinking on the conception of the state—the latter construed beyond a neutral "guard" and more as a collective power around which common interests could coagulate. Rousseau's ideas instruct the thinking of that other great tradition, Marxism.

Marxism. By the 19th century, the inexorable forces of "commodification" and industrialization brought forth new conditions that revolutionized our senses of nature, self, and society. With the crystallization of new divisions of labor and the deepening of class structure, it was only a matter of time before Locke's premise of "life, liberty, and estate" as the raison d'etre of the state was to come under heavy intellectual as well as activist onslaught. Karl Marx and Friedrich Engels, though not exactly disputing the unique attributes of the individual,[38] railed against (1) liberalism's emphasis on the individual as a starting point of social analysis, and

(2) the state as a removed structure designed to offer a modicum of mediation between equal and free citizens in pursuit of their private desires. In the case of the former, Marx and Engels saw the individual, in the final analysis, as an "ensemble" of both the social relations that constitute the very basis of everyone and the primary linkages with the larger society. The latter (i.e., the state), equally a structure of social invention, was interpreted in two ways: (1) an instrument of dominant classes, and (2) an autonomous agency.

The instrumentalist conception of the state in the Marxist tradition is predicated on a particular reading of social arrangements, surrounding human needs, productive capacity, and resources.[39] Marx and Engels argued that the material existence of human beings drives historical processes. With the eclipse of communal (and, consequently, reciprocal) social systems and the inception of private ownership of resources, the stage was set for the alienation of collective power and decisionmaking in the setting of society's priorities. The state, in this view, is therefore a creature of this class structuring of society and is subject to the interests of those dominant in this social order. Armed with the monopoly of coercion and the "mandate" to design and enforce the laws and regulations that govern the social relations of production, the state is heavily implicated in the fundamental struggle between two warring classes: the producers and the owners/controllers of the means of livelihood. In short, the state, immersed in the tug-of-war over the material basis of society, does not represent the general welfare; nor is it a trustee of societal interest. This is an echo of the earlier assertion in *The Communist Manifesto* that "political power . . . is merely the organized power of one class for oppressing another."[40]

The state as a social structure beyond the grip of one class and, consequently, an autonomous force is also part of the Marxist conception of the state.[41] In this interpretation, the independent identity of the state results from (1) the role and function of the bureaucracy and (2) stalemate circumstances between classes. Because no state structure can act without specialized organs, it is not possible to have this permanent feature of the state always follow closely the narrow interests of the dominant class. Rather, the intrinsic interests of the members of the bureaucracy and the coordination of the myriad activities of the state, both of which include order and acquiescence by the rest of society, require a measure of independence.[42] Without that degree of separate identity, then, alienation of the political moment becomes more severe, reducing the bureaucrats to automatons and the state to nothing more than a naked force for compulsion.

But if the nature and function of the bureaucracy buys the state a modicum of autonomy, certain exceptional situations could also arise whereby the correlation of forces between opposing classes is rather even, through either built-up power or mutual destruction. In such peculiar moments in history, the state holds the balance, seeing itself as the organ that can best keep the society together, as well as lead it out of the prevailing impasse. This is to be accomplished without undermining the material foundations, on which the state depends, that sustain existing social relations. Moreover, although contentions between distinct classes are normally the hallmark of societal cleavages, intraclass competition and antagonism are fertile soil for social disruptions. Beyond the broader assignment of managing societal operations, within the confines of the accepted norms, the task of the state is to ensure that conflicts among factions of dominant classes and rival blocs do not result in mutual ruin.

Postcolonialism.[43] Interpretations of the life of the state, like other social phenomena, are historical tasks. Consequently, if classical Marxist perspectives brought forth the unappealing side of the celebration of individualism and the crowning of the private, colonial expansion and conquest were bound to create a response, too. With some adaptation of the key analytical equipment of the critical tradition (e.g., class exploitation) perspectives of postcolonialism address two primary issues: the colonization of the political moment through the imposition of alien rule, and the inception of postcolonial governance. Although there are numerous voices within the postcolonial literature, two broad variants can be discerned: neo-Marxist and nationalist.

Appropriating the central concepts of Marx, but at the same time extending Marx's Euro-focused optic to capture the trauma of Third World societies, the arguments of scholars in this field are well represented by world-system analysis—best known through the works of Immanuel Wallerstein and Samir Amin.[44] Proponents of this school, despite their internal disagreements, form a position that holds that, with the demise of earlier social systems such as the reciprocal and tributary ones, the last half millennium has witnessed the rise of the first global system: the capitalist world-economy. Driven by an inexorable logic of private accumulation through profit and, therefore, expansion, this world order is characterized by one global economy, multiple states, and multiple cultures. Because the internationalization of capital gives the world-system its cast and modality, all states and cultures are identified not only according to their internal traits but, more importantly, according to the place each occupies in the global structure.

Consequently, despite their multiplicity on the surface, states in this modern world-system can be classified into three types: core, semiperiphery, and periphery. Core states are the few that are the most industrialized (i.e., highly capital intensive), bureaucratized, militarily powerful, and strategically located at the heart of the system—the dominant ones in the global economy. Semiperiphery states are those few (perhaps a dozen) that possess some elements of "coreness" (e.g., a notable degree of industrialization/manufacturing, autonomous capital, bureaucratic and military capacity) but also have a dependency relation with some core state(s). States in this category also share some of the attributes of peripherality. The third type of state is the one to which the vast majority belong. Peripheral states are the least technological and have large agrarian sectors, coercion-driven labor processes, very low wages, and weak bureaucratic and military capabilities.[45]

For world-system analysis, then, "stateness" is a function of the international division of labor.[46] Those who perform the most highly valued productive work and trade are closest to the center and, therefore, to power, whereas those whose skills are least valued are furthest toward the margins. This world-system is a highly European-centered order, and colonization was one of the strategies by which both the expansion of the system and the ranking of the states and societies took place. The imposition of the colonial state sealed the peripheralization of most of what is now called either the Third World or the South.

As for the coming of independence, neo-Marxists acknowledge the rise of local social forces to challenge colonialism. However, although decolonization movements won some political power by capturing the state, they did not, by and large, affect the deep structures of the world-system or question the nature and form of politics that were bequeathed[47]—those of the postcolonial state. In view of all of this, the contemporary state in decolonized societies is either a neocolonial project or, at best and under special circumstances, an insurgent structure crippled by the enormous buffeting of the whole system.

The anticolonial struggles of the 1940s and 1950s in Africa were instigated by broad and loose coalitions.[48] Viewing external and European rule as an offense against cultural identity and a source of economic deprivation and political subjugation, these coalitions were led by aspiring bureaucrats, merchants, and political cadres. Their project was driven by a combination of personal ambition, group interest, and popular sentiments that, in their sum total, were conceived to be identical with the general interest and well-being of their respective societies. The ideological husk that held together the endemic contradictions of this assortment of interests and therefore focused collective energy against colonialism was nationalism, with political power as the acme of independence.[49]

Because the rise of nationalism was seen as the antithesis of colonialism, and the winning of political power as the vanquishing of colonial rule, the postcolonial state, in its initial conception, was interpreted by nationalists as a retrieval of positive history and the beginning of revival and mutuality. Substantively, then, this meant equity, prosperity, and peace. The celebratory lyrics at the beginning of this chapter speak to that especially heady moment in Africa. Of course, attached to the affirmative sense of the state was a far less conspicuous but deadly challenge—one destined to be pushed forward by the waiting historical realities: the capacity of the state either to stay on course and deliver on the nationalist project or to become an utter liability, one destructive for both its own long-term interest and that of the society at large.

Postcolonial perspectives on the state are very useful in that they undo Eurocentric conception of the political moment. By foregrounding the pivotal impact of imperialism, colonialism, and the restructuring of the political, economic, and cultural life of Third World societies, this optic has opened up vistas through which we may examine the peculiarities of this experience. In the end, we have an alternative reading of both the order of the world and the making of the state.

Despite these major contributions, however, the postcolonial tradition has a number of deficiencies. The most critical for this project are (1) neither neo-Marxist nor nationalist interpretations say enough about the state as a complex phenomenon—a point taken up later; and (2) both underplay the less visible dimension of their conception of the state. Consider this second point. Neo-Marxist thinking sees the postcolonial state in essentially negative terms; that is, as a creature of the collaborative but unequal relationship between the dominant social forces of the world-system and the rulers of peripheral areas. The nationalist angle, on the other hand, sees the state too positively, as proactive, in pursuit of societal interest. Consequently, neo-Marxism overlooks the possibility of the state as a condensation of collective efficacy, whereas the nationalist pitfall is most discernible in that its proponents overload the apparatus and/or likely conflate narrow middle-class interests and state responsibilities.

Having given a brief review of some of the more foundational thinking on the state, I now bring these discussions to the Somali milieu.

The Somali Context and the State

The most immediate feature about Somali political history is the oft-noted fact that, until the imposition of the colonial state and the dawn of independence, Somali society was quintessentially state-less. Moreover, a chief trait of the culture was acute segmentation based on patrilineally traced blood affinities. This propinquity-ordered identity divided the population into kin families that were redivided into subkin units that, in turn, were further broken down into smaller units, ending at the household (i.e., *reer*).

But the absence of a state, in addition to the segmentation, did not mean a complete lack of public authority or the absence of a sense of political community. On the contrary, like all reciprocal social systems, Somalis of the precolonial age organized and managed their political life through kinship associations, conjoined with religious laws. Figure 5.1 illustrates the makeup of this moral order.

Kinship, an essential part of the ideology of communal societies, and Islamic law (the *qanoon*) together set the basis for decisionmaking and also formed a counterforce to the centrifugal propensities of blood-based identities. Extending arguments I made in other writings,[50] I postulate that kinship, in essence, was composed of two principal elements: (1) blood ties that referred to shared identity, primarily through common male lineage (*tol*) and, to a lesser extent, marriage ties (*hidid*); and (2) a general code (*heer*). Blood ties of tol defined one's place in an exclusive line of male ancestry, and hidid set obligations to the kin of a wife that, for the offspring, stipulated deference to the mother's family and relatives. Heer, an unwritten legal and social practice, delineated directives that guided conduct in intra- and interkin relations.[51] The specific concerns of heer included the following: protection of the folkways and habits of community, stipulation of reciprocal duties and rights, and administration of criminal justice (e.g., identification/definition of legal and illegal acts and regulation of feuds and acts of vengeance).

Any separatist tendencies that *tol* may have promoted were kept in check by hidid and heer, which underscored interdependence and inclusiveness. The combination of blood ties and heer, embodied predominantly in the person of the elder, was one of the two pillars of indigenous political authority; the other was the

Figure 5.1   Basic Elements of Somali Traditional Moral Order

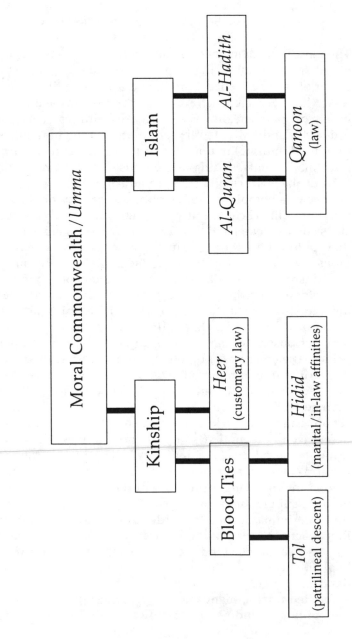

qanoon (derived primarily from the *Al-Quran* and *Al-Hadith*) of Islam, the purveyor of which was the learned and holy, i.e., the *shaikh*. *Qanoon*, like the heer, emphasized reverence for life, dignity, patience, obligation, and, more than the heer, fellowship of all believers, piety, truth, and penance.[52] Together, heer and Islam, in particular, gave the stateless Somalis a rightful political center of gravity capable of controlling capriciousness, managing intersubjectivity, and offering order and continuity.

In short, Somalis of precolonial times might not have seen themselves as a nation, in the now familiar sense that nations are invariably associated with the state. However, they did have a moral commonwealth (or *umma*),[53] despite the incessant feuding, constant competition over very limited resources, and gender inequalities. This is drastically different from the oft-repeated and rather unreflective proposition that Somali society never had much in the way of sustainable social institutions or political fulcrums and is therefore forever condemned to be fractious and clanistic.[54] In my interpretation, tol, devoid of the hidid connection, heer, and qanoon (the constituents of Somali superego), once introduced to the seductions of state power and private accumulation and consumption, turns into degenerative and narrow patrilineal identity (i.e., clanism) conducive to very pernicious asociality.

The imposition of colonial rule disturbed this delicate balance of tensions.[55] Before foreign rule came, of course, the introduction of trade and commerce began to erode gradually some of the adhesives of the old moral order.[56] Very slowly but surely, a process of social differentiation began to take hold with the establishment of regional trade and urban centers. With that change already under way, imperial Europe descended on Africa. The infamous Treaty of Berlin in 1884 and the subsequent scramble had particularly noxious effects on Somali society. To telescope a critical and complex period, I present the following as perhaps the most discernible elements of colonial impact: the sharing of Somali territories by three European imperialists and an African bedfellow, Ethiopia (five colonies were created: two for Britain, one for France, one for Italy, and one for Ethiopia); and a memorable and tenacious resistance: i.e., the Dervish movement of Sayyid Mohamed Abdille Hassan.

For the Somalis, the triumph of colonialism was, in a dialectical fashion, an alienating experience as well as an awakening one. It sowed self-estrangement because, obviously, it was designed to establish conquest on the part of Europeans, to induce inferiority and subservience on the part of the Somalis (this was particularly the case during fascist rule in Southern Somalia), and, in the end, to undermine the age-old *mentalité* of umma and the cosmology that sustained it.

Colonial encounter and subsequent conquest were also awakening because (1) they jarred many Somalis enough to think about cultural pride and masterlessness, as well as Islamic holiness, and (2) they brought to the fore debilitating weaknesses that accompany uneven development and, conversely, impressed on the Somalis the peculiar and formidably calculating rationality behind the triumph of colonialism. Sayyid Mohamed Abdille Hassan understood this and so ignited the first fires of nationalism by turning the ordinarily loose and relaxed spirit of umma into a new and zealous identity. Despite his courage and that of his followers, the sayyid lost. However, his ideals did not die. In fact, they continued to press hard on the memory of the next generations of Somalis.

The Somali Youth League (SYL) in Southern Somalia and the Somali National League (SNL) in the North, together with other independence groups, spearheaded the efforts toward ending colonialism in British Somaliland and the Italian trusteeship of Southern Somalia. On 1 July 1960, these two Somali territories joined to become the new Somali Republic. What does this slice of history mean in the context of our discussion on the state? First, stratification and colonialism, particularly the latter, marked erosion and, in the end, the eventual supersession of indigenous political order and community. Second, independence movements— the antithesis of colonialism—were partly an attempt to revive collective identity and, in a sense, reclaim the authority of umma, which had been contaminated by colonialism.

But there was a downside to this historic effervescence. The very groups who acted as the cadre of the drive toward sovereignty (e.g., traders, lowly bureaucrats, some religious leaders) were also progeny of the systemic process of social gradation—including regional trade and colonization. For example, *dilaals* and traders were intermediaries between pastoral producers and growing international transactions. Theologians acted, in somewhat the same fashion, with regard to questions of faith and providence. Auxiliary bureaucrats, more than any other strata of those social species born out of Somali interactions with the outside world, were direct recruits, trainees, and employees of the colonial state. The severe contradictions between these two identities of the cadres of the independence movements became highly pronounced as the end of the colonial order grew nearer.

In short, the new state was seen by some as a vehicle to reenchant a fallen social reality; for others, the conjuncture was construed in more worldly and crassly instrumentalist terms: the acquisition of personal and parochial power and other tantalizing privileges denied by colonialism. Who would win was to be a central element of the history of the postcolonial Somali state.[57]

The First Republic and Liberalism (1960–1969)

The first regime of the Somali Republic was unveiled with the election of Aden Abdille Osman by the National Assembly for a six-year term as president. President Osman, in turn, nominated Abdirasheed Ali Sharmarke as the executive prime minister.

The Osman and Sharmarke period (1960–1964) represented, in a rather chaotic fashion, a contradictory faith in the liberal conception of the state, with a light nationalist touch. In this sense, the new constitution was the bedrock of the order.[58] Among its accoutrements were specific political and civil rights: universal suffrage, freedom of speech and association, protection against illegal imprisonment, and a right to fair trial. Additionally, the constitution set out the limits of political power and prerogatives by delineating the tenure of all political leaders and the specific functions of political institutions. In the case of the latter, a modicum of separation of powers among the executive branch, the National Assembly, and the courts was inscribed. Coupled with the political character of the regime was an acceptance, almost in toto, of the structure of the economy as inherited from colonialism.

But it was not long before Sharmarke's government began to reap the fallout from its own policies. Caught in a creeping trend of pauperism, but remembering the many promises made on the eve of independence, many Somalis began to view the state with a great deal of suspicion. Such feelings were further aggravated by (1) confusing tendencies of the new state's power, (2) a growing spectacle of national corruption and the attainment of political office as a weak alibi for making personal wealth, and (3) a Northern grumble that Somaliland had been hoodwinked.

The fact that only mayors were to be elected by local communities, whereas all other organs of the society's administration were to be dictated by the central authorities, turned into a sore point. Privatization of public life became particularly stark because of the perceived behavior of the members of the cabinet and the national assembly. New terms were added to the parlance of Somali politics to accent the onset of class and status distinctions. For instance, the terms *dibjir* and *dibir* (vagabond and corpulent, respectively) appeared to signify a mounting disjunction between what was seen as an increasing gauntness at a national scale and the suspected gluttony of the political and commercial elite.

Concerns on the part of some Northerners that all was not well in Mogadishu were expressed by two ominous events in 1961: a negative vote against the constitution, which was seen as a cover for Mogadishu's agenda, and a dramatic but short-lived coup in major towns of Somaliland by Northern junior military officers. By 1963, the coalition collapsed, the SYL fragmented, and the Sharmarke government's attention, as well as everyone else's, shifted to the approaching general elections. On election day, 30 March 1964, eighteen parties, most of them hardly more than an individual member with temporary platforms, participated. In the end, the balance between the "minimum" state and the legitimate maximization of individual utilities that sustain liberal conceptions of the state was weakened by the intramural but intense contentions for personal gain within the state class, the politicians' illicit use of state power to enter the private sector, the relegation of nation building primarily to local efforts and international private gifts,[59] and the traders' extremely narrow agenda.

Once the vote was counted, 21 of the non-SYL deputies crossed the floor and joined the majority party, in search of lucrative portfolios. A single-party political system (despite the proliferation of parties around election time) was in the making. It was time for President Osman to nominate the new prime minister. He called upon a member of the SYL and the minister of interior of the outgoing regime, Abdirazak H. Husein, to form the new government.

The brief leadership of Husein will be remembered for a number of new departures: (1) a sense of regional balance in ministerial portfolios was instituted (in fact, Northerners were appointed to senior and prestigious posts in, for instance, departments of foreign affairs, education, agriculture, and information); (2) a code of ethics in the use of state power, as exemplified by a new edict that required all members of the cabinet to declare their private property and business interests, was enacted; and (3) an emphasis was placed on professional competence in the recruitment and promotion of civil servants. Husein's regime was an attempt to reverse the growing disconnection between the society and the state. But his regime did not get much of a chance. In the summer of 1967, President Osman's tenure came to an end, and Sharmarke was elected as the new president. He, in turn, appointed M. I. Egal, the leader of the SNL in 1960 who became secretary-general of the Somali National Congress (SNC) but left it to join the SYL and Sharmarke's group, as the new prime minister.[60]

Sharmarke and Egal's first administration (1967–1969) was in many ways a return to the laissez-faire liberalism of Sharmarke's time as prime minister.[61] Additionally, and more critically, a calculated strategy of narrowing the base of state power was put to work. First, nonsupporters of the new administration were to be chased out of the SYL. Second, the regime changed the structural relationship between the SYL and the state by making Prime Minister Egal the new secretary-general of the party. This crucial step eliminated any separation between offices of the majority party and the administration of the state. Third, what little autonomy the bureaucracy had came under assault as appointments of cronies began to supplant merit. Fourth, Sharmarke and Egal, together with the minister of interior, Y. N. Hassan, pooled their talent and power to ensure total victory for themselves in the approaching general election of March 1969.

Very few national institutions were not violated. Perhaps the most telling actions were these: (1) open raiding of the state treasury (about U.S. $8 million); (2) pressure on the chief of the National Police Corps, General M. A. Musa, to use his forces and their resources to help those SYL candidates campaigning in tightly contested districts; (3) a modification of the electoral rule to favor the SYL; (4) the more than 1,000 candidates put forth by over 60 parties for the 123 seats; and (5) the deaths of nearly forty people—making the election Somalia's bloodiest.

When the dust settled, the new deputies returned to Mogadishu, eager to recoup their large electoral expenditures. President Sharmarke renominated Egal, who in turn began to appoint the new cabinet. Meanwhile, all but one of the non-SYL members of the new National Assembly, in the first meeting, renounced their affiliations and joined the ruling party. The sole exception was Abdirazak H. Husein, who returned to the National Assembly as a founding member of a new party, the Popular Movement for Democratic Action (PMDA).

Sharmarke and Egal's second regime did not last long. Bedeviled by deepening economic difficulties in the face of more demands from a growing population, a popular perception of malfeasance in the management of national resources, and a generalized and growing suspicion that civilian electoral politics had become a nauseating swindle, the liberal Somali state became the object of widespread ridicule and popular execration. Consequently, on 15 October 1969, President Sharmarke was assassinated, paving the way for a bloodless military takeover. Few tears were shed for the end of the liberal politics of the 1960s.

The Military Dictatorship and Neo-Marxist Nationalism

Within a few hours after the seizure of power, the new military order, the Supreme Revolutionary Council (SRC), abrogated the constitution and the Supreme Court, canceled the National Assembly, and forbade any political activity or organization. Moreover, all luminaries and lesser officials of the nine years of civilian rule were arrested.

In what would become known as the First Charter of the Revolution, the SRC articulated its conception of the functions of the state and, indirectly, the state itself. Functionally, the First Charter stipulated that, in addition to undertaking responsibility for the basic infrastructure, the state would become the pivotal mechanism for the overall development of society in the key areas of the economy, social life, and culture. More specifically, the declared ambitions of this highly active state were to guarantee everyone the right to work, strengthen principles of social justice, stimulate economic growth, establish orthography for the Somali language, clean up corrupt behavior, eliminate "tribalism," and conduct free and impartial elections at a suitable time.

In foreign affairs, the SRC embraced a variant of world-system analysis. Colonialism and neocolonialism were seen as the greatest threat to the welfare of the Somali people, and a promise was made to align the country with "national liberation movements" in the region and around the world. By the 1970s, and during the first anniversary of the SRC, scientific socialism was declared the ideology of the state. This announcement ushered in a wave of nationalizations, which extended the function of the state to most aspects of (urban) life. The sole exceptions to this were livestock production and trade and a dwindling banana industry.

In short, in the mid-1970s, the Somali state under the SRC became omnipresent, eliminating most private space. This odd but potent mixture of nationalism and neo-Marxism had a number of immediate ramifications. First, on the positive side, a stunning tide of popular energy not seen since the agitation for independence was released. Partly as a reaction to the deenergizing languor of the latter stages of civilian rule and also as a response to the mobilizing rhetoric of the SRC, most Somalis felt a moment of pride and reconnection with the state, a reawakening of the umma spirit. Second, as a result of the new emphasis on literacy and language, new schools were built, even in some of the most remote areas, and by 1974 an orthography was established for the Somali language. Finally, a new program of improving the basic infrastructure of the country, including the beautification of the capital, was undertaken.

The first few years of the SRC were a time of new earnestness and confidence.[62] But as the accomplishments were being noted[63] and more promises were being announced, serious debilities were also developing. The most critical was the suppression of democratic rights and a quickening constriction of decisionmaking and governance. Right after the coup, the SRC declared itself the sole authority and set forth a calculated policy of silencing any dissent. That in the midst of mobilization a new and foreboding threshold had been crossed was brought home by the public shooting, in July 1972, of two of the most prominent of the SRC generals, Mohamed Ainanshe and Salad Gabeire. They were accused of counterrevolutionary ideas. During this time, hundreds of lesser figures were detained. Another equally instructive event took place in January 1975. Ten theologians who disagreed with the regime on the reach of a new family law were arrested and executed.

With the initial nationwide exuberance slowly evaporating, to be replaced by a deafening self-glorification of the regime, the rot had set in—one that would subvert the development of rational consciousness and popular political maturity. Contrary to what ideologues were telling each other and foisting on the population, by the middle of the decade, Siyaad Barre's leadership and the SRC's synonymity with a horrid style of governance was crystallizing. Increasingly, the state was identified with concentrated power, fear and intimidation, and disregard for any form of law and due process. The Somali-Ethiopian War of 1977–1978 was, ironically, a godsend for the regime. Everyone's deep nationalist and umma sentiments arose as Somalis took the opportunity on that long-awaited day to recoup one of their "missing territories." But this brief moment of national excitement and glory quickly disappeared when the Ethiopians, backed by their new allies (the Soviet Union, Cuba, South Yemen), reorganized and responded with devastating firepower and numerical superiority.

Bearing the triple burden of defeat in the war and the accompanying national humiliation, an economy on the skids, and a lack of superpower patronage, Somali politics viciously turned inward. The national focus became the regime and the state, which were caught in an enveloping atmosphere of acridity and suspicion. In the middle of the 1980s, a new and pro forma constitution and a peoples' assembly notwithstanding, Somali political authority had become little more than a clanistic operation and family property, its rulers having absolutely no compunction about their vulgarization of power. Particularly mistreated were the peoples of the regions of Mudug, Bari, Togdheer, and Woqooyi Galbeed and the farming and industrious communities of the riverine regions in the South.[64] Many of the communities near the rivers had already lost their meager possessions to a land-grabbing state elite and Siyaad Barre's relatives and acolytes.

Nineteen eighty-eight was a key year in the gathering storm of explosive discontent and eventual implosion. At this time, Somalia and Ethiopia were both confronting deadly ecological deterioration, failing economies, and spreading internal strife and disorder. In Djibouti, Siyaad Barre and Mengistu Haile Mariam signed an agreement of nonaggression and cessation of all hostilities. Included in this rather late rapprochement was the termination by both parties of any support for any opposition to the other. The implication of this particular point for Somalis was immense. Such insurgents as the Somali Salvation Democratic Front (SSDF) and the Somali National Movement (SNM) found themselves deprived, overnight, of a patron and bases. To make something positive out of an unpalatable situation, these opposition forces raised the stakes by attempting to move back into Somalia. The SNM, the best organized and a formidable force, implemented the most daring tactics. Its forces crossed the border of the North and fought their way into some of the major cities of Hargeisa, Burao, and Berbera. The regime responded by unleashing the full military capability of the state.[65] Within a few weeks of hand-to-hand fighting and constant pounding by the military garrisons, together with indiscriminate aerial bombardment by detachments of the air force, Burao was reduced to rubble, and large parts of Hargeisa were devastated.[66]

After the initial thrust of the confrontation cooled down, the regime tenuously regained the urban areas, and SNM warriors controlled most of the vast hinterland. In the ensuing years up to January 1991, regime representatives in Hargeisa indulged in daylight looting of private property and wanton killing, deepening the bitterness toward the state.[67] Although the ferocity of the clash between the regime and the resistance in some regions of the North slowed down toward the end of 1988, it did not bring any peace to that area or contain the accelerating corporate dereliction. Rather, most of Northern Somalia became a forbidden territory, with particularly inhuman and wholesale punishment meted out to members of the Issaq community. In addition, tensions rose in the Northeast, and by early 1989, new and armed dissidents appeared in parts of the southern regions. Most notable were the Somali Patriotic Movement (SPM) and the United Somali Congress (USC). The former drew its membership from the Ogadani lineage; the latter constituted a Hawiye organization. The next twelve months were particularly instructive. As more and more regions of the country slipped out of the control of the regime, Mogadishu became isolated. Security and economic survival deteriorated everywhere to the extent that many began to challenge Siyaad Barre and his regime in the streets of the capital.

Midway through 1990, the signs were clear for those who could read them or cared to take notice. In one of the last attempts to salvage the country from an impending total ruin, over 100 eminent Somali politicians and civic and business leaders came together to face up to Siyaad Barre.[68] Subsequently dubbed the Manifesto Group, they confronted Siyaad Barre with a long inventory of the ills that had befallen the country under his administration and suggested that he immediately resign and hand over executive power to an interim committee. Siyaad Barre refused to budge. He told the departing chief of the United Nations Development Program (UNDP), who also advised accepting the counsel of the Manifesto Group, that

> I, Mohamed Siyaad Barre, am singularly responsible for the transformation of Somalia and Mogadishu from a bush country and scruffy hamlet into a modern state and commodious city, respectfully. Consequently, I will not allow anyone to destroy me or run me out of here; and if they try, I will take the whole country with me.[69]

The defiance to the regime quickened as dissident and armed groups closed in on the capital. Sensing an atmosphere of doom, many foreign residents began to depart. Siyaad Barre declared a state of emergency and put what was left of the army on full battle alert. In the meantime, two very late and hurried attempts to diffuse the situation were announced. First, under the auspices of the Italian and Egyptian governments, a meeting was called between the regime and two of the major opposition forces (the SNM and the USC), to be convened in Cairo. This proposal was stillborn because the organized and armed opposition had long seen the regime as rancid and predatory and not worthy of any contact. Second, on 25 December, the regime announced that a free, multiparty election would be conducted in February 1991. This too was rejected and interpreted as a deceitful ploy, given a recently initiated policy by the regime of executing any dissident or opposition member, especially people from the Hawiye lineage, the main support of the USC.

January 1991 became the decisive month: the city exploded, thus beginning four weeks of fierce battles between loyalists (mostly clanistic military forces) and a growing but disorganized urban insurrection. By the end of the first week of January, the remaining expatriates (including 240 Americans and 200 Italians) were lifted out of Mogadishu to waiting U.S. naval vessels. As a final act of despair, Siyaad Barre, still unwilling to relinquish power, appointed another Issaq, Omer Arteh Qalib, as prime minister.[70]

Qalib was the first foreign minister of the military regime (from 1969–1976) and had been in detention from 1980–1988. On 27 January, when Villa Somalia (the presidential palace) was overrun and Barre fled, he lived up to his earlier promise: he left behind thousands dead,[71] many more wounded, the total destruction of state property, and a city and society dazed by the victory but unaware of the horrendous problems that lay ahead of it.

What, then, is the import of this narrative for the concepts of the state and governance? It is my contention that Siyaad Barre's regime and the state it constructed can best be described as a contrived and awkward marriage of neo-Marxism and nationalism—two central tendencies of the postcolonial conception of the state. Despite some early warnings, such a strategy worked the first few years. In the end, however, when the weighty issues (e.g., democracy, law, efficiency, and economic growth) arrived, the experience turned into a costly dead end.

The causal factors are numerous, but I propose the following to be among the chief factors that underscore the downside of a very crude and superficial commingling of these two perspectives: (1) exaggerated promises that necessitated a need for bureaucratic expansion and high regimentation; (2) a means of governance—the state—that turned into a deaf intruder or a tool of dragooning, with a concomitant paranoia about security; (3) replacement of skill and merit with regime/personal loyalty, ushering in a reign of psychophancy and ignorance; (4) neglect of accumulation and a deepening pauperism and dependency on the outside;[72] and, the most burdensome in the long run, (5) self-righteousness and a belief in the indivisibility of the interests of the state class and society, attitudes that banished accountability and restraint from the idea of political life.[73]

The Death of the Somali State: Theoretical Concerns

Most Somalis and many of their friends saw the end of Siyaad Barre's regime as a solemn occasion and a coming of age—one buttressed by a loss of innocence and hard lessons—and a unique opportunity for renascence. However, the years following that fateful time have been marked by total descent into utter lawlessness and peccant localism. I have argued elsewhere that all dissident and opposition forces, though committed to defeating the regime, lacked any well-crafted tactics to get the job done, as well as any vision of an alternative state.[74] Consequently, with the departure of Siyaad Barre, a vacuum appeared. Dissent groups and opposition forces who took over the capital (predominantly the USC) immediately began to quarrel among themselves, with each faction staking a claim to control of parts of Mogadishu.

The situation was aggravated by two ill-conceived events. First, some of the civilian leadership of the USC named a relatively successful motel owner and a lesser known member of both the last elected parliament and the Manifesto Group to be the new interim president. Without any prior consultations with other opposition groups or a full consensus among the high command of the USC, Ali Mahdi Mohamed was sworn in as interim president on 29 January. This unilateral decision was made more offensive by the fact that, during the ceremony, Ali Mahdi was flanked by, among others, some of the closest senior lieutenants of Siyaad Barre, including General Hussein Kulmiye Afrah (the second vice-president) and Mohamed Sheikh Osman, a longtime minister of finance for Siyaad Barre. In a country already reeling from a clanist dictatorship, this was more than a cause for alarm; it was immediately interpreted as a Hawiye grab for power. Second, a harrowing vendetta was initiated against members of the Darood community. They were seen as supporters of Siyaad Barre, particularly during the last murderous days of his regime.

The Morrow of Siyaad Barre's Decampment

The first indication that trouble was on the horizon came when Ali Mahdi Mohamed was challenged by other leaders of the USC—particularly the chairman, General Mohamed Farah Aideed. Foremost of Aideed's arguments were (1) that Ali Mahdi Mohamed had violated the procedure of collective decisionmaking and (2) that Aideed himself was more deserving of the presidency because he was the one commanding the fighters who shed plenty of blood to defeat Siyaad Barre's regime.

Lurking behind these two concerns was a precarious alliance between different segments of the Hawiye. Ali Mahdi Mohamed is an Abgal (dominant around the area surrounding Mogadishu), whereas General Aideed is Habar Gidir (mostly concentrated at the outskirts of Banaadir and further north of the capital). As these quarrels were heating up, Ali Mahdi called for a national conference to convene in Mogadishu immediately. Most of the rebel groups, already fulminating over the hasty way the interim regime was set up, declined the invitation.[75]

In the meantime, in Mogadishu, what started as isolated incidents of revenge against supporters of Siyaad Barre turned into

wholesale massacre of anyone who was identified as Darood. Those
fortunate enough to get away left their property to be looted and appropriated. With the city emptied of most of the non-Hawiye residents, numerous armed factions (some affiliated with the USC, others little more than youth gangs) laid claim to different parts of the
city. Mogadishu was now very much like the Beirut of the 1970s and
early 1980s, a city lacking central authority, experiencing dwindling
food supplies and other amenities, and engulfed by violent anarchy.

In view of this, it is important to note that, in comparison to the
South, Northern Somalia was somewhat calm. Although the SNM
forces did use intimidation and occasional bloody coercion to bring
the whole territory to heel, a modicum of modus vivendi was established with the non-Issaq communities. Consequently, the area
was spared the mayhem and destruction that was gripping the capital city and was to spread into most of the South.

In the midst of this growing ghastliness in Mogadishu, what
hope remained for the resuscitation of the Somali state was dashed
by two new developments. First, some of the armed opposition
groups to the ancien régime (e.g., the SPM) declared war on the
USC, and new clanist organizations (e.g., Jabhad) were formed in
other parts of the country. Second, and perhaps most crippling, the
SNM declared the secession of Northern Somalia (ex-British Somaliland) and the birth of a new nation-state: the Somaliland Republic.
More than any other event, this was the most bewildering. It put
into sharp relief how completely tarnished Somalism (umma) and
the state that was supposed to represent it had become. The degree
of damage is underlined by the fact that, if the breakup becomes an
internationally endorsed fact, the new boundaries would revert to
those designed by colonial conquest.

I suggest four reasons, among perhaps others, why the leadership of the SNM took this hurried disquieting step: (1) the savagery
in the streets of Mogadishu; (2) the manner in which the interim
Mahdi regime was installed; (3) pressure from grass-roots supporters and fighters who were earlier mobilized around clanist and re-
gionalist sentiments; and (4) personal ambition (i.e., the syndrome
of big fish in small waters). Whether all four factors equally affected
this drastic decision is difficult to discern. Regardless, this announcement did not settle the fundamental issues of governance
and the formation of a viable state.

Initial SNM strategies for filling the void left behind by the collapse of the regime were relatively sober and constructive. Preliminary evidence suggests that they rehabilitated some of the traditional methods of dialogue between communities (particularly with

the non-Issaq Somalis of the North) by calling on the services of elders.[76] Moreover, in a long discussion that took place in Berbera (15–27 February 1991) and in others that followed it, a minimum of order and some resuscitation of the elements of citizenship were initiated. For instance, debate among the SNM Central Committee members on a new constitution was opened, the most immediate item being the form of the new government. In a final show of hands, it was decided (by a vote of 46 to 33) to establish an executive presidency—a point preferred by the chairman of the SNM at that time (Abdirahman Ahmed Ali). The full discussion on the constitution was postponed for a later date; in the meantime, a provisional government was to be set up for at least two years. Finally, within weeks of the cessation of hostilities and the return of some normalcy, many literate individuals took advantage of the new freedom. Consequently, a plethora of infelicitous, but interesting, publications appeared in some of the towns, especially Hargeisa. Although all of them aimed their venom at the ancien régime and celebrated the new arrangement, there were some blunt questions about social attitudes under the SNM.

If the early policies of the SNM rule in the North can be seen as a ray of hope for a possible reclamation of the spirit of umma, the first test was the configuration of the interim regime under Abdirahman Ahmed Ali, which was announced on 4 June 1991. Table 5.1 shows the names and distribution of political offices among the kin groups in the newly declared Somaliland Republic.

There are two points that are worthy of immediate attention regarding the new regime of Somaliland. First is the issue of equity among different kin groups. Given the fact that one of the original defining features of SNM ideology was the principle of fairness and the rehabilitation of generosity (essential constituents of umma), it was troubling that eleven of the seventeen ministers and all four vice-ministers were from the Issaq community. This act represented double jeopardy in the sense that in terms of both sheer numbers and importance of portfolio, the Issa, Gadaborsi, Dolbahante, and Warsangali—i.e., the rest of the kin groups in the North—seem to have been relegated to a negligible minority (virtually peripheral auxiliaries) in terms of political presence.[77] Second, for a new state that was supposedly created out of the ashes of a corrupt and dysfunctional one, the idea of appointing such a large cabinet (as large as that in some of the earlier regimes) seemed to miss the imperatives of parsimony and efficiency.

Compounding these two factors was the surfacing of a secret memorandum, on the letterhead of the SNM, that summarizes the

Table 5.1   Formation of the First Interim Somaliland Republic Regime

Position	Name and kin group
President	Abdirahman Ahmed Ali (Issaq)
Vice-president	Hassan Issa Jama (Issaq)
Ministers	
Foreign affairs	Shaikh Yusuf Ali Shaikh Madar (Issaq)
Interior	Suleyman Mohamed Aden (Issaq)
Defense	Mohamed Kahin Ahmed (Issaq)
Finance	Ismail Mohamed Hurreh (Issaq)
Education	Abdirahman Aw Ali (Gadaborsi)
Health and labor	Abiib Deria Nor (Issaq)
Agriculture	Said Mohamed Nor (Issaq)
Fisheries	Omer Issa Awaleh (Issaq)
Geology/water	Mohamed Ali Ateyeh (Dolbahante)
Public works and housing	Mahdi Abdi Amareh (Issa)
Planning	Jama Rabileh God (Gadaborsi)
Information/tourism	Osman Aden Dool (Issaq)
Livestock	Yasin Ahmed Haji Nor (Dolbahante)
Communication	Mohamoud Abdi All (Warsangali)
Commerce	Mohamed Dahir Mohamed (Issaq)
Justice	Ahmed Ismail Ahdi (Issaq)
Rehabilitation	Hassan Aden Wadaadeid (Issaq)
Vice-ministers	
Interior	Ahmed Jambir (Issaq)
Defense	Dahir Shaikh Abdillahi (Issaq)
Finance	Aden Sahar (Issaq)
Justice	Shaikh Mohamed Ali Jama (Issaq)

Sources: Author's fieldnotes, January 1992; Drysdale, *Somaliland 1991*, p. 45.

proceedings of a meeting ostensibly held by the Security Committee of the SNM.[78] The focus of the meeting, according to the memorandum, was to strategize for Issaq domination of every aspect of life in the new Somaliland, including the state. All eight principal points listed underline the ways in which the non-Issaq communities of the North would, in the future, be subjugated and all regions of the North made available for the Issaq kin group only. In a number of recent visits to the Horn of Africa and in many conversations with elders and average members of Northern communities, I did *not* find anyone who knew about the existence of this memorandum. However, a few speculated to the effect that some elements of the SNM were clanistically and personally ambitious and, therefore, such a scheme did not sound farfetched.

Whatever the veracity of the memorandum, Ali's regime in the North expired without any success in turning the declaration of sovereignty and whatever halo that surrounded it into a viable state; the spirit of umma was not revived, and recognition by the outside world was not attained. That such tasks were proving tough and the future beginning to look like the past were intimated by other incidents: First, the SNM leadership refused to participate in a national reconciliation meeting sponsored by the government of Djibouti. The meeting (the second of its kind) was held in Djibouti from 15–21 July 1991 and was chaired by three elder statesmen from yesteryear (Aden Abdille Osman, Abdirazak H. Husein, and Mohamed Ibrahim Egal) and attended by representatives of six fronts (the SSDF, USC, SPM, Somali Democratic Movement [SDM], Somali Democratic Alliance [SDA], and United Somali Front [USF]).[79] Second, there were confirmed reports of intra-SNM fighting that first broke out around Berbera on 23 December 1991 and, more seriously, a major clash in Burao in January 1992 in which scores are reported to have been killed; there has also been a growing lawlessness in the region.[80] Third, the emergence of very serious accusations of undemocratic and dictatorial behavior by Abdirahman Ahmed Ali, the president of the interim regime, caused many to resign from the cabinet.

During early 1993, a Somaliland meeting was convened in Boroma. There is very little public information on the nature of the agenda, who was invited, and through what procedure. In the end, A. A. Ali was replaced as the "leader" of Somaliland by M. I. Egal, the prime minister of Somalia from 1967–1969. The hope for this change was that Egal could bring his experience to valorize the idea and existence of the Republic of Somaliland. Despite some accomplishments toward the establishment of a meager but self-help–based administration and an infant tax and legal system, things have not moved much. At the time of this writing, politics in Northwestern Somalia (or the Somaliland Republic) were rather contumacious, and the people there seemed unable either to give credible and competent institutional substance to declared sovereignty or to assume their share of the awaiting responsibility for national rapprochement.[81] Equally in the Northeast, although a rudimentary degree of security and order had been established by the SSDF, there was little energy or will to pick up, in earnest, the great questions of resurrection.

By the autumn of 1991, the bloodletting in Mogadishu rose to a new level. The two main factions of the USC, each propelled by the ambition of its respective leader, turned their already grisly confrontation into "a mad form of collective self-genocide."[82] These battles were most acute during the last two weeks of November, when General Aideed's forces, in an effort to destroy those loyal to

Ali Mahdi, started a full-scale attack on parts of Mogadishu occupied by Mahdi's supporters. This strategy did not succeed, but the destruction was colossal. The city became a landscape of charred buildings, with dead bodies strewn everywhere. From the start of Aideed's offensive to the end of February 1992, it was estimated that nearly 14,000 people lost their lives in Mogadishu, 27,000 more were injured,[83] and nearly a third of its 1.25 million inhabitants sought temporary refuge on the perimeter of the city or in other parts of the country.

But Mogadishu's plight was not solely the consequence of the USC splinter; rather, this problem was compounded by the daily terror and intimidation carried out by the thousands of armed youths (some of them as young as nine or ten) scavenging for food or anything else they could get their hands on, "amidst," as Vico would have expressed, "the putrefaction of their dead."[84] Moreover, with nearly 30,000 armed men and teenagers roaming different quarters of the city, coupled with an ever-present anxiety of acute hunger, as well as delirium induced by constant chewing of qat, cavalier killing had become the norm.[85]

The rest of Southern Somalia was not spared such gruesome factional warring. From Kismayo and Baidoba to the Northeast in Galcaio, numerous clanistic battles have been fought over diminishing resources, territory, and strategic advantage in the event that a semblance of national order is eventually reconstituted.

In the end, it is the average Somalis (particularly women and children) who have borne the cost, with nearly 4.5 million (about 60 percent of the total population) confronting hunger and starvation.[86] The death of the state and the wretchedness of Somalis were so total that the welfare of those inside the country, and many hundreds of thousands of refugees across the Ethiopian and Kenyan borders, was in the hands of various NGOs and humanitarian/relief organizations.[87] In the midst of the gloom, perhaps the only heartening tidings that had come out of Somalia by the end of 1992 were the achievement of a temporary cease-fire in Mogadishu to allow food to be delivered to the hundreds of thousands who are marooned in the battered city; the docking of ships carrying 5,000 tons of wheat, which were added to 12,000 tons sent in by the Red Cross;[88] the posting of 500 Pakistani troops in Mogadishu by the United Nations to protect the air and sea ports where relief supplies are unloaded; a decision by the U.S. administration to airlift 140,000 tons of food to other parts of Southern Somalia;[89] and the dislodgement of Siyaad Barre from his stronghold in the Gedo Region of Southern Somalia, forcing him into exile in Nigeria.

During early December 1992, in the wake of deteriorating conditions in Somalia, a multinational military force of over 34,000 troops (24,000 of them from the United States) landed in Mogadishu and other famine-struck areas in the country. Somalia's disruption was so complete that these troops were dispatched to secure the delivery of food to hundreds of thousands of Somalis reduced to starvation by the actions of armed factions and their "warlords." By mid-1993, with this mission largely accomplished and heavy U.S. military presence replaced by diverse UN forces, attention was turning to larger and more daunting issues: the disarmament of private militias and individuals, national reconciliation, and the rebuilding of vital institutions.

In the pursuit of these objectives, the UN sponsored a conference on reconciliation, held in Addis Ababa in March 1993. The participants included delegates from fifteen clanist organizations and a few representatives for women, intellectuals, and traditional leaders. After two weeks of cantankerous posturing by many of the factions and relentless pressure from the international community (particularly President Zenawi of Ethiopia), an agreement was reached.[90] The key feature stipulated the creation of a Transitional National Council to become a prime political authority. This arrangement would be in place for two years, then a new national government would be established. Other important institutions agreed upon were the Central Administrative Departments, Regional Councils, and District Councils. The Transitional National Council would be composed of seventy-four representatives from the eighteen previously designated regions. In addition, five delegates would come from the capital and one from each of the fifteen factions that were present. Each region would have three delegates, one of whom would be a woman.

All of this was certainly in the right direction. However, there were two factors that immediately triggered cause for concern. First, leaders of armed and clanist organizations dominated the conference and felt legitimated by the process. This is both perverse and dangerous. Such legitimation undermines any accounting of the massive human rights abuses that must take place, as well as the introduction of genuine democracy. The centering of human rights and democratic habits are indivisible and intrinsic to a successful transition and renewal. Second, the SNM turned down the invitation and instead sent an observer delegation. This act underscores the degree of alienation of some members of the northern communities from the process.

The promise of both UNOSOM II and the Addis Ababa Agreement was damaged by developments during the summer and autumn of 1993. First, on June 5, twenty-two Pakistani soldiers were ambushed and killed. General Aideed and his new Somali National Alliance (SNA) were accused of the act. UNOSOM announced a bounty of $20,000 on General Aideed's capture. Soon, southern Mogadishu became the scene of a new war between Aideed's supporters and UNOSOM. Many Somalis were killed as the whole UN project became fixated on Aideed. Second, in September 1993, the president of secessionist Somaliland, M. I. Egal, accused the UN of making vacuous promises while undermining the progress of the new state. He asked the UN to depart.

Third, the most dreadful event (especially in the eyes of the United States) happened in early October, when eighteen U.S. troops were killed and around seventy wounded in a clash with armed supporters of Aideed. Moreover, hundreds of Somalis lost their lives. After watching a horrid display of the remains of an American soldier being dragged through the dusty streets of Mogadishu and faced with another soldier taken prisoner, the disgust and indignation of the American public compelled President Clinton to announce a deadline for full withdrawal. The date was set for 31 March 1994. In the meantime, American military presence in Somalia was temporarily strengthened while Ambassador Robert Oakley was sent with the diplomatic responsibility to reorient the mission toward the search for a political settlement. Oakley flew to Addis Ababa in the hope of asking the African leaders of the region to take over the task of reconciliation in Somalia.

For those Somalis who expected UNOSOM to disarm the warring factions, the inordinate focus on General Aideed and subsequent lack of resolve to punish him for his vainglorious and violent ways, together with the announcement of the date for withdrawal of U.S. troops, amounted to defeat. Many were resigning themselves to a return of violent anarchy and starvation. Finally, despite reports that some District Councils were established and a few thousand policemen recruited, none of the major elements of the Addis Ababa Agreement have come to pass.[91] As a result, observers of Somalia were skeptical or unconvinced that Somalis, on the whole, had learned much from their recent past. The absence of an ethical ordering of human relations and effective public institutions continues to be at the heart of Somali misfortune.

Rethinking and Remaking the State

Critical threads that run through the preceding narrative are the complete shattering of the Somali state, the loss of national compass, and the consequent, unprecedented, broad indulgence in communal immolation. If these harrowing conditions are ever to be arrested, let alone reversed, Somalis cannot avoid picking up the challenge of imagining and building a life of "political goodness."[92]

To move in this direction, then, two relevant issues present themselves forthwith. The first is that political goodness is contingent on a cognitive distinction and distance between capriciousness and dutifulness. The former is the height of degenerative expediency or willfulness and is therefore ruinous of social affinity and cohesion; the latter, at the other end of the spectrum, is akin to a categorical imperative—it embodies both obligation and right, which are so elemental in any communality or *civitas*. A society that fails to make such a separation in its operational code, even momentarily, is liable to descend into moral entropy, with brutality as the only means to act politically.[93]

Furthermore, such a civilized mode of thinking and acting (i.e., a routinization) cannot be left solely to cognition alone; rather, the whole exercise must emerge from deeper mores and a worldview (i.e., cosmology) that are the bedrock of any belief system and the work of every generation. Consequently, culture itself has to be continually made, unmade, and remade, for as Berlin tells us, "values are not discovered, they are created; not found, but made by an act of imaginative, creative will, as works of art, as policies, plans, patterns of life are created."[94]

It is one of my lateral arguments that at the heart of the Somali catastrophe is a full breakdown of culture (e.g., heer, Islam), which has resulted in the onset of murderous whimsicalness and meanspiritedness. These are among the factors most culpable in the evisceration of the Somali state, a process that produced its share of social and political morbidities that, in time, sealed its own fate.

This brings me to the second point—the state itself. Given the interdependence of culture and governance implied in this discussion, I suggest that successful rehabilitation and invention of viable values are, to a large extent, conditional on envisioning the idea of the state, in Cicero's sense, and acting on that vision—i.e., making the state. On both accounts, current Somali society is in deep trouble. How, then, does one imagine as well as discern the place and moment of action? Obviously, different vantage points elicit different theories and strategies. For me, the vision starts with a conception of the state as combination of agency (social force), site (institution), and mindset (consciousness). The interplay of these three elements of the state and their relationship with the private sphere are shown in Figure 5.2.

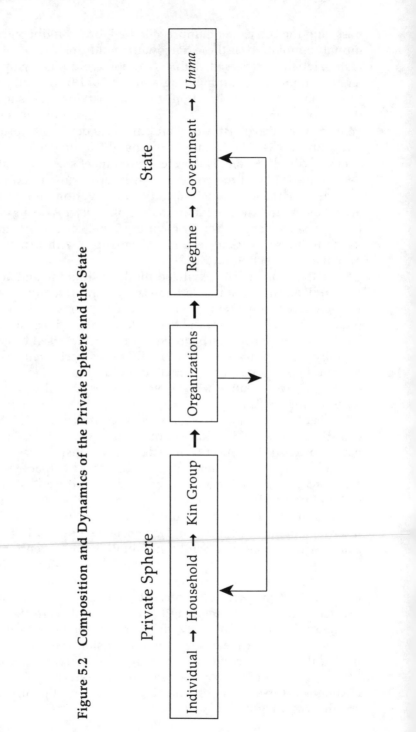

Figure 5.2 Composition and Dynamics of the Private Sphere and the State

The private sphere begins with individuals, who are products as well as producers of households and kin groups. In all three, identities and values are made that are obviously most intimate at the intersection of the individual and household. But as the boundaries of primary associations are crossed, larger but secondary identities (e.g., kin) are formed. Contrary to the argument by some scholars that traditional self-consciousness and mutuality stop here, I suggest that common language, faith, and material existence link self-knowledge to a world beyond family and kin. Of course, the range and intensity of such an extension are subject to the nature and force of any intervening variable that could be either supportive and enriching or subversive and deleterious. In nonreciprocal social systems, particularly those that are commodity-ordered, new identities are born that sometimes supplement, but usually supplant, traditional self-definition. For instance, given the separation of economic and political life, class distinctions appear that when they mature and are organized, turn into trade associations (e.g., unions, management associations, professional organizations). As these associations enter the public sphere, they form the basis for political parties or other forms of political organizations that in turn join the competition for regime formation—one of the sites where civil society meets the state.

The state as an agency is best represented by a regime. Essentially a condensation of the winners, a regime embodies first the face of power and sectarian interest, and only secondarily the collective welfare. This is where the Marxist rendition (i.e., the instrumentalist conception) of the state is most acute. But a regime's capabilities to carry out its project cannot be limited to its immediate membership; rather, as a result of earlier battles, in which even those who lost left behind their mark, a machinery for the execution of policy comes into being. A government, then, is to be seen as a congeries of public bureaucracies that monitor the structures of the state. Each regime presses hard on this machinery to have its way, for instance, by appointing its supplicants and intimidating those unwilling to cooperate. In this sense, clashes between members of a regime and the machinery of the state could be one of the nodal points at which the struggle over the degree of state autonomy takes place. According to one theorist,

> One reason why the concept of the state is such a vexed concept . . . is because it is predominantly at the level of state operations that intellectually and morally ambitious conceptions of the political good intersect with the consecutive, and sometimes quite drastic, shaping of social life.[95]

But regimes or bureaucracies cannot maintain any semblance of hegemony—which is essential to the health and viability of public order—by focusing only on the promotion and protection of their respective interests. In fact, a regime that hopes to come to power through any legitimate means must articulate some sense of the general concerns and a promise of policies set to achieve commensurate goals. Anything less is bound to accent exclusive agendas and imperil claims of leadership.

Government machineries, on the other hand, are even more beholden to the idea of collective well-being; their inception and ends are only justifiable with close reference to public good. In fact, one could further argue that, without overlooking the self-interest or inertia of bureaucracies, government machineries are a major link between regimes and the common good. As a result, effective governance, to a large extent, depends on the caliber and professional integrity of those who operate these institutions. In the end, both regimes and bureaucracies have to speak the lexicon of political goodness to sustain their credibility with the larger society.

The third element of the state, and the most pivotal, is the idea of polity itself, or in Benedict Anderson's more original terms, "imagined community."[96] Group identity depends on, among other things, a memory of collective vulnerabilities and an inclusive sense of the public good, which are buttressed by a distillation of common history and shared fate. In this way, the state is much more than the sum of physical structures and regime personalities; it is, to borrow from Edmund Burke, "moral essence"[97] and an embodiment of "ideal normative agreements"[98] among the vast majority of the membership.

Here, some insights of the liberal tradition as well as Rousseauan thinking on the state come to mind. The notion of political goodness is similar to that of *fides*, which is, according to Dunn, "the duty to observe mutual undertaking and the virtue of consistently discharging this duty."[99] In turn, both concepts sit comfortably well with umma because all three underline an intimate connection between the ethical endowment of a regime, the degree of dedication of government functionaries, and the broad cultural foundations of private life. Without a continuous nourishment of the ideals of community and civic sensibilities (e.g., mutual respect, sympathy, concern for the rights of others) emanating from deep intersubjectivity and reinforced by everyday conscientious conduct of public affairs, the state is reduced to an unhinged coercive apparatus to be used licentiously by whomever wins a manifestly feral contest.[100]

From this angle, the mental construct of governance and the private sphere are highly interdigitated, with regime and regulatory mechanisms seen as material representations of the relationship. Consequently, failure to engender the idea of state or the mounting of a fatal assault on it (even in the face of an odious regime) is to cross a crucial line and, in the process, loose uncontrollable demonic forces that are likely to damage or destroy collective virtue. John of Salisbury, recalling the intellectual bequest of the classical world, reminds us of this seemingly eternal wisdom:

> Since one cannot even imagine how any kind of happiness could exist entirely apart from mutual association and divorced from human society, whoever assails what contributes to establish and promote rightful order in the latter, would seem to obstruct the way to beatitude for all.[101]

Such, we may surmise, is the tragic lesson of the Somali condition.

To recapitulate, then, successive Somali regimes hardly understood their mission or, as was the case with the last one, willfully jettisoned their obligations—desecrating, along the way, the principles of traditional order and hopelessly failing to replace them with workable substitutes. This in turn deprived government offices of professional probity and led to the swift deterioration of competence. Combined, these degenerate traits of the operational side of the state have smothered any idea of state or of civic bonding, leaving behind a stunted and poisoned society riddled with fissures and too disabled even to protect its members from the basic adversities of daily life.[102]

Conclusion

Somalia is in a condition of physical and mental exhaustion. Anyone who dares to prescribe ought to tread very carefully, lest false hopes are raised that can only aggravate the prevailing sense of utter dejection. But to make sobriety a touchstone of any cogitation upon the Somali situation need not hamstring creative exploration of possibilities for collective resurgence. In fact, it is important to remember that crises are not only times of acute misery but also opportune moments for daring. Transcendence, however, is contingent upon an intelligent mixture of dispassionate analytical thinking and a long-range outlook. The former is the key to reclaiming discussions about the present for the sake of reason and sensibleness (with a particular eye on recent history); the latter is needed to hear the voice of a better future, which is desperately calling for magnanimity and imagination.

The moral of the argument of this chapter is this: a resurrection of Somali society is dependent on, to a great extent, the (re)construction of both the operational and spiritual dimensions of the state. Although effort in each direction is necessary, I suggest that the ethical (i.e., *umma*) element is the most urgent as well as basic. As a result, a question arises: what options are available to start this historic undertaking? Below, I sketch four possibilities for the future, comment very briefly on each, and bring forth the scenario I deem most sensible—maybe even necessary.

The Present as the Future

The present as the future is really not an option. With chaos, death, and a generalized hunger stalking many parts of the country, to let the present circumstances expand into any measure of the future is to surrender and accept total defeat and infinite damnation. It is a continuous resistance to barbarism (a condition not dissimilar to what has been happening in Somalia) and the degree of success that accompanies such an effort that determines the ripeness of a given culture. Postcolonial politics in general, and the past twenty years in particular, have left behind very little to be proud of and a great deal of grief and shame. Somalis have failed miserably to capitalize on whatever potential there was for independence. Hence, as the tired cliché has it, the big chickens have more than come home to roost. Like much of Africa, then, the best legacy of the contemporary time is as a basis for a new realization and sobriety—one linked to an unfaltering urge to soar above or at least move away from the sordidness of it all.

But lest this cast of mind and attitude be interpreted by others as license for a customized Olympian detachment, there is a correlate to the proposition: an equally impelling conviction that organized and purposive human agency is the single most significant factor in the making of positive history. Within this formulation, the present is put in its place and into proper perspective, and the summons of a different future is heard.

Return to Kinship

A return to kinship has some merit if it means a conscious and careful recovery of what is civilized (i.e., ethical) and usable of the Somali tradition. Respect for the wise, honesty, fairness, and reciprocity were critical elements of kin-ordered life. Furthermore, the addition of Islamic precepts such as piety, kindness, and discipline enabled Somalis to survive, in a spirit of umma, in an otherwise difficult environment. All of these are rich sources for reconstitution. However, there are a number of critical caveats to be noted: (1) kinship ought *not* to be confused with clanism—the latter is an ugly and calamitous perversion; (2) Somali pastoral culture has gone through numerous transformations—including an inescapable insertion into a complex world—which require new macrostructures (e.g., a state) that can be successfully created only at some expense of more intimate relations and primordial ties; (3) women's equality, so much hidden away in Somali history, (as brought forth in Chapter 8) cannot wait anymore and, as a matter of fact, is one of the few ready-made weapons to show clanism for what it really is— male Hobbesian egoism and deformed vanity running amok; and (4) the last generation that has full awareness of the significance of Somali lore is approaching death; mostly sexagenarians and older, their disappearance will deprive present and future Somalis of the major connection to that valuable past.

Annulment of Unity

An annulment of unity denotes acceptance of the breakup of Somalia into two separate and sovereign states and a return of Northern and Southern Somalia as established by colonialism. Some aspects of the rationale for this (as the declaration by the SNM presented it) would be the maintenance of distinct colonial heritages, ethnic filiation and subcultural differences, and the perception that the thirty years of union were a basis for nefarious rule best symbolized by Siyaad Barre's regime.

It is true that Northern and Southern Somalia had two colonial experiences, each leaving behind a somewhat distinguishable, although by now hardly visible, ethos. It is equally valid (though a rather banal claim) to argue that a proximity of settlements breeds some affinities that create an impression of "us" and "them." Finally, the disappointment of earlier regimes and the malignancy of Siyaad Barre are incontestable.

Despite these arguments, however, the annulment of the union is hard to sustain. First, distinctions between colonial heritages (from Britain and Italy) had some relevance only during the early years of independence. For instance, although both the English and Italian languages gave the educated elite of each territory a sub-identity, thirty years of union have had an impact, and many Southern Somalis have learned how to speak English (Italian is less frequent). More significantly, both colonial languages and their cultural accoutrements were limited to a very small group on both sides; the bulk of the population spoke and still speaks Somali. In the years since 1974, when Somali became the official administrative language, competence in all foreign languages declined precipitously. Ironically, exile could bring back to life some of that identification with a different metropole.

Second, although spatial closeness fosters affection and intimacy—including intermarriages—it can also create anxieties and mutual antipathies (especially in an environment of very scant and dwindling resources). Moreover, many Somalis have, at one time or another, crossed kin boundaries and found the experience pleasant and enriching.

Third, neglect by the liberal civilian regimes was, by and large, nationwide; the exceptions were places such as Mogadishu and commercialized spots in the riverine areas. The brutality of the pseudosocialist/nationalist regime of Siyaad Barre touched many, although the destruction of Hargeisa and Burao were unmatched until the implosion of Mogadishu.

Finally, Somalia cannot cut itself into smaller pieces (it is not the USSR, or even Yugoslavia) and survive well in a world that is furiously competitive. If Northwestern Somalia goes, what will stop the rest of the country from breaking up, including Northwestern Somalia itself. Needless to say, smallness, coupled with underdevelopment, is *not* beautiful, but rather hideous.

Rehabilitation of Liberalism

Essentially, proponents of a rehabilitation of liberalism suggest exhuming the constitution and resetting the political clock to the 1960s. Key features would include a resumption of the basis of the old union defined by two regions, the same districts, and a parliament with the same number and distribution of seats.

That the liberal constitution, with its emphasis on legal and political rights, has a great appeal and relevance to the needs of the times cannot be gainsaid. But it was the Somali brand of liberal experience that delivered Siyaad Barre's regime, and I have offered some explanations for this in the course of this chapter. Suffice it to note here that the liberal order ended with three things: it disempowered local communities by centralizing authority in Mogadishu and its representatives in the provinces; it normalized venality and ineptitude, turning the country into a bottomless pit for foreign aid; and it perverted parliamentary politics into a flea market for the buying and selling of votes and public privileges. Perhaps the fate of the return of an insipid liberalism in places such as Ghana under Hilla Liman, Nigeria under Shehu Shagari, and Sudan under Saadiq al Mahdi in the mid-1980s is a warning too important to overlook.

Imagining the New State

The agony and the depletion of most means of livelihood notwith-standing, this is a historic conjuncture for Somalis. It is time to for-get—and forgive—yet remember; to unlearn yet learn; and to con-serve yet dare. It is important to forget and forgive because privileged grief and vengefulness are cancerous to *civitas;* at the same time, memory keeps alive moments of individual humiliation and collective horror for the sake of durable alertness and vigi-lance.[103] It is critical to unlearn some habits because they have out-lived their usefulness, becoming dead weight on the present as well as crippling any future-oriented initiative; by the same token, a new appetite for learning is the surest way to engage a frenzied world that brings forth both deadly temptations and enabling opportuni-ties. Finally, this is a time to conserve, because frugality, in all areas of life, balances needs of the present with those of posterity; curios-ity and courage are gateways to inventiveness, key ingredients for any likelihood of local empowerment and successful participation in the world order.

To bring about a new governance presupposes an envisioning or return of the idea of state. Like the labor of Sisyphus, this is a continual task for all societies—including the most accomplished, which have amassed large intellectual and cultural provisions. The making of umma and a practice of fides can never be put on hold or laid to rest; rather, solidarity (i.e., responsibility for and to each other), if it is to be protected from the fraying strains of everyday tensions and disagreements, requires an anchor (i.e., a metaphysic) weightier than the drifting sands of immediacy or factional interest. Putting deep foundations for a moral life and continuously shoring it up are the hallmarks of cultural and political maturity. It has been my argument that the state is one of the most crucial platforms to under-take that endeavor, as well as its best gauge at any given juncture.

For the Somalis, then, the assignment is both clear and ominous. Clarity comes from the vantage point of one who has been com-pletely stripped, with no more veils to hide behind or places to retreat to, and the combination of the herculean and intricate dimen-sions of the work ahead is foreboding. In the end, moral resurrection (the basis for a reconnected community), the constitution of a human rights–centered *democratic* yet strong polity, and the creation of specific institutions and leadership that embody these new departures (which should be pluralistic and based on informed consent) seem to be the only intelligent responses to the existing foul and bitter reality. Very briefly, I suggest three possible sources that could be mined for this purpose: Somali kinship, Islamic teachings,[104] and secular political theory. A successful synthesis of these three sources of culture is, admittedly, very exacting. But the enormity of the task need not unduly intimidate the imagination. Because historic transitions in the lives of a people are carried forth only through exceptional feats, this is perhaps the greatest of all challenges, one that requires extraordinary and persistent intellectual sagacity and practical effort. Here lies one of the key features of and assignments for leadership worthy of this conjuncture.[105]

It is important to stress that the wisdom of kinship and the precepts of Islam need not be antithetical to secular political thinking. Rather, I suggest that whatever tensions between them (which are bound to be many and fierce) can be turned into positive energy and opportunities for invention or innovation. In my mind's eye, I can see the companionship of kinship and Islam, for instance, used as a bulwark against both metaphysical dislocation and a possible degeneration of worldly desires (e.g., power) into a generalized unethical and violent greed. On the other hand, secular thinking and practice protects tradition from itself by underscoring logicality, adaptability, and individual engagement in the temporal project of human development called forth by modernity. Finally, all three elements can converge on the much-needed capacity to manage the dialectic of utility and justice that lies at the heart of any *civitas*.

In the end, kinship and Islam are well suited for the coming of a novel social myth conducive to the healing of wounds, the return of piety through new encounters with divinity, and the revival of generous as well as generative soul equal to these times. Secularity is a well-tested ambiance for the eminence of reason, as well as practical experimentation. In view of this, the challenge of the transition is the challenge of synthesis.[106] This age, then, is not as totally lost as the thick darkness of its most distressing moments implies. More positively, there are also opportunities for a new hope. The grand and historic question is whether Somalis of this generation are up to the task. Will they be daring pilgrims eager to begin a new time? An affirmative response will start with alteration in attitude and direction, to be followed by resolute assumption of the burdens of building necessary organizations and institutions.

Notes

1. Perlez, "How One Family." This is the story of one Somali peasant family near the town of Bardera.

2. Mohamed, "Calanyaho." Two caveats are in order here: First, most Somali balladeers do not compose the words to their songs. This is an area usually reserved for those whose talents lie in lyric composition. Among Somalia's greatest lyricists are Husein Aw Farah, Ali Sugulleh, and Hassan Sheikh Mumin. An exception is Abdillahi Qarshi, Somalia's first modern composer, as well as singer, of patriotic ballads. Second, exact dating of songs is problematic, so the best one can do is approximate the year.

3. Suliman, "Wa Mahad Allah Madaxeen Banaan."

4. Mandeeq, "An Togobelney."

5. Naji, "Dalkaygow."

6. Naji, "Qomamo."

7. I distinguish between a strong state and harsh state. The former is a creature, as well as maker, of a delicate balance between civil society and public power—the apotheosis of a democratic governance; the latter represents highly centralized and concentrated power with little, if any, accountability. For more on this, see A. I. Samatar, "Under Siege."

8. For the first category of states, see Tilly, Coercion, Capital, and European States. Tilly's chief concern is to explain why "European states followed . . . diverse paths but eventually converged on the national state." For late developers, see the classic works Gerschenkron, Economic Backwardness; Amsden, Asia's Next Giant. Amsden's well-received volume is a convincing response to the shrill litanies of antistatism and promarket efficacy that dominated the agenda of the 1980s and continue to do so in the early 1990s.

9. Deng and Zartman, Conflict Resolution in Africa. President Olusegun Obasanjo of Nigeria, in the preface to the volume, proposes four categories of difficulties and discontinuities that face Africa: socioeconomic, political, ideological, and institutional. My postulation does not contradict this notion, but adds the environment as another category and underscores the primus inter pares of the political (i.e. , state) moment.

10. For a sample, see my "Somali Studies."

11. Lest this be seen as an unwarranted canonization of the claims of a particular kind of scholarship, this point is made equally by one of the luminaries of social anthropology and ethnography. See Malinowski, Argonauts. Malinowski underscores the necessity of good theory by suggesting that "foreshadowed problems are the main endowment of a scientific thinker, and these problems are first revealed to the observer by his theoretical studies" (p. 9).

12. Isaiah Berlin's reminder to us of the universality of humanness without obliterating diversity is apropos here. Echoing Vico, he tells us that "intercommunication between cultures in time and space is only possible because what makes men [and women] human is common to them, and acts as a bridge between them" (The Crooked Timber of Humanity, p. 11).

13. This position has benefited from Collingwood's proposition, which speaks to the same point. Collingwood writes, "The business of sound theory in relation to practice is not to solve practical problems, but to clear them of misunderstandings which make their solution impossible" (Essays in Political Philosophy, p. 94).

14. Radcliffe-Brown, "Preface."

15. In a recent meditation on the issue of multiculturalism, Charles Taylor calls this private life the "intimate sphere" (*Multiculturalism*, p. 37).

16. Held, *Political Theory*, p. 2. Compare this to David Easton's now classic but narrower conception of politics as the official allocation of assets (*The Political System*). Although Easton's expression is certainly more parsimonious, I prefer Held's more sprawling definition. Despite—or perhaps because of—its tidiness, the Easton proposition can accommodate only one type of authoritative allocation—i.e., command—whereas the advantage of Held's is the possibility of including alternative authoritative means of dispensation—i.e., custom and exchange. Held's definition is closer to Michael Oakeshott's: "the activity of attending to the general arrangements of a set of people whom chance or choice has brought together" ("Political Education," p. 2).

17. This side of the equation of politics (i.e., danger) is foregrounded by the works of Karl Marx and C. Schmitt. The first focuses on internal (i.e., class) divisions; the latter emphasizes the external (i.e., existential "us" against "them"). See Marx, *The Eighteenth Brumaire*; Marx and Engels, *The Communist Manifesto*; Schmitt, *Political Theology*.

18. Hegel, *Lectures on the Philosophy*, pp. 94–97. See also Hegel, *The Philosophy of Right*.

19. Tilly, "Reflections," p. 70. A similar and influential suggestion is made by Skoçpol, who conceives of the state as "a set of administrative, policing, and military organizations headed, and more or less coordinated by, an executive authority" (*States and Social Revolution*, p. 29). Some scholars—particularly historians of civilizations—would argue that the state appeared with the earliest of large human organizations, as far back as the ancient civilizations of Sumer, the Indus Valley, and Egypt. The conception of the modern state, however, is to be seen as a phenomenon associated with this millennium of the masses and social transformations. A distinctive consequence of these changes is the shift—sometimes gradual, at other times revolutionary—of authority from individual or dynastic ownership to more public, territorially based organization. For more on the rise of the state by the beginning of the seventeenth century as a crucial subject of political analysis, see Skinner, *The Foundations*. The thoughts of two thinkers who can be seen as early markers of the coming shadow of the state are found in Khaldun, *The Muqaddimah*; Machiavelli, "Lo Stato."

20. Hintze, *The Historical Essays*.

21. Young, "Patterns of Social Conflict," p. 72.

22. Ibid.

23. Resnick, *The Masks of Proteus*, pp. 13–37.

24. Plato's *The Republic* underscores meritocracy, whereas the tenor of his *Laws* is one of preference for a state based on traditional ownership of the land.

25. Bredvold and Ross, *The Philosophy of Edmund Burke*, p. 210.

26. Machiavelli, *The Discourses*, pp. 1–2.

27. Thucydides, *History of the Peloponnesian War*; Hobbes, *The Leviathan*; Machiavelli, "Lo Stato."

28. There are a variety of ways that one can organize this vast literature. For instance, one can speak about "theories" of the state and, in the process, categorize and subcategorize them, depending on the modifications of the general arguments, to create a confounding labyrinth of schematization. A

useful example of this conceptual valorization of the range of theorizing about the state is Vincent, *Theories of the State*. Vincent identifies five types. For this chapter, I prefer the leaner approach, which speaks in terms of broad traditions. For more on this, see Carnoy, *The State*.

29. Riker, *Liberalism Against Populism*.

30. Smith, *The Wealth of Nations*; Nozick, *Anarchy, State and Utopia*.

31. Locke, *Two Treatises of Government*, p. 410.

32. Macpherson, *The Life and Times*, pp. 26–27.

33. Bentham, *Fragments on Government*; Mill, *An Essay on Government*.

34. Held, *Political Theory*, p. 26.

35. This is perhaps best captured by that memorable statement by Rousseau: "Man was born free and he is everywhere in chains" (*The Social Contract*, p. 49). It is important to note here that Rousseau did not completely extol the prepolitical world nor unreservedly condemn the world of civil society. For him, the downside of Arcadian living included the role of impulse and instinct in individual behavior. Civil society, on the other hand, offered opportunities for the transformation of urge into reason and contained the inception of obligation and virtue.

36. Concluding the analytical venom of the "Discourse on the Origin and Foundation of Inequality," Rousseau wrote, "The first man who having enclosed a piece of land dared to say: 'This is mine,' and found people foolish enough to believe it, was the true founder of civil society. How many crimes, wars, and murders, how many miseries, and horrors the human race would have been spared by the man who, tearing out the fencestakes or filling in the ditch, shouted to his fellow creatures: 'Beware of listening to this impostor; you are lost if you forget that all the fruits of the earth are yours and that the earth itself is no one's!' Though it is likely that by then things have already come to the point where they could not continue on any longer as they were" (*The First and Second Discourses*, p. 66).

37. Rousseau, *The Social Contract*, Book II and Chapter 1 of Book III.

38. For more on this particular point, see Marx, *The Critique*.

39. Reacting against Hegel's conception of the state as "rational," higher, and more durable than the vagaries of sectarian struggle, Marx articulated his first sense of instrumentalism in *The German Ideology*.

40. Marx and Engels, *The Communist Manifesto*, p. 105; Engels, *The Origins of the Family*, pp. 229 and 231. See also Miliband, *Marxism and Politics*.

41. Marx, *The Eighteenth Brumaire*.

42. Draper, *Karl Marx's Theory of Revolution*, Vol. I, particularly Chapter 14, "The Tendency Toward State Autonomy."

43. This can also be termed, as Carnoy describes it, "the dependent state" tradition (*The State*, Chapter 7).

44. An early and inspiring work of this "Third Worldization" of the critical perspective is Baran, *The Political Economy of Growth*. See also Wallerstein, "Three Stages," pp. 30–57; Amin, *Accumulation on a World Scale* and *Imperialism*.

45. Wallerstein, *The Capitalist World Economy*, p. 274.

46. Chase-Dunn, *Global Formation*, especially Part Three, "Zones of the World-System."

47. Alavi, "State and Class"; Charney, "Political Power"; Lonsdale, "States and Social Process"; "The State in Africa"; Ake, "Explanatory Notes"; Beckman, "The Post-Colonial State."

48. For a dense and highly profitable review of this vast literature, see Markovitz, *Power and Class*, Chapter 5.

49. Hodgkin, "The African Middle Class."

50. See A. I. Samatar, "Under Siege."

51. For a detailed and original discussion of heer, see Iye, *Le Verdict de L'Arbre*. Iye focuses on the Issa kin group interpretation and use of heer. However, the principles he underscores are common.

52. The following statement by the Prophet testifies to the inherent universalism of Islam, as well as the required piety from Muslim communities: "God removed you from the arrogance of pre-Islamic times and its pride in ancestry. You are the children of Adam, and Adam was made of dust." God said, "Most noble among you in God's eye is he who fears God most" (quoted in Khaldun, *The Muqaddimah*, p. 160).

53. *Umma* is an Arabic word used by Somalis that is equivalent to Herder's *volk* and is therefore similar to "the people." Umma conveys a sense of belonging that subsumes both a community of believers and autochthonous affinity. *Soomaalinimo* could be taken as a new version of umma that accents the nationalist element.

54. Note that the common term for clan is *qabeel* (an Arabic word that is equivalent to clan). The Somali word I find to be closest to the term *clan* is *qolo*. However, this term does not conjure up the sharp exclusiveness and the prominence of the male ego as does *qabeel*. Consequently, a question arises: how did *qabeel* get into the Somali idiom and consciousness?

55. See A. I. Samatar, *Socialist Somalia*, Chapters 1–3.

56. For instance, middlemen (*dilaals*) who linked the pastoral hinterland to the trading centers and export markets became a common feature of this gradual transformation.

57. Although most Somalis see n to have been moved by the ideology of decolonization, some of the surviving participants of the Northern leadership suggest that, as a group, Northerners were much taken in, perhaps dazzled, by the aura and historical significance of the occasion. The evidence for this is based on three facts: First, despite the declaration of 26 June 1960 as the day of independence in British Somaliland, Northerners waited for a week to merge with the South. Second, Northern leaders came down to Mogadishu to push for unification with no guarantees or conditionalities in terms of Northern interest. Third, there was the a priori Northern willingness to accept Mogadishu as a capital, despite its distance from Hargeisa and the rest of Somaliland. My sources added that Southern politicians, including interim President Osman, were surprised, and perhaps even embarrassed, by the zeal of the Northern delegation. Author's fieldnotes, Summer 1989.

58. A referendum on the new constitution was held on 28 June 1961. SNL strongholds in the North campaigned against the constitution, but, in the end, a majority of the people of the country approved it.

59. By 1963, as the magnitude of Somali underdevelopment became apparent and the regime's uncoordinated policies unraveled, a five-year development plan was hastily announced. Estimates for the new state investments in social overheads (e.g., transport and communication) and some agricultural and industrial projects were put at $200 million, all of it to come from external borrowing and aid (Republic of Somalia, Planning and Coordinating Commission for Economic and Social Development, *First Five Year Plan, 1963–1967*).

60. There are two important points that are forgotten in the midst of heated and confused discussions over contemporary Somali political history. First, President Osman willingly handed over the presidency after his defeat—making him perhaps the earliest (postcolonial) African head of state to leave office peacefully and in an orderly fashion after an electoral defeat. Second, the Somali constitution of the time stipulated that a former president should be given a lifelong seat in parliament. Together, these two points underscore a lesson: the goodness of a confluence between personal obligations and societal responsibility. That is, President Osman accepted defeat gracefully while the society planned ahead for a dignified retirement of a statesman.

61. It is well worth remembering that Egal had some successes in foreign relations. He began to work on establishing a friendly dialogue with Ethiopia and Kenya as well as the United States and Britain.

62. Perhaps the most concrete manifestation of this renewal was the growth in self-help (*iska wax ougabso*) projects all around the country, especially for agriculture.

63. I have documented in a more comprehensive manner the early achievements of the SRC in *Socialist Somalia*, especially Chapters 4 and 5.

64. Prendergast, "Somalia's Silent Slaughter." Also, Dowden, "Skeletons"; Amnesty International, "Somalia: The July 1989 Jezira Beach Massacre."

65. "Not a Nice Way to Come Home."

66. To this day, no one knows the exact number of casualties. Some estimates have put forth a high of 10,000 dead, 30,000 wounded, and over 350,000 refugees who crossed the border into Ethiopia (Lindijer, "Mayhem in Northern Somalia").

67. It is estimated that thousands of homes were despoiled in Hargeisa and stripped of roofs, furniture, and other household items. Hospitals, schools, banks, factories, and shops were subjected to the same treatment. To add to this unprecedented depredation, hundreds of thousands of mines and booby traps were planted in many parts of the North (particularly the Hargeisa, Berbera, and Burao triangle) and continue to claim lives to this day (Drysdale, *Somaliland 1991: Report and Reference*, p. 38).

68. For a full text of this, see *Bayaanka Muqdisho ee Koowaad*.

69. Telephone conversation with Dr. Osman Hashim, Country Representative, UNDP, on 19 March 1991, by Dr. Hashim.

70. In the mid-1980s, amid persistent complaints of personalized power, Siyaad Barre created the position of prime minister. Largely symbolic and bereft of any clout, this post was first occupied by General Mohamed Ali Samantar, who was succeeded by Mohamed Hawadleh Madar, an obscure member of the *Issaq* community. Madar, despite what happened in Northern Somalia, threatened the residents of Mogadishu with the fate of Hargeisa by ordering the Somali air force to bomb if USC dissidents did not put down their arms ("Somali PM in Threat to Bomb Capital," *The Nation*, [Nairobi], p. 1).

71. No one knows the exact death toll, but the first estimates put the figure at an astounding 20,000 people (Biles, "Starting from Scratch"; Nemeth, "City of Slaughter"; Nelan, "A Very Private War").

72. For more on the issue of the regime's acute dependence on external contributions, see the insightful analysis in Chapter 6 of this book.

73. This last point, it seems to me, is at the heart of any repressive order. Echoing Vico's sagacity, Caponigre writes, "Tyranny . . . is essentially

the displacement of the common good by a private utility strong enough to become dominant" (*Time and Idea*, p. 215; the most relevant chapter for my purpose is Chapter 11, "The Theory of the State").

74. A. I. Samatar, "Under Siege," p. 32.

75. The SNM resented what they saw as a unilateral act. More seriously, they were dismayed by a statement attributed to Omer Arteh Qalib, Ali Mahdi Mohamed's new prime minister, to the effect that the USC won the final battle against Siyaad Barre and, consequently, deserved the head of the table.

76. Author's fieldnotes, interviews in Djibouti, January 1992.

77. That a new political and communal conviviality was not in hand is signaled by the vehement denouncement of the declaration of the new state by the United Somali Party (USP), an organization representing some of the non-SNM kin communities in Northern Somalia. For more on this, see United Somali Party, "The Truth."

78. Somali National Movement, "Shir ay Yeesheen." Though the contents of this memorandum are vicious and ugly, reminiscent of the tactics of Siyaad Barre's lieutenants in the North, we need to be extremely cautious of its authenticity because its author(s) could very well be bent on sowing discord among Northerners.

79. Dubbed a congress for the reconciliation of the Somali people, the meeting produced a document signed by all parties, which included the following objectives: (1) a national hunt for Siyaad Barre that would bring him to stand trial, (2) a cease-fire among warring fronts, (3) agreement on the sanctity of Somali unity, (4) an interim government (for two years) headed by Ali Mahdi Mohamed, (5) restoration of the 1960 constitution (for the interim period), (6) restoration of the number of districts before 1969, (7) constitutional provisions for regional autonomy, and (8) constitutional acknowledgment of Somali membership in the Arab League and of Somali and Arabic as official languages of Somalia. For more details, see "Shirweynaha Dib-U-Heshiisiinta."

80. Mbitiru, "Fighting Breaks Out"; Goldman, "Stand-Off."

81. Four points merit notation. First, Egal, his stature notwithstanding, was a central figure in the death of the liberal Somali state. Second, the contest for leadership in Somaliland smacks of an undemocratic recycling of a small cadre of old politicians (particularly from the Issaq community) as the only candidates, including, instructively enough, Omer Arteh Qalib. Earlier, he served Siyaad Barre well. Later, as Mahdi's interim prime minister, he roved the region as spokesman for Somali unity. Third, strong exceptions to the secessionist declaration continue to come from many quarters, including traditional leaders of some of the principal communities of the area. On this last point, see Ali Shireh, *Conference Communique*, p. 1. Fourth, The Somaliland leadership (SNM), thus far, has refused to officially participate in any of the efforts toward national reconciliation, including the U.N.-sponsored meetings held in Addis Ababa in January, March, and November 1993. At the important March conference, the SNM came as an observer.

82. "Somalia: Nasty, Brutish, Split"; Perlez, "Factional Fighting."

83. Physicians for Human Rights, "Somalia: No Mercy in Mogadishu," p. 8.

84. While these Vichian words were penned for another occasion, they nonetheless seem fitting for the situation in Mogadishu. Vico, *The New*

Science, p. 99; Amnesty International, *Somalia: A Human Rights Disaster*, particularly pp. 2–4.

85. "Somalia: Death by Looting"; Smith, "Mogadishu Diary."

86. Kramer, "Suffering Rises."

87. At a time when even the United Nations decamped, it is important to note the tenacious energy and dedication of such groups as Medecins Sans Frontieres—France, International Medical Corps, International Committee of the Red Cross, Save the Children Fund—U. K., and CARE. Their work, in Mogadishu in particular, has made the difference between life and death for many Somalis.

88. Lange, "Horn of Misery."

89. Perlez, "U.N. Let the Somali Famine Get Out of Hand."

90. While the Addis Ababa Agreement opened with a preamble that emphasized peace, disarmament, collaboration with UNOSOM and restoration of property, its main and concrete parts dealt with the establishment of four transitional structures. The full spirit and serious practical elements of the agreement await to be experienced and implemented. *Addis Ababa Agreement.*

91. For a more sanguine review on the fate of the agreement, see United Nations, "Somalia Progresses," p. 4.

92. Political goodness implies a way of being that underscores self-conscious individual and social uprightness, undergirded by a legitimate, democratic, and effective legal order. According to Collingwood, "Political goodness [is] the goodness of life which is lived under good laws well administered" (*Essays in Political Philosophy*, p. 96). Also, Ignatieff makes the same point, but with an emphasis on the way we speak about it. He writes, "A decent and humane society requires a shared language of the good . . . [one] which requires acts of virtue unspecifiable as a legal or civil obligation" (*The Needs of Strangers*, p. 14).

93. Expressing a similar point, Machiavelli writes, "There are two ways of fighting: by law or by force. The first way is natural to man, and the second to beasts" ("Lo Stato," p. 66).

94. Berlin, *The Crooked Timber of Humanity*, p. 42.

95. Dunn, *Interpreting Political Responsibility*, p. 125.

96. Anderson, *Imagined Communities*. Two of Anderson's propositions are relevant: (1) "members of even the smallest nation will never know most of their fellow-members, meet them, or even hear of them, yet in the minds of each lives the image of their communion"; and (2) a nation "is imagined as a *community*, because, regardless of the actual inequality and exploitation that may prevail in each, the nation is always conceived as a deep, horizontal comradeship" (pp. 15–16). A philosophical school that converges on the same conception is communitarian political philosophy/theory. For more on this, see, for example, Taylor, *Philosophy and the Human Sciences*, Vol. 2.

97. Rafferty, *The Works of Edmund Burke VI*, p. 28. Conceiving of the idea of the state in this way is not limited to Burkean celebration of tradition; rather, I argue, it is a fundament to most serious thinking. For an intellectual tradition quite distant from that of Burke yet in agreement on this issue, see Wolfe, *Whose Keeper?* (particularly Chapter Four, "The State as a Moral Agent").

98. Held, *Models of Democracy*, p. 238.

99. Dunn, *Interpreting Political Responsibility*, p. 34.

100. Collingwood writes, "The right to rule is also a duty to rule; and hence politics is so far a branch of ethics that duty is an indispensable part of the concept of rule" (*Essays in Political Philosophy*, p. 44).

101. John of Salisbury, quoted in Huizinga, *Men and Ideas*, p. 172. A recent landmark work that accents the tight link between ethics/moral inquiry and social science, as well as the imperatives of communitarian politics, is Selznick, *The Moral Commonwealth*, particularly Chapter 16, "Covenant and Commonwealth."

102. Stingle, "Eyewitness to Horror"; Wallace, "Somali War"; Perlez, "A Somali Place."

103. This point recalls W. Benjamin's beautiful aphorism that "hatred and its spirit of sacrifice . . . are nourished by the image of enslaved ancestors rather than that of liberated grandchildren" (*Illuminations*, p. 260).

104. Contrary to the pervasive but simplistic and reductionist characterization of any appeal to Islam as "fundamentalist" in these times of trouble, my preliminary observations among Somalis suggest at least three types of appeals: monastic, zealous, and pragmatic. The first is essentially apolitical stoicism. Formed by a combination of feeling aghast and visions of afterlife, this perspective sees the world and the current situation as demonic and unworthy (or impossible) to salvage. Consequently, refuge is sought in full detachment, if not resignation, and hyper-worship. Zealous appeal captures the literal (and usually superficial) interpretation and hurried application of selective pieces from the *Al-Quran* and the *Al-Hadith*. Accordingly, this Islam does not limit itself to setting up the parameters but, most distinctively, tries to penetrate and rule over every aspect of life. Increasingly assuming a reactionary extremism, zealousness becomes a theological imperialism that is antithetical to any alternative thinking. Pragmatic Islam calls for the reemergence of the divine and the propagation of love of learning and the humility and uprightness that accompany it. Furthermore, this brand of political Islam gives to contingency its due, and to reason and inquiry their autonomy. It is this type of Islamic revival that I have intimated above. For some interesting insights into political Islam in contemporary Somali politics, see Abdillahi, "Tribalism, Nationalism, and Islam"; and Aqli, "Historical Development."

105. For more on the unexplored aspects of the pivotal issue of leadership in Somali Studies and among Somalis, see my "In Search of the Somali Wazi."

106. Mumford calls such an effort, in its intellectual form, "polyphonic or contrapuntal thinking, thinking that carries a series of related themes together so that in the process they simultaneously work upon each other and modify each other." Mumford, *The Conduct of Life*, p. 260.

6

Dealing with Disintegration: U.S. Assistance and the Somali State

David Rawson

The *Washington Post*, in a 24 September 1992 dateline from Mogadishu, reports: "Just thirty years after it officially became an independent nation, Somalia essentially has ceased to exist. The land mass on world maps that define the Horn of Africa is now a dangerous and chaotic place of clan-based warfare, feudal fiefdoms, marauding free-lance gunmen and widespread famine that kills thousands each day."

One almost forgets that Somalia was once a leader in the nonaligned world, envied for its progressive socialist policies and proudly hosting the 1974 Summit of the Organization of African Unity (OAU). It is hard to conceive that Somalia once had one of Africa's best-equipped armies and almost succeeded in conquering the western third of Ethiopia in the Ogaden War. Even the last decade, when donors set forth ambitious development programs and put Somalis among the world's top recipients of development assistance, has faded into memory.

Why did the Somali state disintegrate into such anarchy? What, during its last decade, was that state's relationship with the international donor community? Were donors aware of Somalia's intractable problems? Did they unintentionally aggravate those problems? These are the questions this chapter will attempt to answer by delineating briefly the key features of the Somali state in the 1970s and 1980s, characterizing the environment in which donors operated, and analyzing strategies and programs of a major donor, the United States. The perspective from which this is written is that of a policy implementor, looking for lessons that donor interaction with

Somalia's economic and political system can offer for other areas where difficult development issues are posed within weak or disintegrating state structures.[1] One can learn from disasters as well as from successes.

Somalia as an African State and Third World Country

Dilemmas of the State in Africa

Although the human dimensions of the Somali tragedy touch the heart and stagger the imagination, it is no surprise to students of African politics that societal tides could thus rip at the foundational structure of the state. The disenchantment of African societies with central governments has been documented for two decades. In his groundbreaking work, Robert Bates showed how African peasants have escaped the efforts of central governments to tax their production. Goran Hyden, in the early 1970s, watched peasant resistance to *ujamaa* in Tanzania and launched his pioneering studies on the failures of governance in Africa. Janet MacGaffey has plotted the disengagement of traders and merchants from the formal economy in Zaire and the resistance of petty producers to domination and exploitation by the state-based ruling class. Naomi Chazan detailed the rise of local political arrangements in Ghana as state legitimacy withered and the central state receded.[2]

Diagnosing the pathology of African states has thus become a scholarly vocation. Some consider Africa's societal body to be strong but the controlling nervous and skeletal structure of its states to be weak. Numerous studies detail the capacity of African society to adjust to this debilitation by disengaging from central state direction. Others find that a concentration of power at the center has led to a withering of the supportive limbs of civil society. For still others, the current state malady is but an expected incubatory stage in the developmental process of state formation and capitalist penetration. Yet others locate the problem not in the nature of state structures but in the (curable) condition of being overweight—i.e., bureaucratically bloated. Some suggest that radical surgery may be required to bring political health to African society.[3]

Recent events in Africa no longer make us wonder, as Jackson and Rosberg did, why Africa's weak states persist.[4] Instead, we find that sometimes they disintegrate. Somalia is one such state, though some commentators now question whether Somalia ever attained real statehood. Certainly, those who hold that the state-making process is incomplete in Third World "quasistates" would find much in Somalia's independent history to justify their thesis. Since 1960, Somalia's independent status has been as much confirmed by international convention as by realities of internal control. The state system there depended on international financing; an international security net of relief food undergirded its population's subsistence. In the weakness of Somali bureaucratic mechanisms, the unconstrained power of its military, and the state's disregard for the rights of citizens, the Somali state and its leaders often illustrated the image evoked by Robert Jackson of "statesmen civil (and dependent) in their international relations but abusive and coercive in their domestic conduct."[5]

However, the optic of such perceptions is distorted. Not even the most developed Western states fully enjoy the presumed attributes of positive sovereignty, "able and responsive rulers and productive and allegiant citizens." Contrary to Jackson's claim, many states of the Third World do possess "wherewithal to provide political goods for [their] citizens."[6] Certainly the Somalis, already a nation, organized in 1960 a state and government that asserted supremacy over all other authorities and peoples within its territory and independence of authorities outside it.[7] Even Jackson lists Somalia as an example of the "nation-state" in Africa. Commentators who now characterize chaos on the Horn as "typically Somali" should not, because of current disintegration, deprive the Somalis of their historic achievement. Although its exercise of authority and independence vacillated, Somalia did function as a state for over three decades.

Somalia in Global Perspective

The tides that thus sweep the shores of all states have inundated Somalia. This fact belies the notion of uniqueness that strikes outsiders when they first land in Somalia and persists the longer they stay—namely, that these proud people who have lived so long in this haunting, inhospitable land are somehow different from people elsewhere. Do not the very habitat of Somalia and the structure of Somali society make Somalia unique on the African continent?[8] In short, is not Somalia sui generis, the lessons (if any) from its tragic history inapplicable elsewhere?

Although Somalia is a fascinating place and its people distinctive, the Somali nation shares with other Third World countries a peculiar nexus between its state and its society, as well as a particular dependency between its state and the outside world. When we strip away the exotica and focus on the process of state creation, we find that Somalis, like Africans everywhere, inherited from colonial powers a public structure (the postcolonial state) and transformed it into an instrument of authority across the territory they administered. Somalia entered into a series of relations with greater powers in order to give international position and significance to that independent state. The developed world in turn implemented in Somalia developmental and strategic policies that it also projected elsewhere in Africa.

The impact of those global policies on a particular state structure carries lessons, at least for the developers and the strategists. Somalia is distinctive but not unique. That being true, was Somalia, then, nothing more than another pawn of Cold War competition for power and position? The U.S. and Soviet powers certainly were present in multiform relations, at different times, on both sides of the Ethiopian/Somali divide.[9] Further, the disintegration of both these client states seems to coincide with the dwindling interest of either superpower in each. Superpower decisions regarding military or economic assistance certainly played a critical role in the turns of history during this period. However, the U.S. confrontation with the Soviet Union was not the controlling factor in the regression of the Somali state. Rather than superpower rivalry, it was the internal dynamic of elite competition, militarization of state institutions, and growing autocracy of Siyaad Barre's regime that set the course of the Somali state.

The perspective offered here does not deny that the Somali state is also the product of modernity, confirmed by international convention and highly influenced by external factors: regional competition, superpower rivalry, or donor demands. Nevertheless, however one looks at it, three things are clear: that there was in Somalia a political entity that we may accurately term a state; that that state had a history and organizational extent that surpassed Barre's patrimonial domain; and that that state has now ceased to exist, despite the best efforts of the donor community first to reinforce it and then to restructure it.

Democracy, Socialism, and Decline

Independence came to part of the Somali homeland in 1960. States in the international community quickly recognized the independence of the new Somali Republic. But other parts of the traditional Somali lands remained under alien jurisdiction; therein lay some of the seeds of its tragic history.

For those parts that had been set free of colonial domination, however, independence was not trivial.[10] The voice independence gave to Somali national aspirations brought legitimacy to inherited colonial institutions of governance. The new republic's authority was quickly accepted across the land; its sovereign jurisdiction was affirmed by the international community. The new state's police and the military were adequately organized and endowed with sufficiently superior arms to assert coercive hegemony within the country. Thus, the new Somali state carried out essential functions mirroring those of the Weberian ideal state and met the standards of recognition and effectiveness by which states are judged under international law.[11]

Despite colonial imprint, the Somali state was more than a political entity constructed to the designs of British and Italian constitutional lawyers and granted sovereignty by the society of states. Underlying the structure of this postcolonial state were the foundational myths of Somali politics. What gave dynamism to that structure was the energetic quest of Somali elites for national unity and group identity. As Bayart has noted, "An apparatus of control and domination . . . is not just what the holder of power or imperium wishes for it, but what the actors, even if they are subordinates, make of it."[12]

The Somali State and Siyaad Barre

We may take the years 1974–1976 as the high tide of the Somali state system. Somalia held international stature by building bilateral ties with African and Arab states and putting Somalia solidly behind the nonaligned agenda. In 1973–1974, Siyaad Barre was named chairman of the Organization of African Unity and traveled widely across the continent, touting the accomplishments of Somalia's revolution. Somalia hosted both the OAU Summit and the Pan-African Games. Thus, Somalia became a regional power. At the same time, Somalia strengthened ties with the Soviet Union and used its resources to build up one of the best-equipped armies on the continent. At home, the institutions of the revolution had expanded to the far corners of the land. Elaboration of a national political party in 1976 was but a gloss on a text already inscribed "Siyaad Barre rules."

This was the state apparatus that pushed Barre steadily toward the national goal of liberating Somali homelands in Ethiopia: the Ogaden and the Haud. After Haile Selassie was deposed in Ethiopia in 1974, the Somali government increased support for the Western

Somali Liberation Front (WSLF). This guerrilla movement expanded its area of operation and reorganized its structure to permit coordination with the regular Somali army. Soon, Somali regulars were resigning to join the WSLF ranks. Then, in July 1977, thousands of regular Somali forces pushed across the border and moved by September into control of 90 percent of the area. That war turned the energies of the state and its peoples from the social aspect of state making, which had been Barre's innovative focus, toward the political lodestar of unifying national homelands. Although its early successes brought ecstasy, the war's ultimate failure and the Somali retreat in March 1978 destroyed Somalia's national vision. Furthermore, the war failed to deepen the state's capacity to mobilize its people or round up their resources toward collective goals.[13] Rather, having accumulated a certain amount of material, expertise, international prestige, and popular support, Barre's regime spent it all on a mad dash into the Ogaden.

Initially, Barre erroneously believed that he could carry out his war of national liberation without losing Soviet support. The Soviets certainly knew who their enemies were and against whom they were arming the Somalis. Soviet maps at the Somali Military Academy were marked in terms of a red force and a blue force in the customary military manner, but there was no mistaking who those forces were or which territory they were contesting. The Soviets designed and taught military tactics with Ethiopian objectives in mind. Further, the Soviet Union had sunk an enormous investment in Somalia, not only in provision of military equipment, but in meat and fish factories that supplied the domestic Soviet market and in naval and air facilities at Berbera that included a big regional hospital for Soviet armed forces and fishing fleets.

It may well have seemed unlikely that the Soviets would intervene to upset Barre's plans. But they did. In retrospect, several reasons may be advanced: Ethiopia was bigger, it was more geopolitically significant, and its Marxism seemed more pristine, untainted by Islam as Barre's was.[14] Only now evident, highlighted by the breakup of the Soviet Union, is a more primal fear that drove the decision: the Soviets simply could not countenance a war of national consolidation, even in minor client states; irredentism threatened the very structure of the Soviet state. Further, Ethiopia's imperial domination of subject peoples better fit Soviet patterns of state than did nationalist Somali ambition.

Barre's second miscalculation was that he could quickly induce the West to take over for the Soviets as Somalia's patron. He had good reason for thinking that. The events in the Horn presented the

Carter administration with a major opportunity to prove its foreign policy resolve. President Carter desperately wanted to turn this geopolitical shift to U.S. advantage. In April 1977, he was overheard telling Vice-President Mondale, who advocated U.S.-Somali rapprochement, "Tell Cy [Cyrus Vance, secretary of state] and Zbig [Zbigniew Brzezinski, national security advisor] that I want them to move in every possible way to get Somalia to be our friend."[15] Through the private channel of Barre's personal physician, Carter offered the secret, vague, and easily misinterpreted promise that if Somalia would renounce its territorial claims to northeast Kenya and Djibouti, the United States would consider sympathetically Somalia's legitimate defense needs.

This was reinforced by a promise from Carter to the Somali ambassador on 16 June that the United States would "encourage its allies to help Somalia maintain its defensive strength." On 26 July, Secretary of State Vance announced Carter's decision to supply Somalia with defensive arms.[16] Barre, desperate to launch his bid for the Ogaden, chose to credit the assurances and the meaning of "defensive arms" for more than they were worth. In mid-July, regular Somali forces entered the Ogaden to support the war already launched by Somali insurgents. When their presence was discovered by Western observers in August, the United States reneged on its promise of arms.

But the issue was far from settled within the Carter administration. The U.S. State Department and powerful political figures in the administration, such as Andrew Young, felt that negotiation, restraint, and sensitivity to African nationalism would solve this local conflict.[17] Secretary Vance had posited as a cardinal policy assumption that Africa was unique and that success there depended on "U.S. ability to help Africans resolve their disputes."[18] The way to do that in this crisis, in the State Department's view, was to take an "interested" but neutral stance and embargo arms shipments to either party in this local conflict. That remained U.S. policy until Barre announced, on 8 March 1978, his intention to withdraw from the Ogaden.

Ten days later, Assistant Secretary Richard Moose arrived in Mogadishu to explore the possibility of U.S. military assistance to Somalia. However, Barre was not able to give the assurances Moose needed regarding Somali intentions in the Ogaden; all Moose could then offer was a $7 million economic assistance agreement.[19] When the State Department heard that some Somali regulars might still be in the Ogaden, it put the arms-to-Somalia question on hold. If patience and "localism" reigned in the State Department, however, the imperatives of global confrontation loomed at the U.S. National Security Council (NSC). In January 1979, the Shah of Iran fell; in November, Iranian revolutionaries stormed the U.S. embassy and took American hostages, at about the same time the Soviets reinforced their position on the Gulf of Aden with military construction on the Dahlak and Socotra islands.

At the NSC, Brzezinski, always impatient with the State Department's low-profile approach to the Ogaden crisis, perceived a Soviet threat to the "arc of instability" reaching from the Persian Gulf to the coast of Somalia. To counter this threat, the Carter administration designed its Southwest Asian Strategy and the Rapid Deployment Force. At a meeting of the National Security Council on 4 December 1979 President Carter decided to seek military facilities for this force in Kenya, Oman, and Somalia.[20] Global issues had finally given Barre the Western attention he coveted. But negotiations for the facilities would drag on for months. Ever the camel traders, the Somalis asked for an exorbitant arms deal worth U.S. $1 billion. In the end, they accepted the promise of increased economic assistance and some vague assurances of military assistance up to U.S. $40 million annually.

Certainly, Barre had vastly overestimated the strategic importance of Somalia to the West; he also had no qualms about becoming part of U.S. military contingency planning. These attitudes stayed with him to the end of his regime. In his view, he gave the West an open door. To the last, he solicited a larger American military presence in Somalia and tried to sell the utility of a base at Susciuban. He volunteered the entire Ras Hafun peninsula as a free-fire zone for amphibious training and welcomed U.S. military construction at facilities in Berbera and Mogadishu.

Among the client states of the U.S. Central Command, Somalia was by far the most accommodating to exercises of various kinds. Yet, Somali expectations bore little relation to the realities of the strategic marketplace, even in a world without a shah. Paul Henze reported that NSC visitors to Somalia in the late 1970s found Barre living in "an unreal world."[21] Barre's expectations could not help but be dashed by the realities of the world scene. But he persisted and endured. Clearly, he needed succor in those dark days of defeat in the Ogaden; the bailout he received from conservative Arab states may have saved his regime. Military assistance from the West was inordinately slow in coming, but what Barre really needed as he slowly pulled back from his Ogaden dream was the support of full-fledged and friendly relations. He sought from relations with the West, especially the United States, the same thing he found in the Treaty of Friendship with the Soviets: an identity as a leader, a place in the international order. In terms of international politics, the switch to the West was, for Barre, both necessary and purposeful.

Zigzagging and Eventual Disintegration

Barre emerged from the Ogaden War with new putative international partners but the same personal vision of what Somalia should become. Imperative in that vision was his continuation in power, an idea that Majerteen officers were soon to challenge through a coup attempt. Barre's response was quick and brutal: mass executions and decimation of the offenders' homelands. Other disgruntled officers, mostly Issaq, took note and fled. From then on, Barre's survival took precedence over other issues of international stature or national mobilization. That personal ambition drew Barre to maneuver political forces and structures so frequently as to eventually weaken the very framework of the Somali state.

Throughout the decade, Barre juggled institutions and persons in a fashion that played off centers of power to keep himself in ascendancy. The Supreme Revolutionary Council, the Somali Revolutionary Socialist Party, the Peoples Assembly, the Politburo, and the government were each given their day in the sun, only to be quickly superseded by another political constellation. Barre's tactics not only neutralized political opponents, they also paralyzed his administration and undermined state institutions. Instead of working toward political objectives, he made mere survival the goal within the Somali body politic.

But there were moments of good news for Barre in the mid-1980s. Recovering new vigor after his lengthy recuperation from an automobile accident, he mobilized the Party with meetings of the Politburo, the Executive Committee, and regional organs to prepare for the Third Party Congress on 16 November 1986. As expected, the Congress nominated Barre for Somalia's first directly elected president. It also diminished the powers of the Politburo and the Executive Committee, while electing a deputy secretary-general to handle party affairs so Barre could concentrate on the presidency.[22] He was overwhelmingly elected to a new presidential mandate, winning, as with the constitutional referendum, more votes than there were people of voting age in Somalia.

These events had their parallel on the economic front. Somalia was following IMF guidelines and moving into a World Bank agricultural sector adjustment program, under which foreign currency could be bought at market prices through an auction. Exports in bananas and other fruits, in fish and shellfish, and in livestock were growing. There was talk of refurbishing Mogadishu's seaside hotel and expanding the tourist trade. At the Donor Roundtable in May 1987, statistics suggested a slight increase in gross national product (GNP) and demonstrated progress in major areas of donor initiative. The Somali government document prepared for the 1987 Paris Roundtable entitles its first chapter "The Promise of Somalia."[23] Donors, holding grand dreams of progress, examined plans for the Bardera dam to irrigate vast areas in the Juba Valley and provide electricity for the first stages of industrialization from Kismayu to Mogadishu.

Encouraged by the good report that Somalia received from the IMF and the World Bank, donors raised contributions to Somalia's development to new levels. The Italian Emergency Fund program was so generous that it changed the immediate circumstances. The United States, though starting a decline in military assistance, maintained its project assistance under the Development Fund for Africa and provided extraordinary support to the World Bank programs through cash grants. Britain, though skeptical of Somali progress, kept on trying, and along with high-level visits by Princess Anne and Undersecretary Chalker, provided U.S. $7 million over two years in budgetary support. Germany's methodical two-year programming hit all-time highs in terms of technical and financial assistance.

A darker side to this sunny picture passed almost unperceived by donors. Even as it reached the point of maximum cooperation with donors, the Somali state was restless. Adherence to IMF guidelines was ad hoc and arbitrary at best; the apparent economic growth was being fueled by uncontrolled credit expansion by the Commercial Savings Bank. Somali and foreign private investors were allowed to expand operations, but the Damoclean sword, in the form of an authoritarian state and socialist legal code, hung over their investments. It took five years to revise the investment code; finally, the government, at the donors' insistence, pushed it roughshod through the Peoples' Assembly, but it came out with key elements of national control and socialist doctrine still intact. An investor might start up a profitable business only to be shut down by archaic provisions of the socialist code.

Had they been candid with each other, Barre and the donors would have agreed on one thing: the market-oriented economy toward which donor conditionality pushed Somalia was undercutting scientific socialism, key to Barre's historic vision for the Somali state and essential to the wealth and privileges of his cohorts. While donors convened in Paris, Barre was mobilizing the Party, not to broaden political participation, but to get himself elected and to use the Party as a tool to combat further erosion of the "socialist" structure.

Somalia very soon fell off the stabilization and structural adjustment wagon and attempted a return to fixed currencies and state controls. When that happened, the state discovered that the production of Somali shillings to provide counterpart currencies for donor inputs in commodities and foreign exchange had so pumped up the economy that inflation went through the roof. The demand for goods—fueled by intakes from false invoicing, inflated contracts, and outright appropriation of donor funds—sent the Somali economy into a deep trade-and-payments imbalance. Foreign exchange was gone within three months, and the accretion of debts, both public and commercial, left Somali creditless. This time, donors could not cover the gaps because there was no IMF-certified program. The U.S. Agency for International Development (USAID) had to put a hold on U.S. $20 million of economic support funds that were destined to pay off Somalia's debt to the IMF in order to launch a second standby agreement. Getting into the development business meant pushing Somalia back on the IMF wagon; this became the major preoccupation of development strategy.

There were other troubles brewing. The growing influence of the Party was portrayed as a democratic measure but was really a means of increasing the influence of Barre and his clan. Barre put his kinsmen, the Marehan, in top leadership positions within the Party, including the office of deputy secretary-general. To top off the process, in January 1988, Barre named a new government that changed many portfolios but, more importantly, put a Marehan at either the highest or second-highest position of all ministries where money was to be made. In sum, Barre's political reforms narrowed rather than broadened the political base and channeled power and its perquisites into the hands of his kin and cohorts.[24]

Finally, Barre was in deeper trouble in the provinces than even he realized; his security machinery had lost its ability to intimidate and coerce: skirmishes over land rights broke out between Hawiye and Majerteen nomads; Islamic fundamentalists claiming SSDF affiliation briefly took over the town of Los Anod; a dispute between Marehan and Ogadani groups in Kismayu put the town under mob siege for a week. And in the afterglow of the Ethiopian Peace Accord in April 1988, when Barre went to the North to capitalize on the new tranquillity, Isaaq youths booed and tossed stones at his procession. In the melee that followed, security forces killed several youths. Barre rushed back to Mogadishu to revise his plans for political consolidation in the North.

He never had the time to launch a new Northern strategy. Whatever strategy he had was overtaken by Somali National Movement (SNM) attacks on parts of Northern Somalia. Soon, the whole region, and, gradually other parts of the country, were engulfed in chaotic violence that would usher the full disintegration of the state.

The preceding discussion outlines elements of the state's disintegration: elitist politics, militarization, and the drive for autocracy within a narrowing patronage base. The elitist politics, without any channeling through democratic competition or accountability to the public, became an obsessive struggle for status and aggrandizement through tenure in public office. The only limits on ambition were the opposing efforts of other elites and the whimsical will of the president. Development programs became channels for winning that struggle for power and perquisites, rather than investments in Somalia's welfare and economic future. The 1969 coup was a military takeover of state channels for elitist competition. The process of militarization proceeded apace in the 1970s and, ironically, accelerated after the Ogaden War. Officers returned home to nurse their wounded psyches on the benefits of public office. Throughout the 1980s, an ineffective civil service undermined development efforts in Somalia; critical to that problem was military (or ex-military) dominance of top positions in the Party, administration, and government. These officers did not delegate authority or share power. The progressive popular disenchantment with Siyaad Barre's regime correlates closely with the progressive militarization of government services.

U.S. Assistance: The Security/Development Mix

Each bilateral donor had a special history and particular interest in its own assistance orientation. This was particularly true of the United States. From 1960, the United States was determined to make its mark in meeting the developmental challenges of the new Somali state. The 1969 revolution blocked those intentions until, in 1977, Siyaad Barre made his switch from East to West. Because of Barre's unwillingness to fully withdraw from his Ogaden adventure, however, it was not until the 1980s that the United States pushed forward into significant development activity. When the United States took up developmental assistance again in Somalia, it did so to protect its security interests. This collusion between security and development gave U.S. bilateral assistance a peculiar twist. If the U.S. program was the most unique because of the security dimension, it was also the most consistent in supporting the IMF/ World Bank agenda. The foundations of that story, however, were laid down in the 1960s.

The Early Years

The United States welcomed with unusual enthusiasm the creation of the Somali Republic. Recognizing the striking advance in self-government that Somalia had made as a trust territory, the United States had cosponsored a resolution in the UN Security Council advancing the date of independence by six months. On the date of Somali independence, the U.S. representative in the council commended Italy and the United Kingdom for "their aid in furthering the aspirations of the Somali people."[25] Given its tendency to see the new African republics through the prism of its own constitutional experience, the United States was particularly pleased to see in Somalia an act of political amalgamation of formerly divided colonies, rather than the schism created by artificial boundaries elsewhere on the continent.[26]

The political achievement of independence brought with it economic challenges. The United States recognized that Somalia's major problem would be in the economic field and offered to assist Somalia in maintaining economic stability and achieving a proper level of development.[27] Those remained the U.S. goals in Somalia throughout the 1960s. Recognizing in Somalia's livestock and drylands a developmental challenge for U.S. expertise, USAID, by 1967, was budgeting U.S. $4.7 million in agricultural services and U.S. $2.1 million in water resource development. Infrastructure was then still considered a developmental objective, and the United States undertook to build the port at the Southern town of Kismayu. Some U.S. $10 million appears in the U.S. congressional presentation for this project in the fiscal year (FY) 1968. Another objective was human resource development and public management training. The 1968 program had four different projects with this focus, including a U.S. $4 million investment in Lafole Teachers' College.[28]

In the pre-Vietnam era of nation building, police training through USAID's International Police Academy was a valued tool in development. U.S. support through this program for the national police won high marks and lasting memories among Somalia's top policemen. The 1968 program had U.S. $4.4 million reserved for public safety.[29] The United States refused, however, to provide military assistance to the newly formed national army, in part because of a desire to limit military assistance programs in Africa and concentrate on nation building, and in part because of sensitivity to the opinions of Somalia's neighbors and close U.S. friends Ethiopia and Kenya, whose territory was the object of Somali irredentist claims.[30]

The developmental challenges that Somalia posed, coupled with the political will to help the new republic achieve a proper level of development, made the U.S. assistance effort to Somalia in the 1960s a growth industry. The total USAID budget for FY 1968 came to U.S. $30 million; there were at that time some 44 USAID officials and contractors resident in the country, as well as an additional 104 who participated in USAID-Somalia programs.[31] Reading between the lines, one can assume that growing Soviet influence through the Soviet Union's military assistance program may have stimulated the United States to counter with a significant developmental assistance program. If the Soviets would give arms, the United States would outdo them by giving what Somalia really needed: developmental assistance.

By 1974, U.S. assistance programs had ground to a halt. Siyaad Barre's revolutionary regime had made things progressively uncomfortable for the United States. Beginning in 1969, it kicked out the Peace Corps, declared a number of diplomats to be personas non grata, and began castigating U.S. imperialism in official press. When ships under the Somali flag carried arms to North Vietnam, the United States turned off the assistance faucet.[32] By the time Somalia signed its Treaty of Friendship with the Soviet Union, U.S. assistance programs had been closed out except for provision of emergency food. The U.S. embassy, reduced to a minimum size, worked under the constant gaze of Barre's National Security Service agents. To U.S. diplomats, Mogadishu had the closed, hostile air of Eastern Europe.

Getting Back into the Development Business

Memories of those hostile days made it difficult for U.S. policymakers in the State Department to acknowledge Barre's plea for help when the tables turned in the Ogaden War. Politically, Barre's record was a heavy burden that resulted, not surprisingly, in an anti-Somali bias within the State Department. State officers felt that U.S. personnel and U.S. interests had been abused by that arrogant socialist Barre.[33] At the same time, on the development side, USAID's experience had been rather positive. In the 1960s, demonstrable progress had been registered in various development programs. Even in the early days of Barre's revolutionary regime, USAID officials felt they were doing useful things for the people up-country, and they were not at all happy when political exigencies brought over a decade of developmental effort to a halt.

But if development programs had been curtailed for political reasons, they were also to be reinstituted for political reasons. The first of these reasons was U.S. concern about Soviet buildup in the Horn. In early July 1977, Secretary Vance stated that "the United States would consider sympathetically appeals from states which are threatened by a buildup of foreign military equipment and advisers on their borders in the Horn and elsewhere in Africa."[34] Initially, this apparent willingness to confront the Soviets in the Horn was thwarted by Barre's invasion of the Ogaden, an action contrary to long-standing U.S. support for territorial integrity in Africa. Other events were to occur, however, to cause the United States to forsake in the Horn its policy of "keeping the Cold War out of Africa."[35]

Oil was the catalyst of this policy change. The oil embargo of 1973 demonstrated that the United States had lost control of Middle East oil resources and would have to engage politically with Arab states to maintain long-term access. But by 1977, there were credible reports that the Soviet Union's own oil resources were dwindling.[36] Thus, Soviet expansion into the Horn and the Gulf of Aden looked to some U.S. strategists more like a strategic move to encircle Arab oil sources rather than a mere response to the target of opportunity that a revolution in Ethiopia had presented. Then came the Iranian Revolution, the hostage crisis, the Iran-Iraq War, and the culmination of Soviet involvement in Afghanistan. These events clearly defined the West's interests in a strengthened U.S. presence in the vulnerable region. The United States extended to Southwest Asia its global policy of deterrence—to counter and contain Soviet power. After deciding on his strategy in December 1979, President Carter used his annual message to the U.S. Congress in January 1980 to outline the new policy:

> Events in Iran and Afghanistan have dramatized for us the critical importance for American security and prosperity of the area running from the Middle East through the Persian Gulf to South Asia. . . . Twin threats to the flow of oil—from regional instability and now potentially from the Soviet Union—require that we firmly defend our interests. . . . Whether in the Horn or in other areas of the continent, we will also provide to friendly nations security assistance when needed for defense of their borders.[37]

Under the revised policy approach, the United States sought to engage the Somali state in a new partnership, this time grounded not on developmental objectives but on (presumably) shared security and political goals. It was a most ambiguous relationship from the start, as illustrated by the time it took to negotiate a facilities agreement—something both sides wanted for their own security purposes.[38] For the Somali state, the security goal was not only to counter the threat from an Ethiopia backed by massive Soviet and Cuban military assistance, but also to hold on to the dream of territorial unity among Somali homelands. Barre kept Somali forces operating in parts of the Ogaden through 1980, despite the loss of Soviet backing and no substitute aid from the West.[39] The political goal was to preserve and reinforce Barre's regime against both growing disenchantment within Somalia and ethnic insurgencies operating out of Ethiopia.

For its part, the United States sought three different security objectives from the Somali partnership. One was to counter growing Soviet influence in the Horn by demonstrating willingness to engage on the African continent "without building up threatening forces."[40] Another was to guard the Strait of Bab el Mandeb, thus expanding the projection of U.S. power in the Persian Gulf area into the Gulf of Aden and the lower Red Sea. The third security objective was to provide rear-echelon support for the operations of the U.S. Rapid Deployment Force to put out local fires in the Middle East.[41] Policy formulations never fully synchronized these objectives, each of which required different kinds of deployment and support facilities. Instead, the United States carried out limited programs for each: low-level U.S. military presence in Somalia, providing defensive military material and occasional training exercises; no permanent basing in Berbera but periodic visits from ships or aircraft; support for the Rapid Deployment Force confined to refueling stations in Berbera and Mogadishu.

These inchoate security objectives were also circumscribed by the reluctance of the State Department and some political elements of the Carter administration to make security the capstone of U.S. policy in Africa. Strong voices were still arguing that, as in the 1960s, the United States' best suit against the Soviet play in Africa was the development hand. The uncertainty whether Barre could be trusted to stay out of the Ogaden added to U.S. reluctance to launch a security relationship. For this reason, concrete military assistance to Somalia was slow in coming once the facilities accord was signed.

Two things changed that picture. First, policy leadership in the Reagan administration fully embraced the security dimensions of U.S. relations with African states; the new team at the State Department believed it important to confront the Soviets in Africa. Second,

Ethiopian army regulars followed Somali Salvation Democratic Front (SSDF) insurgents into Somalia in July 1982. After clashes with the Somali army, the Ethiopians occupied two border towns. To prove its credibility as a security partner, the United States rushed arms to Somalia in a highly publicized airlift.[42]

Assistant Secretary Chester Crocker's explanation of U.S. purposes shows how carefully the United States drew boundaries around the new security relationship: "The United States has limited our military assistance to Somalia to quite modest levels, geared to the defense of internationally-recognized Somali territory."[43] Crocker saw security in the region threatened from the Ethiopian side: "African security is not served if Soviet arms, Cuban reserve forces, and Libyan money and arms are combined to overthrow legitimate governments in the Horn." Crocker asserted that the United States was not prepared "to countenance subversive action and armed aggression against our friends in the region." At the same time, he recorded the U.S. search for "a wider basis for resolution of the tensions in the region," including promotion of a modus vivendi among countries in the area and support of comprehensive economic programs for Sudan, Kenya, and Somalia.[44]

Following the buildup in 1982, the Reagan administration's requests for Somalia moved up toward U.S. $40 million, giving credence to the view that there was an informal understanding that U.S. access to Somali facilities was to bring Somalia approximately that amount in annual military assistance. (In the best of years, annual outlays were typically below proposed levels—U.S. $33 million in FY 1984 and U.S. $34 million in FY 1985, for example, compared with U.S $41 million proposed for each year.) Requests and allocations dropped markedly from FY 1988 onward, when Congress, in the waning days of the Cold War, began cutting security assistance budgets to peripheral regional areas.

Most significant about the military assistance allocations, however, is how the money was spent. Table 6.1 shows the main categories of the military assistance program.

As the table clearly demonstrates, the Reagan administration carried over from the Carter era the formula that "defensive weapons" were the appropriate type of U.S. arms. Air defense took a lot of the budget. This included provision of new U.S. radars and maintenance or repair of existing Soviet radars, an expensive undertaking that incidentally improved U.S. expertise in Soviet equipment. Maintenance funds for the navy included the rebuilding of a captured "swift ship" and repairs of Soviet patrol boats. This was another expensive technical package that got the ships' motors turning

Table 6.1   Military Assistance Program Allocations, Fiscal Years 1980–1988

Program	Amount (in millions of dollars)
Peace Horn radars	2.5
Maintenance/spare parts	24.1
Vehicles/transportation	21.9
M113 TOW missiles program	18.1
Ammunition	18.0
Peace Cube communications system	15.2
M198 howitzers	11.6
Training	9.5
Troop support equipment	8.2
Small arms	8.0
Radar/missile repair	6.6
Tactical communications	6.2
Freight forwarder costs	6.1
Minor construction	4.8
M47 tank rebuild program	2.7
Total	163.5

Source: United States, General Accounting Office, *Somalia: U.S. Strategic Interests and Assistance*, p. 31.

again but never had the boats seaworthy for long, much to the relief of the landlubbing Somali navy. A command, control, and communications center was a glossy item that the United States built at the personal request of the Somali minister of defense, who wanted a replica of the installation he had seen at U.S. Central Command (CENTCOM) headquarters. It came in much over budget after a six-year effort and could be used only in the last two years of Barre's rule. Transportation ate up a sizable part of the funds, providing the Somalis mobility along the border with two-ton trucks and jeeps. The rest of the 1988 budget went for spares and for support in the form of small arms and recoilless rifles, uniforms, and logistics and maintenance training teams.[45]

A close reading of budgets throughout the decade shows that U.S. policy closely followed a formula of modest defensive assistance. The 1985 security assistance proposal to Congress reported that security assistance was "limited to defensive materials and training."[46] Barre used to tweak his U.S. visitors for believing that "if you give a Somali a gun, he will go out and shoot an Ethiopian." With usual canny insight, President Barre was not far from the mark. The United States purposely spent its military assistance on high-tech items that ate up the assistance budget and gave Somalia only a modest increment in defensive capability. The figures (and how they were allocated) reveal the following high policy goals of expanded regional security that repeatedly graced each congressional presentation on security assistance to Somalia:

- Enhance cooperative defense and security.
- Preserve U.S. access to Somali military facilities.
- Counter East-bloc expansionism in the Horn of Africa.
- Enhance national stability and progress.
- Encourage economic reform.[47]

The last objective enumerated above encompassed the other side of the security assistance package: economic support funds (ESFs). They were proposed for Somalia because of the security partnership; in some way, they were meant to repay Somalia for the facilities access that the United States enjoyed. ESF grants to Somalia during the 1980s were, by comparison with other countries in Africa, very generous. But these funds were never spent for security purposes; every dime of ESF money spent in Somalia went to development projects or to program assistance in the development sector, such as the commodity import program.

Ultimately, the advocates of using development aid as the means of expressing U.S. interests in Somalia won out. Even though the top U.S. interest there after 1980 was security (presumably that of both countries), development funding (buttressed by ESFs) far outweighed military assistance. What Barre's regime most desired, however, was military assistance in support of Somali security concerns; the high-tech, high-cost U.S. defensive equipment only partially fulfilled that desire. Instead, given the way the United States chose to structure its security assistance, the largest part of that assistance funding, economic support funds, went directly to development purposes. In the early 1980s, ESFs went in large part to cover deficits in the balance of payments through such instrumentalities as the commodity import program or the foreign exchange auction of the World Bank's agricultural sector adjustment program. As development assistance funds dwindled in the last part of the decade, ESFs increasingly covered the budget requirements of ongoing projects. It was ESF grants that gave significant weight and dimension to U.S. developmental assistance to Somalia. The development agenda thus determined the use of ESFs; the dynamics of the development environment circumscribed the effect of ESF funding on the economy and its impact on the bilateral relationship.

The Somali leadership sought above all from the United States the comfort and guarantee of a security relationship. What they wanted was military assistance approaching the scale of previous Soviet aid; what they got out of the U.S. relationship was modest assistance with defensive military equipment and a hefty injection of funds into the development program. That program, though well intentioned and carefully conceived, was not without its problems. A review of the dilemmas that U.S. planners faced will expand this picture of developmental assistance to Somalia.

Constraints on Developmental Assistance

The years 1986 and 1987 marked the high tide of U.S. assistance to Somalia. The U.S. embassy and its USAID mission nourished ambitions for a growing relationship, but back in Congress funds were being cut both for military assistance and, to a lesser extent, for developmental aid. With growing accounts elsewhere, USAID was reluctant to spend generously from its development fund for Africa on what it considered to be the "political" programs of Somalia. FY 1987 saw a precipitous decline in project funding, obliging USAID to tap ESF resources for the continuing costs of major projects. By FY 1989, such project initiatives included programs for the following: Shabelle water management, U.S. $22.6 million; Somali management training and development (SOMTAD), U.S. $18.5 million; livestock marketing and health, U.S. $19.4 million; and policy initiatives and privatization (PIPs), U.S. $10.45 million. Of these, the Shabelle program, SOMTAD, and PIPs had mortgage requirements on future funding for the next several years.[48] As USAID sought to justify its programs and cover its commitments in the face of dwindling resources, it had to confront several dilemmas that had not been present in more generous times. These included Somali malversation and misappropriation of development funds, the impact of human rights concerns on U.S. support, and the increasingly active interest of Congress in U.S. policy toward Somalia.

USAID was in the forefront of donors in using commodity and cash grant assistance to bring about economic and institutional reform. It also tracked more closely than did other donors the flow of counterpart currencies through the Somali Ministry of Finance to the respective development projects or programs. Although the record is impressive, it has a downside. Despite USAID's best efforts to move commodity flows away from government warehouses into the private sector, the Somali authorities tried to manipulate commodity auctions to the advantage of its clients and in some cases simply appropriated commodities for government institutions.[49]

Moreover, although local currencies used to buy these commodities were transferred to the Ministry of Finance, where a USAID team tracked disbursements to specific development projects, USAID had little control on overinvoicing, exaggerated costs, or misappropriation of project resources once disbursements were made. Somali authorities skimmed off development investments in a number of little ways.

More significant were structural problems caused by the effect of large-scale commodity imports on Somalia's economy. For example, the U.S. $490 million made available to Somalia between 1985 and 1989 in commodity imports and cash grants supposedly funded construction, transport, and salaries in development projects through transfers from the Central Bank to the development budget managed by the Ministry of Finance.[50]

There were three problems, however. First, although the counterpart currencies that paid for these commodities (or matched the cash grants) were tabulated on ledgers in the Central Bank, there was never any audit on the movement of these funds. Much of the funds, instead of being put into productive investment, was simply recycled through the commercial economy, thus increasing money flows and fueling inflation. Second, when commodities were put on the market or foreign exchange was auctioned, the Commercial Bank, which Siyaad Barre directly controlled, would issue letters of credit called "circular notes" without collateral to favored members of the ruling elite. These notes could then be traded for the cash needed to buy commodities or foreign exchange. The Commercial Bank thus became the "black hole" of Somali finance, the most direct means of bypassing IMF-imposed credit restraints that sought to keep inflation in check.[51] Finally, once counterpart currencies (except for the U.S.-monitored PL 480 funds) reached the Ministry of Finance, they were either used to fund the ordinary budget or held for extraordinary expenditures. A World Bank review at the end of the 1980s, however, noted that the government made no accounting of ordinary expenditures and that the "Ministry of Finance prefers to leave a large portion of counterpart funds outside the budget to finance extraordinary expenditures."[52]

From the Central Bank, the Commercial Bank, and the Ministry of Finance, counterpart currencies flowed into private hands, fostering demand for imported goods, creating an acute trade imbalance, and generating inflationary pressure within the economy. The foreign currency auctions somewhat relieved this pressure, but the economy imploded when Somalia went back to fixed-rate exchange in 1988. Thus, although the weight of commodity and cash grant programs leveraged reforms, they also produced paper money that helped undermine Somalia's economy.

Since the revival of its relations with the Somali state in the late 1970s, the United States had been concerned about the human rights record there. The U.S. embassy's annual human rights report usually gave Barre a poor score. He held prominent intellectuals and former politicians, plus several hundred other political prisoners, in miserable prison conditions; detention without trial, torture, and summary execution were not uncommon. Word of Barre's repressive tactics had contributed to the tentativeness of the State Department's embrace and to congressional reluctance about the budding security relationship. After the 1982 airlift, Barre wanted to come to the United States to formalize the partnership symbolically; the U.S. ambassador made it clear to Barre that such a trip would be extremely difficult unless there was evident progress in human rights. Shortly before making that visit to the United States in 1983, Barre released from prison former Prime Minister Egal and General M. A. Musa, both of whom had been detained since the 1969 coup.[53]

Human rights remained a U.S. concern throughout the 1980s. U.S. voices joined the growing chorus of concern over the continued imprisonment of former Vice-President Abokor and Foreign Minister Arteh. The release of imprisoned intellectuals such as Professor Abdi Yunis became the object of massive letter campaigns. But human rights remained a quiet part of the official U.S. agenda until Ambassador Crigler came to post and publicly put it among the top U.S. objectives. In presenting his credentials to Barre in 1987, Crigler conveyed the U.S. intention to include "measures for protecting, preserving and enhancing the human rights of all persons, wherever they may be" among the "opportunities for bilateral cooperation."[54]

This commitment was put to test shortly thereafter when a high-level mission from the National Academy of Sciences came to Mogadishu to express concern regarding continued imprisonment of scientific colleagues. Crigler and his staff won kudos from the academy for "their vital and invaluable assistance to the mission."[55] This activist stance, which induced the government to bring long-detained political prisoners to trial in early 1988 and secured the release of many of them over the next year, nonetheless failed to deter a more aggressive congressional interest in the course of U.S. relations with Somalia.

Growing U.S. involvement in Somalia after Barre switched sides in 1977 was of particular concern to a few Congressmen who held a continuing interest in U.S. policy toward the Horn. Since the late 1970s, the Democratic majority in Congress had never been happy about closer U.S. relations with Somalia. There were critical congressional investigations or visiting missions to Somalia in 1977, 1979, and 1981. In the early 1960s, hearings held by Congressman Tony Moffett contributed to a "great stall" in the provision of the military assistance promised in the Facilities Agreement of 1980.[56] Even Republicans who supported the security arguments of official Southwest Asian strategy had a difficult time embracing Somalia, a country that blazoned its socialist credentials. As Lefebvre had detailed it, Mogadishu's public relations problems on Capitol Hill included a visceral distaste for Somalia, ineffective lobbying, and the fact that influential members of Congress "personally disliked Barre."[57]

In the late 1980s, Congressman Howard Wolpe led the fight against the assistance relationship. Somali officials saw him as an inveterate friend of Ethiopia, a man who could see no harm in Mengistu Haile Mariam and no good in Siyaad Barre. In early 1988, Wolpe's staff engineered a hold on ESF allocations to Somalia in FY 1988.[58] Barre's human rights record was their justification, even though (in relative terms) that record had improved under prodding from donors, especially the U.S. embassy. What Wolpe was really after, however, was revision of the U.S. security posture on the Horn. He had never considered the U.S. relationship with Somalia to be justified, and he used a congressional hold to dismantle the FY 1988 allocations development program after the U.S. embassy had engaged the Somali government in planning that program. Because so many of USAID's projects were programmed beyond the limits of the Development Fund for Africa allocations, that hold on ESFs curtailed a broad range of U.S. development activity in Somalia. Just as the administration had previously used the security argument to leverage large allocations for Somalia's development program, Wolpe, in a reverse twist, used the human rights argument to stop the developmental assistance that undergirded U.S. security relations with Somalia. Although the Washington foreign affairs community saw the hold only as a troublesome obstacle along the course of continuing U.S. aid, it was in fact the first stage of a process that, in two years, brought the U.S. assistance relationship with Somalia to an end.

U.S. Assistance: Security or Development?

The United States built its relationship with Somalia in the 1980s on security interests but keyed that relationship to developmental objectives. U.S. developmental assistance outweighed military assistance by a ratio of 4:1; by 1987, there were only ten permanent U.S.

military personnel billeted in Somalia, with fifteen to twenty U.S. contractors, whereas USAID had twenty-eight direct-hire positions and some seventy contractors. (This does not include the various temporary duty missions that were at post in any given period.) The nature of U.S. developmental aid evolved over time. In the late 1970s, the United States rushed into providing developmental aid by joining in multidonor projects and offering commodity assistance. By the mid 1980s, USAID's strategy turned toward sector programs and technical support in private-sector promotion. From 1987–1988, the U.S. development program was undergoing administrative restructuring and conceptual reorientation. In the course of this process, USAID wrapped all projects and programs into the overarching purpose of structural reform and wrote strong terms of reform conditionality into every agreement.

From July 1988 to June 1989, it appeared that Somalia might at last be seriously listening to donor advice; the bureaucracy was meeting IMF targets, and Siyaad Barre seemed open to political reform. Nonetheless, the Somali economy had lost its dynamism; human rights concerns and the lack of a full-fledged IMF stabilization program were throttling the development flows from which so much of Somalia's economic activity was derived. Within this stagnant economy, old patterns of malversation took on a more desperate pace; Barre's family took the goods of state to be their own. Donor demands in terms of human rights and political reform came up against the brutal reality of a country disintegrating into civil war.

The nature of that conflict posed special problems to Somalia's partners in security assistance. The United States and Italy were training and equipping Somali armed forces to defend the security and independence of the Somali state, but not necessarily against their own citizens. As the Somali state began to lose control over its provinces, the security dimension of its relations with major donors was inevitably called into question. How the United States dealt with the disintegration of state power in Somalia and what lessons can be drawn from a decade of donor assistance to the Somali state constitute the last considerations of this study.

Dealing with Disintegration

The Somali State in Perspective

This study has attempted to trace, in brief outline, the changing course of the Somali state over its thirty-year history. What began at independence in 1960 as multiparty parliamentarianism turned into revolutionary military rule nine years later. Both parliamentary and military governments tended toward arbitrary rule and control of economic resources for the benefit of the ruling elite. Within the elite of the first republic, individuals struggled for identity and recognition on the basis of kin affiliation, whereas in the second republic, loyalty to Siyaad Barre's regime and its principles of national unity and scientific socialism was grounds for advancement and privilege. Barre sought to fulfill the national dream by conquering Somali homelands in Western Ethiopia; when he failed, he switched international partners and devoted his energies to political maneuvers. In spite of the formation of a national party and the adoption of a new constitution, state institutions in the last decade of Barre's rule were marked by increasing militarization, a drive toward autocracy, and, as the economy faltered, a narrowing base of patronage, channeled to Barre's kin and cohorts. When Somalia finally signed a peace agreement with Ethiopia in April 1988, insurgencies moved from Ethiopia into Somali territory, thus initiating a protracted civil war that culminated in the total disintegration of the Somali state.

Somalia's assistance partners had not realized that disintegration of the Somali state in fact began with the Ogaden adventure. Donors focused on Somalia's economy, not on the quality of Somalia's political institutions, their purchase in the provinces, and their legitimacy as instruments of influence and control. What donors saw when they got back in the development business after the Ogaden War was a Somalia, always poor, but now in desperate economic straits after ten years of scientific socialism. The donors' remedy, chosen from World Bank/IMF shelves, prescribed three treatments for Somalia's ills: a stabilized financial situation based on monetary, credit, and budgetary controls and a market-derived exchange rate; economic growth generated by freeing the natural energies of Somali traders and farmers from the repressive control of the state; and better management of economic institutions through training and further professionalization of the civil service. To make this medicine palatable, donors spent over U.S. $2.5 billion from 1980–1989.

Although Somalia was induced by donor generosity to adopt one or another of these prescriptions at various times in that decade, it did not stay on any medicine long enough to be cured. Siyaad Barre at no time gave up scientific socialism as the organizing principle of his regime, though he was increasingly obliged by reform conditionality to give up central state controls that made "socialism" so profitable to the elite of his regime. Realizing that he was losing his ability to manage the economy to his own ends, Barre retreated from World Bank/IMF measures in September 1987, and into economic disaster. To get back on the reform wagon nine months later, Somalia had to accept more severe prescriptions: liberalization of all export trade, competitive sale of agricultural inputs, and restructuring of the commercial financial sector. By that time, however, civil war had erupted, and the political underpinnings of the economy were crumbling.

Somalia's erratic performance on economic reform was not the only problem donors faced. Within Somalia's weak institutional base, donors sought to generate quick economic growth and rapid structural change. Although coordination was good at the policy and planning level, there were major problems with the implementation of the heavily funded, multidonor projects. Training programs were subverted when trainees failed to return from abroad or refused to work in the provinces for the pitiable pay of Somalia's civil service. Heavy commodity and cash grant assistance, instruments chosen by donors to turn Somalia's economy around, opened broad avenues for malversation and structurally undermined Somalia's economy through their inflationary effect. With the best of intentions, donors with large-scale projects and massive assistance inadvertently contributed to the disintegration of the Somali state. If, in their focus on economic issues, donors had been unwitting participants in state disintegration before 1988, then after civil war broke out, the political nature of Somalia's problem became readily apparent.

U.S. Policy Toward a Disintegrating State

U.S. reactions to the outbreak of civil war in Somalia give an expanded sense of the complexities in donor relations with the Somali state. The United States program in Somalia included developmental goals, political concerns, and security interests. Before 1988, the security interests were primary, though they contributed, as has been noted, to a dominant developmental mission.

After the 1980 access agreement, the United States' relationship with Somalia was based on a commitment to assist in countering security threats to Somalia. The SNM attack in the North in May 1988 was initially viewed as another cross-border incursion warranting continuation of U.S. military assistance programs. The U.S. embassy soon realized, however, that the SNM had come home to stay. Somalia was no longer involved in protecting its borders; it was engaged in civil conflict. Even though the security arrangements included standard language about threats external and internal, the United States did not believe it appropriate to arm the Somali government for war against its own people. As of June 1988, Ambassador Crigler recommended freezing shipments of lethal matériel to Somalia. He also placed national reconciliation as the prime U.S. objective in Somalia, overriding interests in facilities access or regional security; these, after all, depended on a stabilized political situation.

The State Department backed both of those decisions, but the Pentagon was not amused. The U.S. Central Command (CENTCOM) had found Somalia a welcoming training ground for its forces and wanted to maintain a credible military-to-military relationship. This was difficult to do with a drastically reduced military assistance budget, especially if lethal matériel were denied to friends fighting for their very existence. For over a year, the Pentagon demanded a change of policy. Even with the arms prohibition, CENTCOM kept the relationship alive through joint training exercises. There was a Bright Star exercise in August 1988, several small-scale exercises later in the year, and another Bright Star planned for August 1989. A joint training exercise, Operation Eagle Claw, was aborted when street disturbances in Mogadishu in June 1989, followed by the massacre of opposition leaders on Gezira Beach in June, forced U.S. participants to withdraw.

Further, although the facilities in Berbera had not been used in the 1987–1988 Gulf reflagging operations surrounding the Iran-Iraq War (and would not be used later in the buildup for Operation Desert Storm), the Pentagon had money budgeted for a prepositioning depot there. Pressure existed to use those funds for fear of losing them. The Pentagon proposed obligating U.S. $15 million for lease-build construction before the Facilities Agreement of 1980 even came up for renegotiation in 1990. The arguments were that prior leases would sweeten the pot for negotiations, that political instability did not affect U.S. presence at the facilities, and that a depot at Berbera was important to U.S. regional interests. When the Pentagon forwarded this proposal in early 1990, the State Department refused to clear it. The department was not willing to launch new construction or initiate facilities negotiations. But in any case, Somalis were so busy with their own internal problems that they never questioned continued U.S. use of Berbera facilities, even after the lease agreement lapsed.

After the SNM entered the North in May 1988, the difficulties of achieving developmental goals should have been apparent. Barre would have to divert considerable state finances to purchase weapons and proceed with the war. The attention of policymakers was captured by the growing insurgencies rather than developmental objectives. But USAID, tied to an IMF agenda, pressed the dream of putting Somalia back on the reform wagon. Behind the scenes, the United States was intimately involved in pushing forward negotiations on a standby agreement scheduled for mid-1989, a follow-up to the shadow program that the Somali government seemed to be pursuing credibly.[59] USAID proposed using U.S. $25 million of ESF funds that had been blocked in FY 1987 and FY 1988 to help clear Somalia's debt to the IMF so that the standby package could go forward. This, in addition to relief efforts in the North, was the primary thrust of U.S. assistance. Both in program focus and in actual disbursements, USAID concentrated on pushing Somalia back into the IMF/World Bank camp.

The policy establishment in Washington had difficulty with the logic of this strategy. However laudable economic reform might be, was Barre's Somalia a place where such reform could realistically be expected to take place? Could the United States justify a major disbursement of ESFs to a country at war with itself and multiplying human rights abuses by the day? The request to unfreeze ESF funds for Somalia started on its bureaucratic journey in November 1988; it got nowhere. Then, newly rehabilitated Prime Minister Mohamed Ali Samantar came on a mediatory mission to the United States in January 1989. In March 1989, Barre released a few political prisoners and talked of a new constitution. By May, CENTCOM had joined with the Somali military in comradely training exercises, including Operation Eagle Claw. Meanwhile, Ambassador Crigler returned stateside to push the ESF proposal forward. The specter of hope had returned.

It did not take the press long to get wind of the request as it worked its way to Congress. Holly Burkhalter wrote an opinion piece in the *New York Times* questioning how the administration could possibly think of giving U.S. $25 million to Barre's corrupt regime. The coordinated U.S. government answer, sent under signature of the assistant secretary for human rights, spelled out what had been implicit in U.S. funding strategy for some time: U.S. funds to Somalia were designed to dismantle Barre's socialist regime and provide succor to those in either the private sector or the Somali administration who wanted to build a new order. Assistant Secretary Schifter noted that the U.S. $25 million was intended to revive an IMF program so as to help those "who are suffering both from poverty and from human rights abuses."[60] Broadly interpreted, Schifter's letter endorsed the transfer of power away from Barre to the people he was oppressing. That strategy never got tested, however. The June 1989 massacres in Mogadishu brought the violence of insurrection to the capital city. Somalia's unreported civil war was suddenly in the headlines. The U.S. administration dared not push further the ESF request to Congress; without that money, Somalia could not pay its debt to the IMF, and a new standby arrangement and reform program became a dead letter. From summer 1989 on, U.S. developmental assistance in Mogadishu became a holding operation.

After troubles broke out in the North, the United States became increasingly vocal in airing its critical view of the human dimension of these events. Although admitting that the insurgents had been armed and equipped outside of Somalia, U.S. officials insisted that the problem had become one of civil strife inside, for which the only solution was respect for human rights and national reconciliation. Recalling its own searing civil conflict the century before, the U.S. government evoked the tradition of Lincoln and urged Barre to "bind up the nation's wounds."[61] The memorable words of Lincoln's second inaugural address—"with malice towards none, with charity for all"—figured prominently in Ambassador Crigler's televised speech on 4 July. Later in August, marking the arrival of a field hospital, Crigler argued that "political reconciliation is the most desirable course."[62] In the October dedication of the port at Kismayu, he urged Barre toward "a peaceful solution and reconciliation among all Somalis."[63] Human rights and political reconciliation had truly come to the top of the U.S. agenda.

When trouble broke out in the North in 1989, U.S. congressional interest in Somalia blossomed. Congress mandated two General Accounting Office (GAO) investigations, one into the refugee and relief situation in the North and the other, in 1990, into the overall record of U.S. assistance to Somalia.[64] Letters to the State Department on human rights concerns came from congressional representatives across the political spectrum and around the nation. Some thirty representatives signed a letter to the secretary of state asking for a change in U.S. policy toward Somalia. Against such skepticism and hostility, the new Bush administration sought to urge continuity in U.S. relations with Somalia. It argued that assistance had to go forward so that the United States could play a credible role in promoting national reconciliation and bringing Somalia back to economic reform.

In a period of budget crisis, and with the Cold War diminishing as the Soviet Union retrenched around the world, these aid arguments did not gain much sympathy. U.S. administrations under

Carter and Reagan had overcome congressional reluctance to assist Somalia by asserting the country's importance to U.S. security interests in the Gulf Region. Now, by making national reconciliation its top objective in Somalia, the administration undercut the foundation of its funding support from Congress. From 1988, President Bush was asking for funds to save Somalia from itself. A congressional hold had been put on all ESF allocations for Somalia. The last executive charge up Capitol Hill to remove such holds was thwarted by the June 1989 riots and massacres in Mogadishu. Shortly after the massacres, Ambassador Crigler determined that U.S. hopes of playing a major role in changing Somali politics or reforming Somalia's economy had been dashed in the bloody sands of Gezira Beach. Crigler concluded that the United States would not be able to fund a reform program, Bright Star exercises should be canceled, and the U.S. in-country presence should be radically reduced to better manage the crisis situation.

Washington agencies were unhappy. They countered that they needed to hold onto current staffing to prepare for contingencies and to maintain programs until a better day emerged in Somalia. The Pentagon, for example, argued that Crigler's policy concerns could be accommodated with minor changes in personnel and programs. Agencies saw the ambassador's proposals in the latter part of 1989 as threatening their ability to secure minimum funding to guarantee their survival in Somalia. But with violence in the streets and no hope of an early reprieve from political instability, Ambassador Crigler staged a drawdown of U.S. personnel. Undersecretary for Management Ivan Selin visited Mogadishu and supported the ambassador's approach. Implementation of this plan for progressive withdrawal between October 1989 and June 1990 reduced the U.S. presence in Somalia from about two hundred U.S. officials and contractors to less than one hundred.

The State Department's public position was that this reduction reflected cutbacks in various programs and that the United States would still have a significant presence in Somalia, consistent with its interests. With a lean but experienced staff, the U.S. embassy would seek the national reconciliation that was so clearly needed. Unfortunately, though, trend lines pointed toward disintegration rather than reconciliation.

Why Donors Kept Trying

The vision of donors pushing forward the agenda of economic and political reconciliation against the unfolding drama of the Somali state's demise is almost surreal. One cannot help but wonder why the IMF, the World Bank, the United States, and other bilateral donors persisted in attempts to turn the situation around. Why did donor staffs remain, albeit in reduced ranks, after violence broke out in Mogadishu in June 1989, holding on until the last moment, when a daring helicopter mission rescued them from descending anarchy?

There are reasons for this persistence. Donors kept trying because of usual concerns about maintaining leverage with the host government. Without programs and funding, how could donors get a hearing from the Somali government? How, for example, could they keep in the game of pushing for national reconciliation? Donors needed inducements to draw Siyaad Barre toward that objective. Leverage through promises of aid could also keep economic reform on track; Somalia needed to be rewarded so that a momentum for reform could be maintained. For the United States, good relations with the Somali government were also required to keep access to Somali facilities.

Donors may have persisted because they were taken in by the studied ambivalence of Barre's tactics. He would free political detainees in Mogadishu even as his troops were carrying out outrages in the North. He would offer consultation with the opposition and then scuttle meetings with them. At times intransigent, at times amenable, at times conniving, Barre made just enough moves toward reconciliation to keep donors hoping—witness the release of prisoners in October 1988 and again in March 1989. But his string had run out. The tactics of bluster and about-face that had kept Barre in power for twenty years could no longer hold the Somali state together.

Another reason that the donors kept trying was the apparent seriousness with which the Somali state seemed, at last, to be addressing economic reform. Its careful adherence to standards of an IMF shadow program from July 1988 gave hope that Somalia could get back into IMF good graces. By this time, though, "development" had become something of a shell game in which donors collaborated to clear each others' accounts. Bilateral donors would forward funds to pay off the accumulated Somali debt to the IMF; in turn, the IMF would certify a program that permitted donors to restructure or forgive debts and restart aid flows. By 1989, some U.S. $268 million, including U.S. $78 million of overdue balances to the IMF, were outstanding.[65]

There was concern about who might step in should the Western presence not be asserted in Somalia. True, the West no longer feared

Soviet influence; discussions on regional issues had long since revealed a narrowing of the gap between West- and East-bloc perspectives on the Horn. Somali efforts at upgrading relations with the Soviets were treated with equanimity in Washington; if the Soviets could do something to help, so much the better. However, outside interference from Libya was a danger. SNM claims that Barre received chemical weapons from Libya in August 1989 raised a firestorm on Capitol Hill, as well as in the quarters that were generally critical of U.S. assistance. U.S. persistence in Somalia was said to be required to forestall Libyan intrusion.

Finally, bureaucratic inertia figured in how donors dealt with the disintegrating situation; it was business as usual in development aid agencies. Significant numbers of people found daily purpose and monthly wages from carrying forward established assistance programs. As evidence that the state was crumbling became irrefutable in late 1990, donor bureaucrats justified continuing programs in terms of establishing good credentials with likely successor regimes. Money to support a restructuring program was required in order to hand a viable economy to whatever group might replace Siyaad Barre. Military matériel and training should still flow to keep a military-to-military relationship through the transition period until a new political order was established. Donors simply did not foresee that there might not be a successor regime, that the Somali state might just vanish.

Conclusion

I have outlined above the pattern of donor assistance to Somalia as that state lost control of the hinterland and eventually found itself in civil war. Because I have posited that Somalia is not unique and that there may be lessons in its developmental experience for states and donors elsewhere in the Third World, what does the history of donor relations with the disintegrating Somali state teach us?

Ambiguities of Security Assistance

The United States was the only donor to claim that security interests were basic to its relationship with Somalia. The nature of U.S. security interests evolved during the 1980s. Competition with the Soviets for regional influence turned to collaboration on regional issues. The Soviet residual presence in Ethiopia and Yemen no longer threatened sea lanes of communication. Facilities at Berbera and Mogadishu were still considered important but not critical to Southwest

Asian logistic support. Moreover, in defining how it would support Somali security interests, the United States had to distinguish between its policy of respecting Ethiopian sovereignty over the Ogaden (or, inversely, denying Somalia's territorial ambitions) and its policy of assisting Somalia's defense against destabilizing threats from Ethiopia. The solution was found in providing "quite modest levels geared to the defense of internationally-recognized Somali territory."[66] This finesse worked as long as threats to Somalia's security came from across the border. But when peace was established with Ethiopia and insurgency threats to Somalia's security moved from Ethiopia into Northern Somalia, the relationship broke down. Somalia could not count on U.S. military assistance in conditions of civil war.

The problem is also one of definition. U.S. policy pronouncements and planning documents genially mixed notions of strategy, security, and politics. For example, in a speech entitled "Challenge to Regional Security in Africa," Assistant Secretary Crocker used the phrases "strategic significance," "security concern," and "important political and security interests" interchangeably.[67] By classic definition, strategic interests are those for which a nation is willing to employ power and deploy armed force. A state may have concerns about the security (i.e., stable relationships of power) in a region or in the political makeup of particular governments of that region without those concerns entailing "strategic interests." Mixing these notions offered the impression that regional stability on the Horn was of strategic value to the United States, something for which it was willing to fight.[68] When push came to shove, however, the United States was not willing to fight for the political future of the Barre regime, the security of the Somali state, or stability on the Horn.

Moreover, the United States was not willing to pursue a security arrangement with a state regime in a situation of internal conflict. In a bipolar, state-centric view of the world, it was easy to forget the lesson, drawn by Drew and Snow, that "insurgencies are, first and foremost, internal struggles for power and only secondarily East-West confrontations." Such struggles are "fundamentally different" from the conventional warfare toward which U.S. security assistance programs are geared. Furthermore, Drew and Snow find that "research on this subject is in its infancy in the U.S. military."[69] The lessons are twofold: U.S. policy requires clearer definitions of strategic interests and security concerns; claiming strategic interests where one is not willing to exert force only leads to policy quagmires. Moreover, insurgencies always complicate security assistance programs; ascertaining the nature of security threats to a

Third World partner is key to determining whether an assistance relationship can be sustained.

Dilemmas of Development

Part of the finesse in the security assistance game with Somalia was
to take security assistance funds (ESFs) and use them for developmental purposes. Although this gave great weight to the developmental effort, such heavy assistance brought real problems as well.
First, there was developmental bugaboo: coordination. Western
donor assistance to Somalia was well coordinated at the policy- and
project-definition level. The problem, as the World Bank survey revealed, was in implementation. Multidonor projects, a favorite
mode of assistance, combined cooperative effort with heavy financing. However, most such projects were colossal failures because implementation was poorly staged; once the project began to fail, its
very complexity made it difficult to revive. The World Bank survey
found that Somalia's twelve largest projects had an 83 percent rate
of implementation slippage; the implementation rate for smaller
projects was much higher.[70] The lesson is that large cooperative en-
deavors can be too cumbersome for fragile development environments. In countries like Somalia, with limited infrastructure and a
weak institutional base, development requires experimental, innovative projects of modest scale that can quickly be adjusted to account for emerging realities.

Commodity assistance provided another dilemma. Somalia was
so poor and needed so much that providing food and other commodities seemed the logical way to revive the economy. But these
commodity flows generated tremendous inflation within the economy. The counterpart currencies that paid for them had no relation
to the value of production or trade, but were instead generated by
recycling notes through the Central Bank or unlimited credit from
the Commercial Bank. Thus, manipulating counterpart currencies
and hedging on foreign exchange transactions became the most accessible avenues of corruption for the Somali elite. The lesson is
this: do not try to jump start a desperately poor economy. It takes
time and sustained, but measured, effort in traditional economies to
turn them toward market production.

Narrow Analysis: Hopeful Policy

Although issues of governance are high on the development agenda
in the 1990s, donors' principal focus during the 1980s was on

economic reform. Donors had a rather singular indicator by which they judged the state: was it on the economic reform track? Conformity to IMF standards was taken as sign of health in the body politic. To evaluate that condition, donors primarily consulted with the ministries of foreign affairs, finance, and planning, as well as technical ministries administering aid programs and, in extremis, Siyaad Barre himself. Thus, donors misjudged Somali policy intentions in the summer of 1987 because they were listening to ministers who told them what they wanted to hear about economic reform, rather than to party officials who might have instructed them about the brewing political revolt against structural adjustment. A large part of economic and political life, not only in the provinces but also in the capital city, eluded, in this manner, the donors' analytical scope. In focusing on economic reform, donors missed the political forces that were undercutting reform and the larger story of disintegrating state power in the provinces.[71] The lesson here is that adequate development policy requires a multidimensional analysis of social, economic, and political factors—not only of bureaucratic choice in the capital city, but also of popular will in the regions where the state is presumably carrying out economic change.

Realism Versus Optimism

Finally, there was a curious blend of hard-core realism and policy optimism that infused analysis of the deteriorating situation in Somalia. If donors had been politically oblivious before the events in the north, they became deeply cognizant of political processes afterward, interacting on the ground with political actors through heroic relief efforts, human rights investigations, close contact with opposition groups, and negotiations with power brokers such as the Manifesto Group. Analysts knew what was happening in its stark reality, and they became able, following the outbreak of civil war in 1988, to rattle off names of kin divisions or dissident military groups with a facility that made Washington dizzy.

Yet, despite the flow of dismal facts, donors were looking for an overall solution to the problem of state disintegration, and they reinforced each other in this futile effort. Long after the United States might have given up on Somalia, Italy, the World Bank, and the IMF were urging greater generosity to save the regime or keep structural adjustment on track. Desperate for a turnaround, donors placed heavy weight on any hopeful sign and kept chasing the specter of peace. In a recent analysis of U.S. Middle East diplomacy, Robert Kaplan suggests that "Foreign Service Officers . . .

become hostage to a professional idealism that blinds them to the obvious."[72]

It is not, however, that such officers are naive idealists, but that U.S. mission planning is structured in a problem-solving, goals-and-objectives approach. (The World Bank and UN agencies have also adopted this management mechanism.) U.S. management planning requires establishing goals and assessing the means to achieve them, but unachievable goals will skew long-range analysis and attendant mission planning. National reconciliation and the survival of the Somali state presented challenges that the best management by goals and objectives could not encompass. This is the lesson: clear strategy, goodwill, and adequate means cannot resolve some problems. However unpalatable the strategy is to problem-solving, developmental functionaries, there may be times when quitting is the best policy.

The people of Somalia need no instruction in the bitter lessons of history. To the outside observer, the shards of their broken state are merely intimations of past forms. Causes of state disintegration in Somalia—militarization, elite competition, misspent patronage—seem to have been constituent elements of its autocratic regime. The disintegration that they engendered might have been arrested if only Siyaad Barre had ceded to a council of elders and if liberty in discourse, movement, and commerce, so ingrained in traditional Somali culture, had become intrinsic to the political ethos of the Somali case.

A more effective state system in Somalia would require a different national vision. Coercive jurisdiction over all Somali homelands was never a viable goal, but deeper cultural bonding among all Somali peoples could have been a practical objective of national aspiration. The international partners of choice should not have been the superpowers, but rather Somalia's neighbors in the Gulf and on the Horn, where ties are so vital to the commerce and livelihood of the Somali people. In short, Somali leadership should have pictured the state's future in regional terms particular to Somali aspirations, rather than as a partner in global strategy and an avatar of scientific socialism. All this suggests that the bluster and wiliness of Siyaad Barre should have given way to the craft of statemanship, which could have better analyzed the realities of the world arena and defended Somalia's interests in it, not merchandising the future of the country's people but making hard choices for them among real alternatives.

A more effective Somali developmental strategy would have assessed proffered "assistance" with a practiced eye. Were projects managed to their stated objectives or to the personal gain of project directors and the corporate benefit of aid consultants? Was commodity assistance limited to real need, or had it become an easy substitute for domestic productivity? Would proposed aid unleash and enhance economic exchange among individual Somalis, or would it merely offer a channel for easy enrichment of money managers? Were the Somali people, in their scattered localities, to be involved in determining their economic future, or were they merely assumed participants in large projects designed by capital city planners? One lesson from the 1980s is almost tautological: the greater the levels of foreign assistance, the deeper the dependence and indebtedness of the Somali state. Two corollary lessons are (1) no amount of assistance would have leveraged reform that the leadership did not want, and (2) no fortune could have bought what Somalis needed most: reconciliation among themselves and a purchase on their own economic future.

From our safe distance, we are too much at ease to appreciate the moral of this tragic tale. In post–Cold War perspective, it is facile to observe that the United States, having stressed the strategic importance of Somalia, was not as sensitive to political and social impediments to Somalia's development as it should have been. It is easy to criticize the nearsightedness of donors' singular focus on economic reform, but that was the common objective to which they covenanted at Paris roundtables. Although the tale shows that coordination had its hazards, including monumental (but coordinated) failure, it is hard to fault donors for too much consultation and coordination, the summum bonum of developmental dogma.

Had donors not been so determined to do good (or at least to disburse assistance allocations), they might have understood that their agenda did not coincide with that of the Somali state under Siyaad Barre. His aim was that of retaining power through crafty exercise of central authority, not through building the economy and reconciling social divisions. Although the record shows a growing popular dissatisfaction with the state's performance during the 1980s, donors found no alternative to dealing with the Somali state, even a disintegrating one. That is why they persisted against increasing odds. The experience of Mogadishu may, at least, help donors in the future better judge when the game is really over.

Shall the chaos in Somalia now be rethought? Must Somalis wait for the passions of war to be spent and exhaustion to set in before they can hope for a better day? Should they, as Fay Weldon's Joanna May, look to "shame and rage, fear and desire" as the four saving and refining passions of the universe?[73] Or can Somalis, with their own resourcefulness, find the creative power to trace out a civic space wherein to construct a new order? Imagination is key to making sense out of chaos.[74] That possibility exists in human society as well. As Vico noted long ago, "The world of civil society has certainly been made by man. . . . Its principles are therefore to be found in the modifications of our own human minds."[75] If the Somalis can find the creative power to reorder their society, polity, and economy, let us hope that this time they can draw, together with donors, their own blueprint.

Notes

1. In describing Somali political culture, this chapter draws necessarily on secondary sources (in that least literate of bureaucracies, all documents have now been destroyed), on interviews, and on personal impressions (my team served in Somali during the high tide of donor assistance). To capture donor intentions, I have broadly consulted World Bank, International Monetary Fund (IMF), and U.S. Agency for International Development (USAID) documents, as well as congressional testimony and other public statements. European development officials actively working on the Somali account in the 1980s have graciously commented on programs of the other major donors.

2. See Bates, *Markets and States in Tropical Africa*; Hyden, *Beyond Ujamaa*; MacGaffey, *Entrepreneurs and Parasites*; Chazan, *An Anatomy of Ghanaian Politics*.

3. See Migdal, *Strong Societies*; Chazan, "Patterns of State-Society"; Ayoade, "States Without Citizens"; Callaghy, "The State"; Diamond, "Swollen Bureaucracies"; Chazan, *An Anatomy of Ghanaian Politics*. A study of particular relevance to these considerations sees the state corpus levitated, "suspended," between the pull of international financing and the tug of the populations it is supposed to govern (A. Samatar and A. I. Samatar, "The Material Roots of the Suspended African State").

4. Jackson and Rosberg, "Why Weak African States Persist."

5. Jackson, *Quasi-States*, p. 154.

6. Ibid., p. 29.

7. Bull, *The Anarchical Society*, p. 7.

8. A notion that begins with Burton, *First Footsteps*, and carries on through Hanley, *Warriors and Strangers*.

9. A. I. Samatar, *Socialist Somalia*, pp. 128, 136, 154.

10. Jackson, *Quasi-States*, p. 139.

11. Jackson and Rosberg, "Why Weak African States Persist," pp. 260–261.

12. Bayart, *L'etat en Afrique*, p. 61.

13. The Waranleh warrior culture was pervasive in traditional Somali society. This ethos, however, is quite distinct from the military takeover of state administrative positions, a process that became more acute after the Ogaden War (A. I. Samatar, *Socialist Somalia*, p. 152). The war essentially weakened Somali state infrastructure, thus contradicting Tilly's general thesis about war making and state making but confirming his secondary

point that military organizations "acquired from outside" will overshadow other state organizations (Tilly, "War Making and State Making," pp. 169–191).

14. Lefebvre, *Arms for the Horn*, p. 180.

15. Ibid., p. 175.

16. Ibid., p. 176.

17. Ibid.

18. "Address by the Secretary of State."

19. Lefebvre, *Arms for the Horn*, p. 197.

20. Ibid., p. 199.

21. Remarks by Paul Henze, former NSC staffer, at the Sixth Michigan State University Conference on Northern Africa, 23–28 April 1992.

22. *Africa Contemporary Record, 1987–88*, p. 393.

23. Somali Democratic Republic, *National Development Strategy and Programme, 1987–1989*, pp. 1–12.

24. *Africa Contemporary Record, 1987–88*, p. 305.

25. "Statement Made in the Security Council by Francis O. Wilcox," p. 151.

26. President Kennedy set the pattern for two decades of speeches by likening African decolonization to that of the United States (Kennedy, "Remarks").

27. "Statement Made in the Security Council by Francis O. Wilcox," p. 151.

28. United States, Agency for International Development, *Congressional Presentation for Somalia, FY68*. The FY 1968 proposals, revised 28 April 1969, show the direction and levels of developmental effort in full-fledged U.S. collaboration with the first Somali Republic.

29. Ibid.

30. Lefebvre, *Arms for the Horn*, p. 197.

31. United States, Agency for International Development, *Congressional Presentation for Somalia, FY68*.

32. Lefebvre, *Arms for the Horn*, p. 193.

33. Ibid., pp. 192, 195.

34. "Address by the Secretary of State."

35. The notion that Africa was distinct and separate from the regular arena of world politics goes back to Assistant Secretary G. Mennen Williams and his Deputy, Dr. Wayne Fredricks. See "Address by the Deputy Assistant Secretary of State." Subsequent administrations subscribed to this formula in policy addresses until, under the Brezhnev Doctrine, Soviet intrusions into Africa took on dimensions that the United States could not ignore. It is ironic that the Carter administration, which most clearly articulated the vision of a unique, apolitical Africa, would be the administration that had to devise the first response to Soviet expansion in Africa (for example, Shaba I and II, Somalia and Chad).

36. Lefebvre, *Arms for the Horn*, p. 199.

37. Carter, "Annual Message to Congress."

38. The agreement was formalized by an exchange of notes on 21 and 22 August 1980. Negotiations took the longest of any access agreements in the region, largely because Somalia demanded an exorbitant price for facilities access and the United States, having secured other ports of access in the region, was not all that interested in Somali facilities.

39. Lefebvre, *Arms for the Horn*, p. 220.

40. United States, Department of State, "Address by Chester A. Crocker."

41. "Statement of Lannon Walker."

42. Lefebvre, *Arms for the Horn*, p. 224.

43. United States, Department of State, "Address by Chester A. Crocker," p. 4.

44. Ibid.

45. United States, Department of State, *Congressional Presentation for Security Assistance, FY-88*, "Somalia."

46. United States, Department of State, *Congressional Presentation for Security Assistance, FY-85*, "Somalia."

47. United States, Department of State, *Congressional Presentation for Security Assistance, FY-87*, "Somalia."

48. United States, Agency for International Development–Somalia, *Country Development Strategy Statement-ECPR*, 9 June 1989.

49. United States, General Accounting Office, *Somalia: U.S. Strategic Interests and Assistance*, p. 25.

50. Somali Democratic Republic, *National Development Strategy and Programme, 1987–1989*, p. 106.

51. In a terse statement, the IMF reported that a detailed examination of the Commercial and Savings Bank of Somalia "revealed substantial accounting irregularities in a number of branches." In 1987, domestic credit expansion was 149 percent, nearly 6 percent of the total domestic product (International Monetary Fund, *Supplement to the Staff Report for 1988*).

52. World Bank, *Somalia: Crisis in Public Expenditure Management*, Volume III, p. 9.

53. I. M. Lewis, *A Modern History*, p. 245.

54. United States, Embassy in Somalia, Letter from Ambassador Crigler. Crigler had laid down the human rights marker earlier in remarks at his swearing-in ceremony, which was carried on Voice of America and publicized by the United States Information Service in Mogadishu.

55. National Academy of Sciences, *Scientists*, pp. xii, 3–8.

56. Lefebvre, *Arms for the Horn*, p. 103.

57. Ibid., pp. 260–262.

58. Ibid.

59. International Monetary Fund, *Somalia—Recent Economic Developments, 1989*, p. 8.

60. Letter from Assistant Secretary Schifter to the *New York Times*.

61. This message was carried to Siyaad Barre in meetings with Ambassador Crigler and in a visit by Assistant Secretary Crocker in July 1988.

62. United States, Embassy in Somalia, Remarks by Ambassador Crigler, October 1988.

63. Ibid.

64. United States, General Accounting Office, *Somalia: US Strategic Interests and Assistance* and *Somalia: Observations Regarding the Northern Conflict*.

65. International Monetary Fund, *Somalia—Recent Economic Developments, 1989*, p. 8.

66. United States—Department of State, "Address by Chester A. Crocker," p. 4.

67. Ibid., pp. 3–4.

68. The suggestion here is that closer attention to meaning is important in establishing sound policy. Confusion even prevails as to what the policy pronouncements meant by *security*—is it U.S. security or African security? As a recent collection of essays records, Third World states view security more as regime holders' interest in short-term survival prospects than as countering territorial threats or perpetuating the state within the international system. This view constitutes a transvaluation of the accepted notions of state security and confuses the purposes of a "security assistance relationship" (Job, *The Insecurity Dilemma*). It is also critical in relating national strategy to any supposed security concern to remember that strategy is "the direction of power so that it serves policy purposes" (Gray, *War, Peace, and Victory*.) As von Clausewitz taught, strategic thinking "must include in this consideration the instrument of this real activity—the armed force" (von Clausewitz, *On War*, Book III, Chapter 1, p. 241). The fact is that the United States has never held, in Africa, an objective for which U.S. policymakers were willing to exert power in a way that might require, as von Clausewitz wrote, "employment of battle as a means toward the attainment of the object."

69. Drew and Snow, *Making Strategy*, pp. 110, 116, 187–190.

70. World Bank, *Somalia: Crisis in Public Expenditure Management*, Volume I, p. 11.

71. The problem with indicators is that they convey "a stylized, flattened picture of processes . . . that were, in fact, multi-dimensional" (Friedberg, *The Weary Titan*, p. 285). When we use indicators in policy formulation, we might heed Aron's advice not just to choose because market mechanisms are more efficient than central planning but to evaluate using "multiple criteria: efficacity of institutions, liberty of persons, equality of distribution and, perhaps above all, the kind of man who is creating the regime" (Aron, *Memoires*, p. 126).

72. Kaplan suggests that foreign service officers can become obsessed with the diplomatic process to the point that they cannot "accept that sometimes it is better for a process to collapse than for it to continue" ("Tales from the Bazaar," p. 59). The determination to keep trying, however, stems not from idealism, as Kaplan would have us believe, but from devotion to duty. It is a matter of policy objectives, not high-mindedness.

73. Weldon, *The Cloning of Joanna May*, p. 187.

74. The technique in mathematics is to create a complex plane wherein real numbers are aligned on a horizontal axis and imaginary numbers are laid out on a vertical axis. The resultant symmetries depend on the state of human imagining. See Field and Golubitsky, *Symmetry in Chaos*.

75. Vico, *The New Science*. Book I, Section III, p. 96.

7

Crises on Multiple Levels: Somalia and the Horn of Africa

Terrence Lyons

The Regional Context of the Somali Crises

The Horn of Africa has been the site of some of the most devastating, prolonged, complex, and rapidly changing conflagrations in the world. Each conflict has its own particular origin and dynamic and must be understood and resolved with respect to its specific characteristics. In addition, all are interlinked into a regional (in)security system and should therefore be seen in their regional habitat. My fundamental argument is that interstate rivalries and the practice of supporting neighboring insurgents, common economic and environmental problems, and flows of political ideas, refugees, and arms across borders make the regional dimensions of each specific conflict important both conceptually and in terms of actions toward amelioration. This chapter will outline the regional context of the Somali crises, explore the historical evolution of Somalia's role in the Horn of Africa, and touch upon potential models for regional relations that have consequences for the Somali people.[1]

The Somali condition is intertwined with the regional milieu, in part because the various territories of the Horn of Africa are connected by common resources and problems. Ethiopia and Somalia share the waters of the Shabelle and Juba rivers, for example, and decisions on water management in one state have consequences for its neighbor.[2] Geographically, Somalia and Djibouti are Ethiopia's natural outlet to the sea, and Ethiopia is hinterland for both. Berbera is the closest port for much of Ethiopia, and Mogadishu and Kismayu have the potential for serving other parts of southern

Ethiopia and northern Kenya. Precolonial trading patterns brought much of Ethiopia's exports through northern Somali ports.[3] The development of the Addis Ababa–Djibouti railroad diverted most of this trade, and in more recent years, Ethiopia developed the ports of Assab and Massawa in Eritrea to control commerce internally. If political differences or security problems limit Ethiopia's use of those ports and stability returns to Somalia, Berbera's historical importance for Ethiopian trade may be restored.

The permeability of borders in the region means that violent contestation in one state has spillover effects in neighboring territories. One of the most devastating consequences of regional instability has been the massive numbers of refugees and displaced persons generated by the conflicts. Refugee populations in northeast Africa are proportionately the highest in the world, with Sudanese fleeing to Ethiopia; Ethiopians, in turn, seeking safety in Sudan, Somalia, and Djibouti; and Somalis escaping to Ethiopia and Kenya. Even before the upsurge of chaos in 1991 and 1992, more than 350,000 Somalis, 780,000 Ethiopians, and 700,000 Sudanese were refugees.[4] The inability or unwillingness of regional governments and international organizations to develop long-term policies to repatriate or integrate these vulnerable populations has drained away very scarce resources and resulted in the creation of large and alienated groups susceptible to manipulation by unscrupulous leaders.

Weapons also move freely from armories in one state to combatants and bandits throughout the region. The Horn of Africa has been the recipient of weapons either bought by the various regimes in a generally futile search for security or provided by external powers in an equally ineffectual pursuit for influence. According to one estimate, a total of U.S. $7.5 billion in weapons was delivered to Ethiopia, Kenya, Somalia, and Sudan between 1981 and 1987.[5] Many of these weapons have been lost to insurgent groups or sold by soldiers. Following the defeat of Mengistu Haile Mariam's army in 1991, desperate Ethiopian soldiers sold their arms for next to nothing to rebellious groups in the region. Former Ethiopian soldiers streamed across the border into Djibouti in 1991 with enormous quantities of weapons, helping to spark antiregime activities in that small country. Much of the population across the region is armed, and caches of weapons in private hands are large. By the early 1990s, the entire area was so awash in weapons that international efforts to impose an arms embargo will have little effect on the level of fighting for years to come.

The black market in the Horn has been thoroughly regionalized. Following the destruction of Hargeisa in 1988, the Ethiopian city of

Diredawa was filled with inexpensive electronic goods and vehicles sold by Somali refugees cashing in what assets they were able to take with them. Even in times of conflict and state collapse, trading in coffee and, most notably, *qat* continued to thrive among Ethiopia, Djibouti, and Somalia through informal channels.[6]

The porousness of boundaries on the Horn of Africa applies to political ideas as well as refugees, arms flows, and contraband. The literature on Africa has generally focused on the demonstration and diffusion effects of coups d'état and conflicts.[7] Political values other than conflict, however, may also be transmitted across national borders. The series of national conferences leading to democratic reforms in Francophone Africa were clearly connected to the activists in Cameroon, Congo, and elsewhere who came to understand the potential of this form of activity from their neighbors in Benin. Political change can snowball across a region as reform in one state carries its message and momentum into neighboring states.[8] Khadiagala has suggested that security may be conceived as a learning process as contagious as coups or conflict.[9]

With regard to Somalia, the manner in which conflicts are settled and new forms of political organization created by its neighbors can be expected to add new ideas to the thinking of Somalis seeking security. The success or failure of novel ways of organizing politics in an ethnically structured, highly decentralized manner in Ethiopia will instruct the tactics of Somalis trying to recover from the heavy costs of the overly centralized ancien régime. The breakdown of Somali state into competing clanistic groups in the 1990s may have influenced the political programs of Somalis in Ethiopia. Some Ogaden Somalis have reportedly objected to designating their new region "Somali" because it legitimates the participation of rival, non-Ogadeni Somali kin groups.[10] The outcome of the pro-democracy movements in Kenya and Djibouti will also play a role in shaping political ideas in Somalia. The international community's decisions with regard to the recognition of independence in Eritrea, the Somaliland Republic, and potentially Southern Sudan are all connected. External actors view each case with serious concern for the implications of setting precedents.[11]

It is impossible to judge in advance how the lessons of the region will be learned (or mislearned) and applied in Somalia. It is clear, however, that the regional context and the relative success of the reform processes in Ethiopia, Kenya, and Djibouti will influence this thinking and that future developments within Somalia will affect discourse in neighboring states. Furthermore, no state in Africa can cordon itself off from the changes sweeping the continent.

Somalia's Historical Role in the Horn of Africa

The Somali state, from independence in July 1960 until the late 1980s, was in nearly continuous conflict with its neighbors. The historical evolution of the region left the Somali people divided and the postcolonial state dedicated to their reunification, thereby conditioning the policies of independent Somalia toward others in the neighborhood. During the colonial period, the Somali people were separated into five territorial parts: Britain claimed a strip along the Gulf of Aden and maintained jurisdiction over Somali populations in the Northern Frontier District (NFD) of its colony Kenya, Italy moved into a region along the Indian Ocean, France claimed sovereignty over the hinterlands immediately surrounding the port of Djibouti, and Ethiopia won recognition of its control over Somalis in the Ogaden. Resistance to the imposition of non-Somali authority over these territories encouraged nationalists to think in Pan-Somali terms and work for the unification of their divided people into a single nation-state.[12]

Geographic and environmental conditions reinforced the desire for Somali unity. Traditionally, the transhumant Somalis grazed their herds over large areas of the semiarid lowlands without regard to borders. Somali herders moved seasonally from the pastures of the Haud, a region that crosses the Ethiopian and Kenyan borders, to year-round wells along the coastal plain. During the scramble for Africa, Europeans and Ethiopians negotiated border agreements, but these administrative lines were meaningless to the pastoralists, "for whom there is one frontier only: the furthest limits to their pastures."[13] The lands inhabited and exploited by Somali pastoralists form a single economic and ecological unit, despite the political divisions.

Reunification of the Somali people served as a legitimizing state principle after independence, and every Somali politician was judged by his or her performance on this "core value."[14] The principle was enshrined in the 1961 constitution, was symbolized by the five-pointed star on the state flag, and dominated political discourse. Prior to independence, the Somali Youth League (SYL) proclaimed that "there is no future for us except as part of Greater Somalia."[15] Somalia, according to Prime Minister Abdirasheed Ali Sharmarke, could not "regard our brothers as foreigners" even if, as a result of indiscriminate colonial boundaries, they lived in a neighboring state. "Of course we all have a strong and very natural desire to be united."[16] President Aden Abdille Osman declared in 1965 that "re-unification of all Somalis is the very reason of life for our nation."[17]

Analysis of the content and evolution of Pan-Somali disposition is beyond the scope of this chapter. The point here is that as an ideology, it encouraged leaders in Mogadishu to pursue foreign policies that inherently led the state into conflict with neighbors that had rival claims to the Somali-inhabited territories. Somalia's arguments under the principle of Greater Somalia were antithetical to Ethiopia, Kenya, and Djibouti's insistence on the principle of territorial integrity and the sanctity of colonial borders, principles these states were prepared to defend by force if necessary. These contradictory and combustible organizing principles of politics and core state values in the Horn led to a series of border clashes, diplomatic contests, vitriolic propaganda broadcasts, mutual subversion, and simmering tensions that sapped the strength of the region, inhibited development, and prevented regional reciprocity. To explain the consequences of the regional environment on the contemporary Somali crises, I will outline the historic evolution of conflict and conflict resolution with each of its neighbors.

Somalia and Kenya

The newly independent Somali Republic tried to win control over its ethnic brethren in Kenya while Britain still was debating the future of its colony. Kenya's nationalist leaders strongly resisted Mogadishu's designs and insisted that the colonial border be respected and the Northern Frontier District (NFD) remain part of Kenya at independence. They argued that the Somali-inhabited region represented "an indivisible part of Kenya."[18] Leaders of the multiethnic Kenyan state could not recognize an ethnic desire to sovereignty without unleashing other centrifugal forces and bringing into question the legitimacy of the state and their rule. Despite a British commission that determined that the majority wanted to join Somalia, London ignored the results of the referendum and kept the NFD within Kenya at independence.[19]

Somali nationalists in the NFD (later renamed the Northeastern Province), with indignant Pan-Somali euphoria and tacit support from Mogadishu, became rebels, or *shiftas* (bandits) as the new leaders in Nairobi called them. The war continued throughout the early 1960s with attacks on state outposts and officials. Kenya blamed Somalia for fomenting the rebellion and claimed that "guerilla terrorism and brigandage . . . covertly sustained" by Somalia had become "an overt undertaking of warfare."[20] As Kenya gained independence and established its rule, however, Mogadishu saw its chances of winning jurisdiction over the territory decline. Somali irredentism shifted its focus to the Ogaden, an area of greater cultural and economic importance to the Somali nation.

Kenya and Somalia negotiated a détente during Mohammed Ibrahim Egal's regime (1967–1969). The process began with meetings chaired by Zambian President Kenneth Kaunda at the Organization of African Unity (OAU) summit in Kinshasa in September 1967 and in Arusha in October 1967. A series of mediations and bilateral meetings in 1968 and 1969 resulted in a normalizing of relations and a lifting of the state of emergency in the Northeastern Province of Kenya.[21] Later, Siyaad Barre met with Kenyan president Arap Moi at the July 1981 OAU summit and reportedly renounced Somalia's territorial claims on Kenya. Ethnic Somalis have entered and participated in Kenya's political system, and such access encouraged Mogadishu to deemphasize its agitation for self-determination. An important test of Siyaad Barre's intentions toward the Somalis in Kenya occurred in February 1984, when Kenyan soldiers killed several hundred Somalis in the northern region of Kenya. Mogadishu allowed the matter to pass as an internal Kenyan problem without making any efforts to assert its role as guardian of the Somali nation. Later in 1984, Moi visited Somalia and signed a border agreement. Conditions for Somalis (whether refugees or citizens) in Kenya deteriorated in the late 1980s when the Moi government imposed harsh restrictions.[22] The Somali question, however, had become an issue of internal Kenyan politics rather than an international conflict.

In 1992, however, the disintegration of the Somali state spilled over into Kenya. Siyaad Barre and troops loyal to him established a stronghold just north of the Kenyan border. Some, including military leaders in Mogadishu, alleged that Barre was receiving support from Nairobi. In April 1992, United Somali Congress (USC) troops overran Barre's base and crossed the border, reportedly looting several towns on the Kenyan side.[23] Bellicose rhetoric and threats rose from the Kenyan government; the USC, in turn, charged that Kenya was supporting remnants of Barre's forces and harassing Somali refugees.[24] The risk of clashes—and further regionalization of the conflict—increased. The issue in the 1990s may not be Pan-Somalism, but the chaos in Somalia itself may still draw Kenya into confrontation.

Somalia and Ethiopia

Independent Somalia also sought to bring its kinsfolk in the Ethiopian-controlled Ogaden region into the Somali state. Emperor Menilek brought the Ogaden under Ethiopian rule in the late nineteenth century, and Haile Selassie attempted to incorporate the local Somalis into his imperial state. Somalis, however, claim that the people of "Western Somalia [the Ogaden] have a distinct history and geography, and their ethnic cultural and linguistic characteristics are completely different from those of Ethiopia."[25] The Ogaden is historically and culturally one of the homelands of the Somali nation, and access to the Haud pastures is critical to the nomadic mode of production.[26]

Incidents began to occur in the Haud within six months of Somali independence. At the 1963 OAU meeting, the Somali and Ethiopian representatives accused one another of seeking territorial aggrandizement across their common frontier, and the Somalis rejected the OAU norm that sanctified colonial borders.[27] In late 1963 and early 1964, armed conflict broke out along the border, including Ethiopian aerial bombing of Hargeisa.[28] Sudan, acting as a third party under the auspices of the OAU, mediated a cease-fire and established a demilitarized zone on both sides of the border. Simmering tensions and occasional flare-ups continued, however, because neither government was prepared to make the concessions the other needed to resolve the issue.

During Egal's regime, Ethiopia and Somalia initiated a period of détente, in part because of the cost to both parties of the extended stalemate and the freedom of action that the new Egal government enjoyed in domestic politics.[29] The Somali prime minister began to eliminate specific sore points with Addis Ababa, demilitarize the conflict, and start a process in which the major issue, sovereignty of the Ogaden, could be discussed. That détente, however, proved to be unstable because the core contradiction was intact. When the Egal government fell to Siyaad Barre's coup in 1969, for reasons unrelated to the Ogaden issue, the negotiating process died.

After the 1974 Ethiopian revolution, Somalia increased its support to the Western Somali Liberation Front (WSLF) insurgency in the Ogaden. Although Somalis long resisted Ethiopia's rule, as in the Bale uprising in the 1960s, the WSLF was organized and supported by Mogadishu. In July 1977, Somalia directly invaded the Ogaden, hoping to exploit Ethiopia's postrevolution weakness to achieve its Pan-Somali goal. Although Ethiopia had a much larger population and army, at that time the balance of forces in the Ogaden seemed to favor Somalia. The Soviets had built up Somalia's army, especially its tank forces, at a far faster rate than the United States had equipped Ethiopia. Moreover, Mogadishu was able to commit all of its forces to the Ogaden, whereas the Derg (the new Ethiopian revolutionary military government) had to fight simultaneously in Eritrea and against numerous other domestic rebel groups.[30] Nonetheless, Ethiopia successfully repelled the Somali invaders with the help of massive Soviet and Cuban assistance.

After this period of intense military struggle, tensions over the Ogaden gradually abated but were not fully eliminated. Mogadishu continued to support Somali separatists, although the WSLF lost much of its power. In return, Ethiopia supported anti-Barre groups such as the Somali Salvation Democratic Front (SSDF) and the Somali National Movement (SNM).[31] The Ethiopian military, in addition, occupied two Somali border towns, increasing the pressure on the regime.

By January 1986, the two sides concluded that the stalemate benefited neither party, and both wanted a settlement in order to concentrate their resources against internal threats to their regimes' survival. Mengistu and Barre met in Djibouti at the organizational meeting of the Inter-Governmental Authority for Drought and Development (IGADD) and discussed the issue. As in the Egal period, the Somalis wanted to concentrate on specific points, such as normalizing relations, whereas the Ethiopians insisted on addressing the core issues of sovereignty, frontier demarcation, and renunciation of Somali territorial claims. The ensuing deliberations of an ad hoc ministerial committee stalled, a military buildup on both sides escalated, and border violations threatened to break out into a new round of fighting.

In April 1988, Mengistu and Barre again met in Djibouti and agreed to reestablish relations, withdraw troops from the border, exchange prisoners of war, and refrain from the use or threat of force against the territorial integrity or political independence of either state. Because of the urgent need to redeploy troops from the Ogaden in order to face the Eritrean and Tigrean challenges, Ethiopia apparently gave up its insistence on settling the territorial issue. It withdrew from the two Somali towns and expelled the SNM units operating in its territory, although Somali officials accused Ethiopia of continuing its support.[32]

Somalia and Djibouti

Pan-Somali nationalism complicated the issue of the ultimate disposition of French Somaliland in the 1960s and 1970s. The French colony voted in favor of continued association with France rather than independence in 1966 and changed its name to the French Territory of the Afars and Issas. Somalia, along with Egypt, championed the cause of independence for the colony in the 1960s and early 1970s.[33] In 1976, following a change in the citizenship law, which allegedly had discriminated against Somalis in favor of the non-Somali Afars, the territory voted overwhelmingly in favor of independence and changed its name to the Republic of Djibouti.[34]

During the lead-up to independence in June 1977, Ethiopia feared that Somalia would seize the new state during this transition and cut Addis Ababa off from the important railroad terminus and port of Djibouti. Mogadishu, however, accepted the vote as a victory for Somali self-determination, despite the fact that the Somalis in Djibouti did not seek reunification with their neighbors. Somalia was the first state to recognize Djibouti and did not press its claims further.[35] The competing interests of Ethiopia and Somalia and the continued presence of French troops allowed Djibouti to maintain its independence.

The Decline of Somali Irredentism

The goal of creating a united Somali nation-state suffered serious setbacks with the independence of both Kenya and Djibouti and the Somali defeat in the Ogaden War. Somalia's neighbors, however, recognized their vulnerability to the policies of intervention-by-proxy employed by Mogadishu in the 1960s and 1970s and continued to regard Somalia as a potential threat. Kenya and Ethiopia maintained a joint security alliance out of a common perception of the danger of Somali irredentism. Regional relations remained guarded, if not openly hostile, following the 1988 détente with Ethiopia.

Within Somalia, Greater Somali ideology served more as a means to obfuscate internal Somali divisions and the narrow social base of the regime in power. The collapse of central authority, following the overthrow of Siyaad Barre in 1991, shifted the focus of politics inward, as various groups used clanistic organizations as bases of support in a political struggle to succeed Barre or gain power.[36] The SNM's declaration of independence for Northern Somalia demonstrates that the breakup of the Somali nation, rather than a concern for the creation of a Greater Somalia, marks the politics of transition in the early 1990s.[37] Nonetheless, Greater Somali nationalism, despite its current eclipse, remains as a potential basis of legitimacy and mobilization that may be adopted by a future regime. This possibility makes Somalia a continuing source of worry and insecurity for its neighbors.

Prospects for a New Regional Order

The Somali crises, I have argued, are interconnected with but not caused by the larger predicaments in Northeast Africa. In the longer term, the Horn of Africa will break the cycle of internal and regional conflicts only when a new, more just order is constructed, accepted as legitimate, and institutionalized. The creation of new forms of governance needs to take place on multiple levels and must involve many diverse actors. Perhaps the most important level will be that of the state, where democratic and responsive governments and healthy civil societies must be created. In the past, centralized, authoritarian bureaucracies seized control of decisionmaking at the expense of both regional/international cooperation and local autonomy. The breakdown of such regimes, most notably in Somalia and Ethiopia, suggests that the old focus on the state as the sole and most appropriate location for regulation of social and economic activities must be reevaluated.

In the future, governance will need to take place in multiple areas, with different structures, rules, and actors playing greater or lesser roles depending on the issue area. Although some legitimate authority and responsibility will continue to reside at the old level of the state, new structures or practices need to be created on the local and regional levels. An increased capacity to govern and coordinate on the local and regional stages will both provide a check on central power and prevent the overburdening of the state, thereby discouraging that institution from becoming either oppressive and/or overloaded. In this scheme, then, one issue area may require more management from the local authority, whereas another could demand a more regional coordination; nearly all, however, have implications and consequences for each of these many sites of decisionmaking. Key questions in the coming years, therefore, will be how these different setups interrelate and reciprocate, who will participate and in what manner, and how each level will be accountable to the citizens who are subject to its ordinance.

Analysis of the critical role of the state and local institutions is discussed elsewhere in this volume.[38] A number of questions relating to the architecture of a new international order that do not apply specifically to the Horn of Africa will have important implications for that region. Agreements to limit and regulate international arms transfers will not remove the underlying conflict issues but may reduce tools of violence and discourage leaders from becoming tempted, by runaway means, to risk conflicts. Recent initiatives to create a humanitarian relief coordinator at the United

Nations may eliminate some of the friction over assistance programs in conflict zones that has plagued the Horn.[39] New guidelines that redefine the role of the international community, especially international organizations such as the UN High Commission for Refugees, in responding to and preventing humanitarian disasters when sovereignty is at issue, will help reduce the degree to which the politicization of humanitarian relief has hampered efforts in the past.[40] In 1992, the United Nations widened its consideration of "humanitarian intervention" in response to the catastrophe in Somalia and the crisis in Yugoslavia.[41] The policies instituted by such international financial institutions as the World Bank and International Monetary Fund will have an increasingly large impact on the impoverished states of the region that lack the leverage to resist conditionalities. Nongovernmental international organizations, such as Amnesty International, Citibank, scientific organizations, Oxfam, the Cable News Network (CNN), and the Catholic Church, all influence different issues globally and will be critical components in the international order.

In addition, the regional level will be an important arena for decisionmaking and the management of the huge challenges facing the peoples of the Horn in the coming decades. Regional cooperation has been derailed in the past because state interests, priorities, and sovereignty have conflicted with regional regimes, gains, and cooperation.[42] In the Horn, states competed on a nearly continuous basis and recognized few norms that might have limited conflict. Even the identity and legitimacy of actors was in dispute. As Harbeson has stated, "The international politics of the Horn of Africa has largely been a struggle of competing actors to establish just such settled identities."[43] Political accountability, extremely limited in the national arena, was nearly nonexistent for regional organizations that often served more as private clubs for authoritarian leaders than as representative institutions.

The Horn of Africa forms a regional system, not because the majority of the people of the area identify primarily with the region, but because their security and material welfare are so intertwined that a change in one aspect in one state has heavy repercussions throughout the area. The region, then, forms what Buzan calls a "security complex" because the "primary security concerns" of the actors "link together sufficiently closely that their national securities cannot realistically be considered apart from one another."[44]

The capsizing of political orders in Ethiopia and Somalia and the challenge to old forms in Kenya and Djibouti may provide a window of opportunity for the imagination and construction of a novel, more broadly defined, and inclusive sense of regional identity that will support greater transcommunal esprit de corps. Giving meaning and institutional form to regional consciousness, however, is a difficult and long-term process.[45] Many observers have enumerated the mutual gains of cooperation, but fewer have analyzed the structural hurdles to obtaining these benefits.[46] In addition, many of the strongest political organizations in the area in 1993 are articulating increasingly parochial conceptions of political identity and advocating modes of organization that are antithetical to those promoted by contiguous movements. Common problems do not necessarily or inevitably lead to regional partnership.

A cacophony of competing and potentially antithetical modalities of political organization have been proposed in the Horn of Africa. Within Somalia, several principles that may be used to structure politics have been advocated. The Somali National Movement (SNM) champions former colonial borders as the legitimate basis for political life and has proclaimed the unilateral independence of the former British Somaliland colony as the Somaliland Republic. The SNM argues that this action is not secessionist, but rather a return to the status quo that existed for four days in June 1960 before the British colony and the Italian trusteeship territory were united. Other Somali political groups have rejected this line of argument and insist that the borders recognized from July 1960 are the appropriate framework for a new state. In addition, many of the numerous movements within Southern and Central Somalia are organized on the basis of kin identification. These highly localized identities are an additional potential (dis)organizing principle of politics. Greater Somalia as a framework seems to be displaced by these alternative models. It is less certain, however, that the ideals and symbols that provided a vision for politics in the 1960s and 1970s have lost their value and energy to mobilize.

Regardless of the relative merit of any of these principles, the colonial status, the independent state, the kin, and the nation are all possible and contradictory forms of political organization. The adoption of any one model, such as the principle of the colonial state as defined by the SNM, is inherently in opposition to other forms, such as the norm of the post–July 1960 independent state.

The picture is complicated further by the existence of additional alternatives, proposed or in effect, in Somalia's neighbors.[47] In Ethiopia, the Eritrean People's Liberation Front (EPLF) insists that the former boundaries of the Italian colony of Eritrea are the appropriate framework for the state. The Ethiopian People's Revolutionary Democratic Front (EPRDF) and the Oromo Liberation Front

(OLF), the two leading parties in the Transitional Government of Ethiopia, accept this principle with regard to Eritrea but have proposed a political system for the rest of the country that relies upon lineal parties in ethnically defined regions to structure politics. Self-determination in Eritrea means self-determination for the former colonial territory; self-determination in Ethiopia after Mengistu means the ethnic group or nationality.

The contradictions of these competing principles may come to a head if the Afar people, who straddle the border of Eritrea, Ethiopia, and Djibouti, decide that self-determination for them means a united Afar region, whether within Ethiopia or independent. In the past, some *Issa* kin leaders, who occupy a region that straddles Somalia, Djibouti, and Ethiopia, have dreamed of creating a Greater Issaland. Such ambitious designs may become more audacious in an environment in which the principal regional states collapse. In addition, there remain Greater Ethiopia nationalists who insist that the only acceptable territorial basis for the state is the historic Ethiopian state that most certainly includes, in their view, Eritrea.

Some groups in the Horn argue that a certain form of government is a prerequisite for legitimacy. In the past, many proffered that only a Marxist or socialist government was legitimate. In the 1990s, such groups as Forum for the Restoration of Democracy (FORD) in Kenya, the Front for the Restoration of Unity and Democracy (FRUD) in Djibouti, Sudan People's Liberation Movement (SPLM) in Sudan, and others argue that democracy is necessary. Few, if any, of the political movements in the Horn can be placed clearly in only one category, and most insist that their movement articulates and represents the only or most legitimate policy. Regardless of the validity or justness of any of these claims, the potential for rival forms of political legitimacy to coexist in the region suggests that regional conflict and disharmony will not disappear with the old leaders.

Potential regional relations in the Horn of Africa in the future fall along a continuum from adversity to cooperation.[48] The implications for Somalia are significant: an openly hostile ambiance and relationship will sap already scarce resources, compound insecurity, and further throttle economic or political development; on the other hand, a more cooperative milieu may provide the margin of security and "peace dividends" necessary to start the reconstruction of Somalia. Potential political leaders who in the early 1990s preoccupy themselves with the bloody struggle to gain power in a specific territory need to consider the implications of different forms of cooperation for the medium to long term.

The current dissolution of the state in Somalia, and potentially in Ethiopia, may trigger an anarchic regional environment that will not facilitate an amelioration or resolution of the material and security problems of the Horn. The separation of Ethiopia and Eritrea seems inevitable and—if both parties are committed to making the transition smooth and building cooperative, mutually beneficial ties—should not prevent political and economic reconstruction. An independent Somaliland Republic also may not inherently preclude development in Somalia if all parties reach agreement on future forms of collaboration. The political map recognized internationally at the beginning of the 1990s need not be the only or best basis for political, economic, and social reconstruction. If powerful centrifugal forces in Ethiopia and Somalia (potentially joined by Djibouti and/or Kenya) lead them to collapse into tiny microstates controlled by independent "warlords," however, prospects for security and development will halt.[49] The potential for a degeneration into a Hobbesian world, where authority is exclusively based on military might, should give competing political movements cause to reflect.

A different model is based on a reaffirmation of central authority by new and more democratic governments and growing regional solidarity and cooperation. A fleeting glimpse of this possibility was seen in the humanitarian summit held in Addis Ababa in April 1992.[50] The Provisional Government of Eritrea participated in this meeting, indicating that this model of regional structure can accommodate the addition of at least certain types of new states. The lack of a recognized government in Somalia, however, prevented their participation. An additional weakness of this process is that the government in Khartoum attended but the Sudan People's Liberation Movement did not, despite that movement's critical role in addressing humanitarian problems in the Sudan. A regional order based on heads of state meeting to coordinate their policies and to cooperate on common problems will succeed only if all governments are constitutional and representative of all communities. Somalia and much, if not all, of the rest of the Horn remain distant from that goal in 1993.

Alternatively, regional relations may be built around strengthening organizations to manage common problems and facilitate cooperation. The example of the Association of South East Asian Nations (ASEAN) suggests that such associations can play important roles in developing regional security by establishing and structuring rules of state behavior. Despite its numerous frailties, the Economic Community of West African States (ECOWAS) demonstrated the ability to become involved in Liberia when the conflict there threatened destabilization of the whole area. In addition, the Southern African Development Coordination Conference (SADCC) demonstrates the potential benefits of regional economic coordination, particularly regarding transportation and infrastructure projects.

The Horn of Africa lacks a strong and competent regional organization. The Inter-Governmental Authority for Drought and Development (IGADD) offers a very nascent structure that, at present, performs some important coordinating functions on ecological policies and may, in the future, develop broader capabilities. The lessons of the now-defunct East African Community, however, caution that neither suspicion and distrust nor uneven development automatically fade with the founding of regional organizations and that functionalism does not always triumph over parochialism.[51] Ravenhill points out that the East Africa Community was plagued by problems typical of cooperative ventures by developing countries, most notably perceptions of unequal benefits and the inability to place regional cooperation above short-term national expediency.[52] In the Horn, some existent cooperation on transportation, such as the Addis Ababa–Djibouti railroad, and on such common problems as locust eradication portend the recognition of some areas of mutual interest. In the past, however, states in the Horn have not been willing to relinquish any significant measure of sovereignty to regional formations.

Regional organizations may also inhibit rather than encourage action toward addressing some of the fundamental problems facing the peoples of the Horn of Africa. Acharya has recently argued that regional organizations are often supported by vulnerable leaders who see such organizations as useful for coping with domestic contentions.[53] This suggests that if these structures are made up of states with authoritarian governments, the building of a more just and democratic order will be inhibited rather than stimulated.

Other continent-wide organizations, such as the Organization of African Unity and the important new process for a Conference on Security, Stability, Development, and Cooperation in Africa (CSS-DCA), may play a larger role in shaping regional relations in the future.[54] The CSSDCA, promoted by former Nigerian head of state General Olusegun Obasanjo, proposes a laudable series of norms to advance security and development and calls for greater participation by nongovernment groups. The plan also recognizes sovereignty and "the rights inherent in the territorial integrity and political independence of all African states" in its declaration of general principles.[55] The critical conflict between sovereignty and new regional norms therefore remains.

In addition, the relationship between geographically focused organizations such as ECOWAS, SADCC, and IGADD and more inclusive, continental institutions such as the OAU and CSSDCA remains vague and open to question. Coordination among such organizations, so that each one does what it can do best, will develop only with discussion and experience over time. In the end, however, regional organizations such as IGADD and continental organizations such as the OAU and CSSDCA are limited in their impact by the nature of their membership. Organizations comprised of states will be only as representative, responsive, and competent as their components.

The issue of federation for the Horn is being considered by some political thinkers and activists in the region. This idea has historical precedents in the brief Italian occupation of Eritrea, Ethiopia, and Somalia during World War II and the later British military control following the defeat of the Axis in the region. Although British Foreign Secretary Ernest Bevin proposed creating a Greater Somalia out of this region, the plan soon faltered on the rival claims of the Ethiopian emperor and the opposition of the other Four Powers.[56] The Soviet Union and Cuba tried to construct a *Pax Sovietica* federation based on a common Marxist-Leninist ideology among Ethiopia, Somalia, and South Yemen in 1977. The scheme quickly failed because neither the commitment to Marxism-Leninism by Ethiopia and Somalia nor the regional dominance of Soviet influence were sufficient to overcome the intense regional divisions.[57] Scholars from the region are reexamining the potential of federated polities to address the Horn's acute problems but, as yet, have not resolved how the advantages of cooperation can be used to overcome petty interests and mistrust.[58]

A final, more speculative, but unavoidable, category that deserves greater pondering is the issue of how regional cooperation may be facilitated by creative new relationships based on redefining sovereignty, the basis of citizenship, the meaning of borders, and other legal abstractions that have been deployed by political elites to control their territories. In the Horn, as in the former Soviet Union and Yugoslavia, the demise of old structures has left analysts scrambling to develop new international norms that reflect the actual circumstances and may be used to reduce deadly tension. For the Horn to develop into a less conflictual region, imaginative and more flexible applications of old principles may be necessary. The International Committee of the Red Cross and the United Nations have had to invent new methods of distributing food in Mogadishu and elsewhere in Somalia, including violating their own rules against providing food to combatants and hiring local security forces, in order to take action in the face of a humanitarian disaster.[59] The Transitional Government of Ethiopia and the Provisional Government of Eritrea have already discussed classifying Assab as a free port to balance Eritrea's territorial integrity and Ethiopia's need for access to the sea. Other norms relating to what defines a state may require similar new thinking to attend to the crises.

Conclusion

The Somali crises, seen in this collective study as a catastrophe, have had a ruinous impact on the Horn of Africa, and the instability within the broader region has complicated efforts to end the chaos in Somalia. For good or ill, the peoples of the Horn of Africa are tied together in a regional system because actions in one segment of the region have direct implications for neighboring parts. Shared resources and common problems, the demonstration effects of events in one state on another, spillover effects from conflicts, and a history of interference and destabilization in neighboring states indicate that one element of a long-term solution to the Somali catastrophe will be a new regional order. As this chapter has suggested, authentic regional cooperation, although necessary, will not develop quickly or spontaneously. Decades of conflict, mutual suspicion, and distrust will impede such efforts. Hard and intelligent work and difficult decisions at all of the multiple levels of governance will be required.

Notes

1. Several authors have analyzed these conflicts in their regional dimension. See Lyons, "The Horn of Africa Regional Politics"; Lancaster, "The Horn of Africa"; the individual works of Assefa and Khadiagala, A. I. Samatar, Kok, Nyong'o, and Iye in Assefa, *Conflict and Conflict Resolution*; Markakis, *National and Class Conflict*.

2. Nyong'o, "The Implications of Crises."

3. Donham, "Old Abyssinia."

4. United States, Committee for Refugees, *World Refugee Survey, 1991*; Ruiz, *Beyond the Headlines*.

5. Henze, *The Horn of Africa*, p. 119.

6. Clapham, *Transformation and Continuity*, pp. 185–186.

7. See Li and Thompson, "The 'Coup Contagion' Hypothesis." See also Hill and Rothchild, "The Contagion of Political Conflict"; Lutz, "The Diffusion of Political Phenomena."

8. Huntington, *The Third Wave*.

9. Khadiagala, "Short Notes."

10. The Transitional Government of Ethiopia has proposed a new provincial map based on ethnic lines, including a Somali province that incorporates parts of the old areas of Harerge, Bale, and Sidamo. See "Ethiopia," p. 7.

11. For a discussion of international policies toward the disintegration of states, see Hopf, "Managing Soviet Disintegration"; Weller, "The International Response"; Markakis, *National and Class Conflict*, pp. 51–57. For more on the historical basis for Somali identity, see Cassanelli, *The Shaping of Somali Society*, pp. 3–4.

12. S. Samatar, "The Somali Dilemma," pp. 157–158 and map p. 154.

13. Drysdale, *The Somali Dispute*, p. 7.

14. Castagno, "Somali Republic," p. 553.

15. Quoted in Markakis, *National and Class Conflict*, p. 75.

16. *The Somali Peninsula*. See also the statement by Somali President Dr. Abdirasheed Ali Sharmarke in Drysdale, *The Somali Dispute*, p. 8.

17. Republic of Somalia, *Somalia: A Divided Nation*, p. 48. See also Legum, "Somali Liberation Songs."

18. Republic of Kenya, *Kenya-Somalia Relations*, p. 6.

19. Drysdale, *The Somali Dispute*, pp. 122–138.

20. Republic of Kenya, *Kenya-Somalia Relations*, p. 61.

21. For a detailed account of these negotiations, see Touval, *Boundary Politics*, pp. 212–245.

22. "Kenya: Forcible Return."

23. Nairobi KTN Television, "USC Forces Raid Kenya," p. 7.

24. Mogadishu Radio, "SLA Condemns Kenyan Aid," p. 6; Mogadishu Radio, "Aidid Decries Kenya's Treatment of Refugees," p. 5.

25. Barre, *Salient Aspects*, p. 37.

26. Cassanelli, *The Shaping of Somali Society*, Chapter 2; Markakis, "The Ishaq-Ogaden Dispute," pp. 162–163.

27. Zartman and Thompson, "The Development of Norms."

28. Gurr, "Tensions." For background and context, see Markakis, *National and Class Conflict*, pp. 169–180.

29. Touval, *Boundary Politics*, p. 235. See also Zartman, *Ripe for Resolution*, pp. 89–90.

30. Gorman, *Political Conflict*, pp. 66–68.

31. A. I. Samatar, "Somalia's Impasse."

32. See the comments by Somali Prime Minister Mohamed Ali Samantar printed in Foreign Broadcast Information Service, *Daily Reports* (10 February 1989); Economist Intelligence Unit, *Country Report*, p. 31.

33. For a presentation of Somalia's case, see Republic of Somalia, *French Somaliland*.

34. Schraeder, "Ethnic Politics."

35. Thompson and Adloff, *Djibouti*; Fenet, "Djibouti."

36. Adam, "Somalia: Militarism."

37. "Somalia: One State or Two?" pp. 5–6.

38. See Chapters 5 and 6 in this book.

39. P. Lewis, "Disaster Relief Proposal," p. A9. For a detailed critique of existing mechanisms, see Clark, *The U.S. Government*.

40. Deng and Minear, *Filling the Moral Void*.

41. For a detailed discussion of the legal issues raised by humanitarian intervention, see Scheffer, "Toward a Modern Doctrine."

42. Stedman, "Conflict."

43. Harbeson, "The International Politics," p. 120. See also Lyons, "The Horn of Africa Regional Politics."

44. Buzan, *People, States, and Fear*, p. 106.

45. For a recent account of the complexities of identity, see Anthony Smith, "National Identity."

46. Kendie, "Which Way the Horn of Africa."

47. Ottaway, "Nationalism Unbound," provides an excellent consideration of similar issues.

48. Stedman, "Conflict," p. 378.

49. The history of the Era of the Princes in eighteenth- and nineteenth-century Ethiopia may suggest what such an outcome may look like. Some suggest that Djibouti is already a microstate, unable to survive without external guarantees.

50. Addis Ababa Voice of Ethiopia Network, "Horn of Africa," in Foreign Broadcast Information Service, *Daily Reports* (19 August 1992): 1.

51. Duffy and Feld, "Wither Regional Integration Theory?"

52. Ravenhill, "The Theory."

53. Acharya, "Regionalism," p. 149.

54. On the potential for the OAU to manage conflicts, see Amoo, *The OAU and African Conflicts*.

55. *The Kampala Document*.

56. Drysdale, *The Somali Dispute*, pp. 67–69.

57. Patman, *The Soviet Union*, pp. 202–203, 213; Clapham, *Transformation and Continuity*, pp. 226–227; Lefort, *Ethiopia*, p. 210.

58. Kendie, "Which Way the Horn of Africa."

59. *The Washington Post*, 5 May 1992.

Part 4

Culture and the Catastrophe

8

Women and the Crisis of Communal Identity: The Cultural Construction of Gender in Somali History

Lidwien Kapteijns

When Benedict Anderson wrote his *Imagined Communities: Reflections on the Origin and Spread of Nationalism*, he defined *nation* as an imagined political community.

> It is imagined because the members of even the smallest nation will never know most of their fellow-members, meet them, or even hear of them, yet in the mind of each lives the idea of their communion. . . . It is imagined as a *community*, because, regardless of the actual inequality and exploitation that may prevail in each, the nation is always conceived as a deep horizontal comradeship.[1]

Amrita Chhachhi, in her essay in *Women, Islam and the State*, takes the idea of a constructed rather than a "natural," or innate, communal identity further in developing the concept of forced identities. She observes that "very often identities are constructed on an imagined commonality which is then given objective existence."[2]

Why is it that Somalis in the ongoing civil war have mobilized their identity in terms of clan rather than, for example, religion or geographic location? Why was the Lebanese civil war waged primarily by groups that identified themselves as religious sects, whereas Yugoslavia is pulled apart by groups privileging their ethnic identity? It is obvious that all these identities are not inherent but socially constructed; that is, they are the outcome of the ways in which these groups shaped, and were shaped by, their specific historical paths and circumstances.

There is no denying that the groups fighting in Somalia after the expulsion of Siyaad Barre have increasingly done so in the name of clan and clan hatred. However, the argument that Somalis' primary identification with clan and clan hatred caused the civil war only restates the question of how and why Somalis forged this particular communal identity. Although clanism is, at the time of this writing, a real historical force, the Somali clan is an "imagined" community in the ways specified in the quotation from Anderson above: for example, in that its members ignore inequalities and exploitation within the group.

The clan is also a social construct, rather than a natural phenomenon, because the decision to reckon descent patrilineally is a cultural one; the group resulting from such a construction of kinship may make sense socially—certainly from the perspective of patriarchy—but not biologically. As a biological group, the community is indeed imaginary. The active social construction of the kin group called clan is suggested by the term *tol*, Somali for "agnatic kin" but also for "to sew together."

Finally, Somalis have constructed their clan identity by defining it as a static, timeless feature of Somali life and as a reality that has remained untouched by social change since ancient times. Thus, Said Samatar, in an otherwise exemplary essay, maintains

> that modern Somali state politics is nothing but traditional clan politics writ large, with the difference that the society is today armed with modern, mass-destructive weapons.[3]

This chapter takes issue with this interpretation and argues (1) that clan is a constructed, not a natural or innate, communal identity, and (2) that this communal identity of today, in spite of a continuity in nomenclature, is *not* traditional and *not* a dead weight inherited from the precolonial past, but rather a modern (late colonial and postindependence) identity forged by Somalis in their interaction with each other and the colonial and postindependence states in the context of patriarchy and the capitalist world economy. It is toward the understanding of this process, and in the face of the current catastrophe, that I hope to make a contribution.

The communal identity prevalent in contemporary Somalia, that of clan, has become a compelling reality for all Somali people, for it is one in whose name people have killed and have been killed. Even individuals and groups who have spent their lives resisting it have found this identity forced upon them. Chhachhi has this to say about forced identities in the context of contemporary India:

Forced identities do not imply that they are false or coerced—it simply implies the lack of real choice in a particular situation. In a communal riot, for instance, an individual identified as a Muslim, or a Sikh, is a target for attack, irrespective of her/his religious convictions or political views. In the context of the general communalization of society, with regular outbreaks of violence, communal identities are increasingly forced upon individuals of various communities.[4]

Thus, clan identity became inescapable for Somalis during the regime of Siyaad Barre and the clanistic warfare that followed his expulsion in January 1991. This same lack of choice is metaphorically described by Jean Said Makdisi in *Beirut Fragments*, her memoirs of the war in Lebanon, a conflict in which the communal identity forged by the warring factions was largely that of religious sect:

> In all of this, I have felt repeatedly that religion has worked rather like the stamp with which cattle are branded [in American cowboy movies]. . . . And so are we all, like it or not, branded with the hot iron of our religious ancestry. Believers and non-believers alike, struggle though we may, we are being corralled into the separate yards of our fellow co-religionists by the historic events of the moment. Belief and political vision have less to do with how one is seen, and then is forced to see oneself, than with external identification—the brand.[5]

Thus, in Somalia, "the historic events of the moment" allowed some and forced others to emphasize and politicize clan identity.

If Somali clan ideology, at least to some extent, manages to mask the deep differentiation of wealth and power and therefore the class divide among community members, its unequal gender ideology is very explicit. By the logic of the definition of *clan* as a community of agnatically related men, women are second-rank members. Considered a temporary member of her father's household, a woman gains only outsider status in the household of her husband. As the proverb has it, "A woman belongs to [the group of] the man to whom she is married" (*Naagi waa ninkay u dhaxdo*). As lists of the casualties of the fighting in Mogadishu and other parts of the country began to circulate in the Somali community in London, I was struck by the fact that the names of women were *not* included.

Although precolonial Somali society was undoubtedly patriarchal, contemporary constructions of the Somali communal identity devalue women's social roles and significance to a greater extent. Locating gender in the cultural construction of the Somali communal identity is the central objective of the following analysis.

Somali Communal Identities
in the Precolonial Era: Pastoral Society

In the precolonial era, Somali people were members of two types of society. Either they belonged to stateless agrarian societies that practiced sedentary mixed farming in the inter-riverine area and pastoral livestock husbandry everywhere else, or they were citizens of the largely coastal city-states, which lived off trade. Since this analysis is based on data from Northern society (which did not include sedentary farmers), its value to theorizing the history of Southern Somalia can be evaluated only by experts in that field. In the North and East, pastoral society and city-states forged different communal identities and developed different gender ideologies and gender roles. This section will deal with the pastoral herding economy.

Pastoral society forged a communal identity phrased in terms of kinship, an ideology that assigned each Somali to a certain patrilineal descent group (lineage, sublineage, major section, minor section, *jilib, reer*), to a specific age group, and to the male or female gender. This communal identity structured four significant areas of social life: access to the factors of production (land, water, and livestock); the division of labor; the exercise of power and political authority; and the moral values that explained and justified the social status quo.[6]

Access to the Factors of Production

Somali people obtained access to land and water through membership in groups that defined themselves in terms of common patrilineal descent. Both men and women acquired membership in a specific kin group and clan by birth. However, although women always retained some of the rights and duties of membership in their community of birth, they were expected, by the rules of exogamy and virilocal marriage, to work and raise children for their husband's group. Thus, a kin group such as a clan or subclan always consisted of "insider" men and "outsider" women—that is, of men who were full members of their group in their own right and of women whose communal identities were ambiguous and whose membership in their marriage community depended on husbands and sons.

The Division of Labor

The division of labor was by gender and age group. Men and women of different ages had specific and distinct labor tasks; very young children, for example, were responsible for young livestock and the unmarried young men for dry-season camel herding. Successful male elders often had considerable leisure from productive labor.

The Exercise of Power and Political Authority

Kin group membership, together with age and gender, also structured the exercise of power and political authority. This was largely the domain of male elders, who had established their economic autonomy from other individuals and had proven their wisdom and impartiality. In theory, all adult males of sound mind and some means could participate in the exercise of political authority; age and married status were not explicit criteria for such participation. However, only after men had established their own households through marriage, and only as they accumulated prestige and influence by giving support to other community members over time, did they acquire the qualifications for leadership. Finally, wisdom and impartiality were ideological imperatives only for older married men and not for the younger passionate bloods. Thus, age and gender informed the processes by which political power and authority were acquired and exercised.

The same is true for the accumulation of wealth and power. Because only men could establish autonomous units of production and reproduction (households), women could gain wealth and power only through, and in the name of, men. For men, however, there were two roads to authority and power. One was the long and slow process of trying to become a wise elder who continuously reinvested his wealth in members of his kin group and thus acquired claims to their future labor and other services. The other was a track for angry young men who, under the leadership of a charismatic and fearless entrepreneur (the *abbaanduule,* or "war leader") decided to intensify their labor efforts and make a bid for quick wealth through raiding or warfare. Although oral tradition contains many references to the clashes between peace parties (often made up of established elders) and war parties (made up of ambitious young men), the ideology that structured the communal identity of precolonial pastoral society offered rationales for both roads to success. Thus, age and gender also shaped access to wealth and power.

Moral Values and the Social Status Quo

Moral values and the standards for correct social behavior also bore the stamp of a communal identity and an informal code of customary law (i.e., the *heer*) based on the ideology of kinship. Members of Somali pastoral society were Muslims, and Islam constituted an integral part of their communal identity and unwritten constitution. However, in relations with other Somalis, communal identity was primarily formulated in terms of kinship; although customary law was generally in accordance with Islamic law, it imposed many rules nonexistent in Islam and disregarded or sidestepped some specific Islamic legal provisions, such as those governing women's inheritances.

What was the moral dimension of the precolonial pastoral ideology of kinship? Although an examination of the standards for proper social behavior is beyond the scope of this essay, it must be emphasized that age and gender were again relevant variables and that standards for proper behavior differed according to someone's age and gender. Elsewhere I have argued that marriage, as the junction of the two crucial axes of social differentiation (age and gender), was the locus in which conformity to gender and age discipline and inequalities was enforced.[7]

Let us take the example of the unmarried young men. They did the hardest work and enjoyed the least material comforts at the time when they were physically strongest and had the least stake in the status quo. The prospect of marriage and the need for the economic contributions (and therefore moral approval) of elder kinsmen gave unmarried young men an incentive to toe the line of the social status quo. Young men could earn economic autonomy and the physical comforts of marriage only by offering obedience and labor services to their kin group. At marriage, a man established his own household and obtained a tangible stake in the status quo. He acquired rights in his wife's (or wives') productive and reproductive labor and could, using the resources of his wife and children, set out on the road to becoming a successful elder. Thus, kin group membership, age, and gender were significant factors in shaping the standards for proper behavior.

As a woman married, she left her community of birth and entered her husband's kin group. At that point, she owed primary obedience to her husband and his relatives rather than to her father and his kin group, and she was to intensify her labor (now including childbearing and rearing) in her husband's service. However, for the first time in her life, she could, within the limits set by her husband, accumulate wealth and power of her own by investing in her own community of birth and in particular her own children. Because daughters would eventually come under the authority of another marriage community and another man, mothers were encouraged to invest especially in their sons and to socialize their sons differently from their daughters. Thus, for women, too, marriage regulated and reinforced the standards for what was the appropriate behavior for their gender and age group.

Precolonial, nonstate Somali society was unquestionably patriarchal in a number of ways. First, as was mentioned above, a woman's position in both her community of birth and that of marriage was somewhat ambiguous because her loyalties were divided among both. However, a woman's value to both groups was institutionalized in the practice of exogamy, which prescribed that men obtain brides from outside their own immediate kin group. Because exogamy, from the perspective of the group, was to promote the likelihood of peaceful conflict resolution and economic resource sharing among groups competing for scarce resources, each married woman became a significant bearer of social capital in that she represented to both communities the rights and duties of reciprocal sharing. Second, women could not establish households. However, although barred from economic autonomy, women's labor was crucial (and was acknowledged to be crucial) to the central economic pursuits of pastoral society. Women in precolonial society were not equal to men, but they were acknowledged to be indispensable to the sustenance of society and its reproduction over time. Third, women were barred from formal positions of political and religious authority. Although they were protected by customary law and bound to uphold it, they were always represented by men and rarely constituted legal persons in their own right. Fourth, although women's productive and reproductive labor was valued, their moral capacities were considered below those of men. Thus, a proverb says, "Knowledge cannot come to reside in a bosom that has contained milk."

This was, in too brief outline, the ideology of kinship governing precolonial pastoral society and shaping its communal identity. Although the ways in which Somalis organized their society and secured its reproduction over time were in many ways unique, some basic features, such as its social stratification according to age and gender and the forging of a communal identity and ideology phrased in terms of kinship, are typical of many precapitalist, agrarian, nonstate societies. The community thus forged was coterminous with similarly structured groups, and it controlled the resources to which it aimed to regulate access and for which it competed with other such groups. This important characteristic was to change in the colonial period. Although women were dependent on and subject to men, they were (and were acknowledged to be) crucial to the mode of production of their community; in marriage, moreover, they represented the rights of political cooperation and economic sharing among groups.

Somali Communal Identities
in the Precolonial Era: The Townsmen

City-states, towns, and federations of towns that were politically autonomous and derived their livelihood from trade have existed on the Somali coast since before the beginning of the Common Era.[8] They were inhabited by people of a variety of ethnic and religious backgrounds. In contrast to the herders of the interior, however, the largely coastal city-states forged a communal identity in which membership in a certain descent or ethnic group played a secondary role. Instead, the inhabitants of the city-state emphasized their civic identity, their citizenship in their town, with all that implied with regard to their way of life, behavior, dress, cuisine, religious observance, and so forth.

Religion was an important part of the townsmen's communal identity; their way of life was considered to be more in line with the legal and other texts of Islam than that of the pastoral producers. Yet Islam seems to have been an integral part of this civic communal identity without dominating it; the case of nineteenth-century Bardera in its conflict with Kismayu seems to have been an exception and might be indicative of rapid socioeconomic transformation.[9] Even today, original inhabitants of Zeila, now residing in Djibouti, still often refuse to identify themselves primarily as Somali, Afar, or Arab; they insist on being Zeilais (Zeila people), that is, people who are sophisticated, urbane, elegant, peaceful, industrious, Muslim, and loyal to that particular town.

Nineteenth-century sources confirm the nontribal and nonethnic communal identity of the towns. In the Merca of the late 1870s, pastoral Somalis were not allowed to spend the night in town and had to offer their goods for sale in a market outside the city walls. Yet the town had both a town market and a Somali quarter! Similarly, although the population of Zeila always included many Somalis of the Issa and Gadaborsi kin groups, these Somalis did not primarily identify themselves as such.[10]

The townsmen constructed their own communal identity, at least partly, in opposition to that of the pastoral producers. In the towns, livestock, labor, and bridewealth came to have monetary value, and accumulated wealth could be stored as money in bank accounts (rather than being reinvested in livestock to be herded by kinsmen), so the townsman's kin group became less relevant to his ability to maintain and increase his capital. The fact that labor could be obtained through the payment of wages, and not by calling on the rights and duties vested in kinship, set the townsman further apart from his pastoral kin. Finally, by embracing Islamic law rather than the heer, a member of the urban middle class could avoid sharing his wealth with, or bequeathing it to, his distant male relatives and could instead privilege his nuclear family (both sons and daughters, men and women).

Although the communal identity forged by the townsmen highlighted their distinctiveness from the pastoral producers, within the city it partially masked the very real internal differentiation of wealth and socioeconomic power. There were at least two social strata inside the town, that of the wealthy merchants (foreign and Somali) and that of the poorer townspeople, who performed manual labor and engaged in seasonal wage labor such as sorting gum. The social roles of townswomen were therefore different not only from those of their rural sisters; within the city, they differed according to class.

In contrast to pastoral women, middle-class urban women performed labor that was *not* defined as crucial to the central economic pursuits of the city-state, that of buying and selling. Apart from their reproductive labor, which continued to be crucial, middle-class women created and maintained the distinct urban lifestyle and household. They embroidered, wove, sewed, mastered the art of a fine urban cuisine, and spared neither time nor effort in beautifying themselves. Because women's labor was relegated to the domestic domain and was not compensated monetarily, middle-class women were economically dependent on their husbands and fathers. This dependence was symbolized by their seclusion inside the house and behind large body veils. Because bridewealth could be paid in money, the acquisition of which did not always depend on the assistance of the extended kin group, urban marriage became more and more a relationship between two individuals and their immediate family. As a result, a wife's role as a bearer of reciprocal rights and duties between two groups became less significant than in rural society. The parallels between these women's lives and the processes of "housewifization" described for bourgeoisie elsewhere in the world are evident.

The social roles and position of lower-class women were very different.[11] Having to work for a living, these women were not subject to seclusion and were not economically dependent on male breadwinners. However, for them, social freedom from seclusion and economic autonomy meant only that they were at the bottom end of urban society. They engaged in petty commodity production (such as making and selling *lahooh*, a kind of pancake, hired out their labor as sorters of coffee and gum, or lived off the charity of fellow Muslims or kinsfolk. Although the secluded, dependent, and elegant wives and daughters of the middle class clearly enjoyed the approval and admiration of their community, more research is needed to establish whether the lower-class women enjoyed such respect or whether they were marginal to the town's communal identity.

The Transformation of Somali
Communal Identities in the Colonial Period

In the last two decades of the nineteenth century, Somali society came under colonial rule. In the decades that followed, it was gradually incorporated into the world economy as part of the Italian, British, and French colonial empires. Northern Somalia became British Somaliland and a protectorate of the British Crown. As the colonial state put its weight behind the urban, commercial capitalist economy, the urban middle class and its way of life, sustained by the returns on capital invested in exchange activities, gradually gained hegemony. Although many Somali communities had only very limited contacts with the colonial state, the direct and indirect results of colonial rule affected all. In the still poorly understood processes of negotiation and manipulation between the British colonial state and local communities, both sides "reimagined" and reforged pastoral communal identity and the kin group.

It may be illuminating to draw a parallel between Somali society and the game of chess. In the colonial period, the chess board (the terrain and resource base of pastoral society) was enlarged. The rules of the game (regulating processes, such as the exercise of political power and the division of labor) also changed. Although the chess pieces (the relevant political units, such as the clan) might still be called by their old names, their basic characteristics had been transformed. How did this occur?

As new forms of wealth and power accumulated in the state sector and the urban economy and began to penetrate the rural economy, the mandate of the kin group (i.e., the clan) changed.[12] The new mandate included regulating access to the state and the state-supervised urban economy, resources that existed outside of the clan's traditional resource base and outside of its control. Clans, which until then had regulated access to the means of rural production (land, water, and livestock), now vied for control of resources controlled by others: export licenses; dhow licenses; the rights to collect *zariba* dues and other tolls; and the rights to dig permanent, privately owned wells, buy trucks, open shops, and so forth. Thus, the chess board had been enlarged.

As individuals, in particular unmarried young men, opted out of the rural economy and moved to town, the clan saw its control over the division of labor and over the age-based discipline it had exercised weaken. Young men could now earn money for bride-wealth without explicitly submitting to the labor discipline and authority of the community; this had grave implications for the traditional authority of elders. Leadership was increasingly vested in those men who could provide access to the state and urban economy or who succeeded in exploiting such access to build up their own wealth and power. The slow and arduous track to power of the local elder who reinvested his surplus wealth in the junior members of the kin group became more and more obsolete.

Raiding, too, became gradually less significant; as a result, the ambitions of charismatic young leaders were often channeled into other ventures outside the pastoral economy. To the extent that raiding continued or (as after the British withdrawal to the coast in 1909) increased, access to the state and the town for firearms became a crucial condition for success. The colonial administration, in its desperate search for community leaders, supported one self-styled leader after another—whoever at any point in time either commanded some local authority or could persuade the colonial state that he did. Thus, much of the warfare and raiding of the period preceding and immediately following World War I was the result of, or had as its objective, special access to the favor of the colonial state. The rules that governed the exercise of political authority and power—the rules of the chess game—were no longer the same.

Meanwhile, the policies and legislative measures of the colonial state were highly contradictory. The economic project of the colonial state was to make money. It therefore encouraged commercial enterprise and closely identified with the urban middle class, particularly the largest import-export companies, such as those of the Indian merchants Haljeebhoy Lalljee and Cowashi Dinshaw.[13] However, the political project of the colonial state was to maintain law and order and therefore to preserve the social status quo in the interior. Thus, the state allowed a middle-class rather than clan-based identity only to a small group of property-owning and tax-paying townsmen and to a few trusted, long-term, political, bureaucratic, or military servants of its administration—the kind of people who, in the Sudan, were called "the better kind of native." Behind protective city walls, and behind the laws enforced in the Islamic and colonial courts, these people were allowed to develop a class-based or even Islamic identity.

For the interior, however, the colonial state negotiated and reimagined the communal identity based on clan—employing a host of "political officers" and even hiring an occasional anthropologist for the purpose! First, as mentioned above, the colonial state confirmed or created clan leaders whose local authority derived ultimately from their links to the state and their access to the political, military, and economic benefits it bestowed.[14]

Second, for several decades, the state responded to economic or political disturbances of the caravan routes in the interior with collective punishment of the clan or subclan.[15] Therefore, individuals who tried to establish a foothold in the urban economy and assume a new urban, Islamic, middle-class identity were unceremoniously pushed back into the arms of the clan and its ambitious new leaders.

Parallel to this was the colonial practice of applying criminal law exclusively in the towns. In the countryside, all offenses were treated as political cases, requiring the involvement of the (sub)clans of both offender and victim. Murderers, for instance, were hardly ever held individually responsible and punished for their crimes, irrespective of any long-standing association they may have had with the urban economy.[16] Thus, the communal identity based on clan (and as a result, the power of the new clan leaders) was continually reinforced and was consistently forced upon individual Somalis, irrespective of their own ambitions and perceptions.

This may have seemed to be traditional practice to the British administrators, but it was not. The old clan had been a community of producers whose economic means and social relations had been regulated in its name. The new clan, reimagined and reconstructed in the context of colonial rule, came to assert legal and political authority over individuals whose productive activities, wealth, power, and prestige depended largely on a world outside the physical domain and control of the clan. The colonial state, in collaboration with new clan leaders, tried to mask the loss of autonomy of the clan by extending its legal and political authority to individuals who were members of the clan in only a very limited sense—for example, as the result of the accident of birth alone. The communal mode of production was dead, but the community was artificially kept alive and, through political negotiations and compromise between the new leaders and the colonial state, reimagined and reinforced.

What implications did the new colonial order have for gender relations? Those Somalis who came to the colonial towns found that most of the new economic niches were reserved for men. Somali men were expected and encouraged to engage in exchange activities, and the lower rungs of the bureaucratic, political, and military branches of the colonial administration were open to them. Women were also present in the towns, but their presence was only selectively acknowledged. First, the colonial state created very few opportunities for women either in state service or in the urban economic scene. When Europeans had first arrived in Somaliland, it had commonly been accepted that only Somali women could be trusted to load camels well.[17] However, even before the establishment of the protectorate, men had proven to be able to do so—for a wage! Men were also considered suitable personal servants, particularly if they spoke Hindi and had some previous experience with British colonial officers in Aden or India. Domestic service did not become a female occupation until much later.

The colonial administration did inherit some old women with donkeys as water carriers in Zeila, and it found that in its dispensaries, Somali women were kinder nurses' aids than men.[18] When first considering building a road from Berbera to Hargeisa, some members of the local colonial administration believed that labor needs might be met by hiring Somali women, who were believed to be both more available and less expensive than men. The project did not materialize.[19] In the 1930s, almost fifty years after the establishment of the protectorate in Northern Somalia, only one woman was listed on the government payroll, as published in the Blue Books: a female prison warder of the lowest rank who guarded female prisoners.[20]

The state tolerated the many lower-class urban women who engaged in petty trade, small-scale service activities, or wage labor. It even showed pity toward the completely impoverished women and children who had come to Berbera and had no source of food and income. However, it insisted on regarding their condition and presence as a temporary result of war and drought and on presenting as a charitable subsidy its own payment of a meager wage to those masaakiin (paupers) it employed on public works. Several times it attempted to send these paupers back to their clans in the interior.[21]

The colonial state never considered women significant to its economic objective of generating income to cover the costs of running the protectorate. This was true even for rural women, in spite of the fact that the main export item (and thus the main source of government income from import and export dues) consisted of sheep and goats, whose husbandry was to a large extent the work of women! In 1937, the export of sheep and goats had reached al-most 105,000.[22]

However, women were considered significant to the two-pronged political project of the state: (1) that of containing social change and preventing it from threatening law and order, and (2) that of creating opportunity for a few privileged Somalis to obtain a middle-class sta-tus and lifestyle. As for the latter, a good example of how the colonial administration created windows of opportunity for a few Somalis is the way in which it cautiously supported a trend toward individual bourgeois marriage. In 1928, it enacted a law that allowed individu-als to obtain dispensation from customary betrothal and levirate arrangements. Although more evidence is needed, it seems that women could reject kin group authority over their betrothal and re-marriage only if there was another willing groom at hand.[23] The place of women in the new, small, Somali middle class envisioned by the British was exclusively that of wives, mothers, and daughters, eco-nomically and legally the wards of their immediate male kin.

The major political objective of the colonial administration, however, was the maintenance of law and order and the contain-ment of social change in the interior. In general, therefore, its poli-cies tended to reinforce kin group and male discipline over women. For rural women, whose goat and sheep husbandry was so crucial to the solvency (never quite attained) of the protectorate's adminis-tration, this meant that although the value of their labor to the state increased, their deepened dependence on men, who monopolized all major exchange activities, was taken for granted and reinforced by the state. After all, the major thrust of the 1928 Natives' Betrothal and Marriage Ordinance was to give legal state sanction to tribal custom (and therefore to kin group and male authority over women) in matters of marriage.

Lower-class urban women were also expected to fit the image of wives and daughters dependent on men. Although the state toler-ated urban women's economic activities, if women were loud and troublesome *and* not clearly under the authority of a man, they might, as was the case in neighboring Aden, be accused of prostitu-tion and punished.[24] Moreover, women were not allowed to chal-lenge the social order by threatening to do well on their own. If the district court in a township felt that there was "a reasonable possi-bility" that a young woman who seemed less than twenty-five years old might become a prostitute, she was to be handed over to her kin and, if she repeated her offense, to be imprisoned and fined.[25]

One might argue that the state was trying to protect young urban women from sexual exploitation, and that may be partially correct. However, the state reinforced kin group and male authority over women without making the men in question economically responsible for them and without offering women alternative opportunities for economic survival. Thus, the British proved unwilling or unable to respond to the social change set into motion or sustained by their own presence in any other way than through the legal or political suppression of its consequences. Because the colonial state presumed that lower-class urban women were economically and legally dependent on men, even when there were no men (or no men of means) on whom to depend, women who found themselves working and living autonomously acquired the extra onus of unrespectability if not illegality. Because the urban economy offered women few respectable economic niches, this image of unrespectability and illegality became a self-fulfilling prophecy and proved to be a lasting and burdensome heritage for working urban women.

One final element of social change affected women and the Somali communal identity in the colonial era. Toward the end of this period, the rules of exogamy were relaxed, even in the countryside. It now became possible and more common for close paternal relatives (even first cousins) to marry each other.[26] This coincided with the "commoditization" of marriage and the trend toward regarding marriage as a bond between two individuals and their closest kin. Whereas the clan (or subclan) had been a community of men who married and had children by women from other communities, by the end of the colonial period, it was in theory a community that could marry itself. As women ceased to be the bearers of reciprocal rights and duties and thus became socially less significant, the warp of the fabric of Somali society was seriously weakened, and the new communal identity, still referred to by the old term *clan,* became a threat to the wider community that called itself Somali. Not only had the chess board and the rules of the game changed, even the chess pieces were no longer the same.

Somali Communal Identities After 1940

The political developments of the period 1936–1960 (from the Italian invasion of Ethiopia to the achievement by British and Italian Somaliland of political independence and unification) had an enormous impact upon Somali society and the communal identity it came to embrace. This period witnessed the transformation of Somalia's middle class and the demise of the colonial administration.

Although the nationalist program of this period included an often explicit rejection of a communal identity phrased in terms of clan, in the context of the new political and economic realities of the 1960s, the state class and the new bourgeoisie began to manipulate clan identity and solidarity to disguise its own economic and political privilege and to secure its own trading profits and access to the state. This is the theme of the following section.

After the temporary (August 1940–March 1941) conquest of British Somaliland by the Italians, many of the foreign members of the middle class in Somalia left the protectorate. Even though some foreign merchants returned, the next two decades witnessed the gradual Somalization of Somalia's middle class, a group made up largely of merchants (in particular livestock traders), civil servants, and bureaucrats.[27] Geshekter characterized the nature of this colonial middle class, which represented Somalis who had done relatively well in the service of the colonial administration or the urban economy, as follows:

> Born in the pastoralist nomadic sector but with subsequent commercial, urban, and even overseas experiences, they were an amalgam of truck owners, truck drivers, traders, clerks, interpreters, teachers, and brokers.[28]

The new middle class differed from the townsmen of the precolonial and early colonial eras not only in the smaller percentage of foreign merchants it included, but also (and more importantly) in its specific economic relations with the pastoral producers and in its new communal identity.

The townsmen's way of life of the earlier period, based on commercial capitalist practice, had seriously impinged on pastoral economy and society,[29] but it had not transformed the productive processes and the relations of production in the interior. This began to change in the late 1920s, with the further expansion of livestock exports, the reorganization of the livestock trade under the merchant-*dilaal-sawaaqi* system,[30] and the beginnings of the commoditization of some of the factors of production in the pastoral interior (i.e., labor and water). The townsmen of the earlier period had certainly used and manipulated kinship (in particular affinal) relations and other long-term bonds with the pastoral producers (such as indebtedness). However, as discussed above, their communal identity (and economic interests) explicitly distinguished them from the nomads. In the 1850s, Burton noted that those townsmen of Zeila who were married to Issa women sent their wives into the interior to buy sheep and goats from their relatives but that they "would not trust themselves amongst their connections."[31] The communal identity the townsmen had forged, an identity boasting urbane sophistication, good taste, an elegant and luxurious lifestyle, and the "proper" observance of Islam, had served to distance the townsmen from the nomad in order to impress him and keep him in his place. This changed after the 1940s with the transformation of the Somali middle class.

First, the new middle class was economically different from the earlier townspeople. Whereas the latter had tried to make producers indebted to them in order to guarantee a continuous supply of pastoral products, the new middle class indebted itself to the producers and used the bonds of kinship to obtain on credit the livestock it exported for profit abroad.[32] Thus, the new livestock traders used the idiom of kinship (and clan) not only to set themselves up in business and raise venture capital, but also to maintain large profits. As profits continued to accumulate at the level of circulation rather than production—that is, as the traders grew wealthy while the nomads did not[33]—the merchants continued to benefit from an emphasis on common kinship identity with their suppliers.

However, the first political and ideological programs of the new middle class often explicitly denounced divisive clan identity and loyalty and emphasized a common Somali and Islamic identity in the face of British pressure to constitute clan-based political parties.[34] Geshekter explains the emphasis on a national, Somali communal identity in the context of the Africa-wide, anticolonial movement for political independence and the specifically Somali nationalist desire for the reunification of the five Somali territories (French, British, and Italian Somaliland, Kenya's Northern Frontier District, and the Ethiopian-ruled Ogaden).[35]

Is it possible that the emphasis on *soomaalinimo* (a national, Somali communal identity) was a distinct part of the ideological agenda of what Abdi Samatar calls "the bureaucratic segment of the petite bourgeoisie,"[36] which consisted of white-collar workers who had at least some modern education? So far, there is no evidence to suggest that the larger and less-educated trading segment of the new bourgeoisie was less committed to a nationalist ideology and a national communal identity. More persuasive, perhaps, on the basis of currently available data, is the theory that distinguishes between the periods before and after the achievement of political independence and explains the reimagining of a Somali communal identity based on clan in terms of the struggle for control of the state among members of the new trader-bureaucrat middle class:

> In the absence of any philosophical or ideological differences among the petite bourgeoisie, clan background was the only factor that distinguished between parties and candidates.[37]

Political candidates used "the tribal ploy"[38] to get votes. They ran up huge debts in cajoling their clan constituencies to vote for them, only to gorge themselves on state resources (licenses of all kinds, foreign aid, and so forth) after the elections. Thus, the politicians and the merchants used common clan identity to mask class differences between them and their clansmen. The only payoff for their clans was a selective clientage and a favoritism extended to a relatively arbitrarily chosen few. The jobs and favors bestowed on some fellow clan members created, to borrow from Spaulding, "an illusion of comprehensive inclusiveness, rather as advanced capitalist societies create an illusion of universal opportunity by awarding astronomical salaries to entertainers and professional athletes and bestowing completely arbitrary bonanzas upon a handful of lottery winners."[39] Thus, the Somali middle class reimagined clanism in the context of its own exploitative relations with the pastoral producers and rural and urban voters.

In spite of these new political and economic realities, however, throughout this period, a large number of Somalis—represented most eminently by the segment of the middle class made up by the new intelligentsia of students, teachers, poets, writers, and composers—held on to the nationalist common identity based on soomaalinimo.[40] They were particularly influential in the first five (some say nine) years of the military regime of Siyaad Barre (1969–1990), which fostered that soomaalinimo and rallied the people around notions of scientific socialism.

However, whatever its public statements, the increasingly tyrannical regime developed a system of clientage based on the divisive manipulation of clan identity. By the time the dictator was expelled from Mogadishu in January 1991, the new communal identity of clanism, in whose name people had been silenced, tortured, raped, exiled, and murdered, had become inescapable for most Somalis. With the exception of groups of Muslim fundamentalists, most Somali men and women seemed unable even to imagine an alternative communal identity or to acknowledge that clanism was not an identity to which Somalis were *genetically* predisposed, but one that had been shaped by human (to a large extent, Somali) actors in the context of specific historical circumstances.

Thus, many Somalis fell prey to the latest type of "clan leaders." These new war leaders, who built up their wealth and influence during the Barre regime, derive their current political power from the manipulation of kin identity, which they call "traditional." Yet their objectives are far from traditional in that they aim to capture the resources that any state of the economic periphery—irrespective of whether its subjects live or die—can attract from the international community.[41] The chess board of Somali society has been extended once again.

What is the gender content of the ideology called clanism? How did women fare as the state developed a system of clientage and favoritism based on clan? It was mentioned above that after independence (in contrast to the precolonial past), women were no longer considered central to society's major economic pursuits, those of market exchange and capital investment. Thus, in terms of the new gender ideology, women had become less valuable. This essay also contends that women, as wives, gradually ceased to function as the bearers of reciprocal rights and duties between two autonomous communities. Women continued to be marginal or ambiguous members of their clans; in the recent bloodletting, women who married outside their own clan were often torn between the clan identity of their sons and husbands and that of their fathers and brothers. Thus, they sometimes killed or were killed by either the former or the latter. A third contention of this essay is that women, in the absence of lucrative or prestigious new niches in the urban economy or state sector, became either more dependent on men or, if they did not have men on whom to rely, gained the extra burden of being regarded as undeserving of respect.

However, some women have been recipients of the political and economic favors handed out by the state and other clan bosses. Siyaad Barre's state feminism, irrespective of the sincerity of its ideological beginnings, became the source of much clan-based—and class-based—clientage extended to a select group of women. Thus, during the Barre regime, some women got to climb the social ladder held up by men, although in general they were not allowed up very far.

Women gained positions largely in three ways. First, they gained positions as female relatives of loyal male clients of the economic or political boss. Second, women gained positions as female relatives of men who needed to be kept out of power. A politician could extend patronage to (or pay off) a clan by rewarding some of its women; because these women did not have their own constituency, real power sharing could thus be avoided. Finally, although this is a reality few Somalis are willing to acknowledge, many Somali women had to compromise their sexuality in order to obtain or hold on to a wage-paying position. In the context of patriarchy in

Somalia, as elsewhere, such sexual exploitation has been directed primarily against women, for, as Janet MacGaffey put it, "sexuality is a weapon that men, by virtue of their dominant position in society, do not generally have to use."[42] In the end, the new communal identity based on clan has devalued women's social roles and deepened their dependence.

Conclusion

This chapter has traced the history of a Somali communal identity based on clan. It has argued that clanism is a modern communal identity forged by Somalis in their interaction with each other and with the colonial and postcolonial states in the context of patriarchy and the capitalist world economy. Precolonial Somali society was an unambiguously patriarchal society in which women were barred from autonomy in production and reproduction, were excluded from formal political or religious leadership, and were not acknowledged as autonomous legal persons. However, as Somali society underwent a political and economic transformation during the era of colonial rule, the new material realities and the new communal identity forged in the crucible of social change further devalued women's social roles, deepened women's dependence on men, and degraded them in ways not untypical of other capitalist countries of the economic periphery.

Notes

1. Anderson, *Imagined Communities*, pp. 6–7.
2. Chhachhi, "Forced Identities," p. 147. See also Vail's theoretical introduction to his edited volume, *The Creation of Tribalism*, pp. 1–19; Chanock, *Law, Custom and Social Order*.
3. S. Samatar, *Somalia: A Nation in Turmoil*, p. 26.
4. Chhachhi, "Forced Identities," p. 147.
5. Makdisi, *Beirut Fragments*, p. 137.
6. The following subsections are based on Kapteijns, *Women and the Somali Pastoral Tradition*, pp. 2–8.
7. Ibid., pp. 6–8.
8. For a fuller treatment, see Kapteijns and Spaulding, "Class Formation."
9. Cassanelli, *The Shaping of Somali Society*, pp. 135–146.
10. Kapteijns and Spaulding, "Class Formation," p. 29.
11. Ibid., pp. 33–34.
12. The following analysis is based on the colonial records (the 535 series) kept in the Public Records Office (PRO), London. See Great Britain, Public Records Office, Colonial Records Office.

13. Great Britain, Public Records Office, Colonial Records Office, Series 535, No. 9; No. 35; No. 40; No. 51; No. 52. In No. 52, Archer, the commissioner, reports that the merchants paid few fees and benefited from the administration's debt enforcement in the interior.

14. Ibid., No. 5: "We must therefore endeavour to arrest the process of detribalisation by restoring the influence and authority of the tribal Chiefs and Headmen. . . . We must pick out the really influential men."

15. Ibid., No. 51, about the punishment of the *Jibril Yunis* in Bulahaar and Zeila; see also No. 8 and No. 9.

16. Ibid., No. 30, in which Archer proposes on 27 June 1913 to apply criminal law in the interior in some circumstances. The proposal is approved on 3 July 1913 (No. 33).

17. Swayne, *Seventeen Trips Through Somaliland*, p. 30; Burton, *First Footsteps*, p. 94; James, *The Unknown Horn of Africa*, p. 31; Also Great Britain, Public Records Office, Colonial Records Office, Series 535, No. 5, Notes on Military Transport.

18. Kapteijns and Spaulding, "Class Formation," p. 34, for more on water carriers; Great Britain, Public Records Office, Colonial Records Office, Series 535, No. 46, for more on nurses.

19. Great Britain, Public Records Office, Colonial Records Office, Series 535, No. 46, proposes a labor force of 1,000 women at Rs. 8 per month and 500 men at Rs. 15 per month. "Women would form the bulk of the labour. . . . The labour which the Commissioner states will be available is composed largely of women and the majority of the total labour locally obtained will be indigent."

20. Kapteijns, *Women and the Somali Pastoral Tradition*, p. 12.

21. Great Britain, Public Records Office, Colonial Records Office, Series 535, No. 51. This contains two pictures of the destitutes.

22. Great Britain, Public Records Office, Colonial Records Office, *Annual Colonial Reports*.

23. Kapteijns, *Women and the Somali Pastoral Tradition*, p. 12.

24. For full reference, see Kapteijns and Spaulding, "Counsels of Despair."

25. Kapteijns, *Women and the Somali Pastoral Tradition*, p. 12.

26. Oral information from author's fieldwork, Djibouti, September–December 1989.

27. A. Samatar, *The State and Rural Transformation*, p. 109; A. Samatar, Salisbury, and Bascom, "The Political Economy," p. 86.

28. Geshekter, "Anti-Colonialism and Class Formation," p. 27, and "Entrepreneurs, Livestock and Politics," p. 282.

29. Kapteijns and Spaulding, "Class Formation," pp. 27–33; Kapteijns, *Women and the Somali Pastoral Tradition*, pp. 9–10.

30. A. Samatar, Salisbury, and Bascom, "The Political Economy," pp. 84–88.

31. Kapteijns and Spaulding, "Class Formation," pp. 20, 31; Kapteijns, *Women and the Somali Pastoral Tradition*, p. 10.

32. A. Samatar, Salisbury, and Bascom, "The Political Economy," pp. 84–88. For more on trade with kinsmen, see I. M. Lewis, "Lineage Continuity," p. 380; Geshekter, "Entrepreneurs, Livestock and Politics," p. 270.

33. A. Samatar, Salisbury, and Bascom, "The Political Economy," p. 96.

34. Geshekter, "Entrepreneurs, Livestock and Politics," pp. 276, 281–282; I. M. Lewis, "Lineage Continuity," p. 385.

35. Geshekter, "Entrepreneurs, Livestock and Politics," p. 281.

36. A. Samatar, *The State and Rural Transformation*, p. 109.

37. Ibid., p. 111.

38. Ibid. See also A. Samatar and A. I. Samatar, "The Material Roots of the Suspended African State."

39. Spaulding, "The Recruitment of the Khatmiyya Leaders," p. 17.

40. For example, Afrax, *Maanafaay*; Mumin, *Leopard Among the Women*. Vail also describes the role of a local, educated middle class but emphasizes their significance in the development of new ethnic ("tribal") ideologies (*The Creation of Tribalism*, p. 12).

41. A. Samatar and A. I. Samatar, "The Material Roots of the Suspended African State."

42. MacGaffey, "Women and Class Formation," p. 174.

9

The Mirror of Culture: Somali Dissolution Seen Through Oral Expression

Maxamed D. Afrax

The human race had the wisdom to create science and arts; why should it not be capable to create a world of justice, brotherliness and peace? The human race has produced Plato, Shakespeare and Hugo, Michelangelo and Beethoven, Pascal and Newton, all these human heroes whose genius is only the contact with the funda-mental truth with inner most essence of universe. Why then should the same race not produce those leaders capable of leading it to those forms of communal life which are closest to the lives and harmony of the universe?

—*Leon Blum*

Reer ba'oow yaa ku leh!
(O, wretched household, to whom do you belong!)
—*Popular Somali saying*

Nearly a quarter of a century ago, a Somali poet and playwright, Mohamed Warsame "Hadrawi," produced a satirical play using the above Somali saying as its title. The plot centered around a poor no-madic family victimized by a member of the corrupt ruling elite. This saying can, however, be more aptly applied to the current up-heaval in Somalia. Indeed, the whole nation could be described as a *reer ba'ay*, a place squalid in every sense of the phrase.

The entire fabric of Somali society has been ravaged. The very existence of the whole nation has sunk in a deep dark sea of unimaginable human and material disaster. Furthermore, in my view, the communal mind of the society seems to be in a coma. No collective responsible effort, voicing national concern or calling for saving the savable, has so far emerged. For a nation proverbially known for its deep-rooted traditions of reasoning and a history of national consciousness, this is an utterly puzzling development. Why and how has it happened? This is the knotty question that persists as Somalia increasingly captures the attention of the world.

Any attempt to deal successfully with this problem requires a better understanding of Somali culture and society. What, in cultural perspective, are the real reasons for this unprecedented collapse of Somali political and civic life? Is it true that the cause lies in the old Somali culture, as repeatedly argued in some recent newspaper articles and other publications? What are the basic characteristics of Somali culture? What are the principal messages conveyed by the major forms of Somali cultural expression, both traditional and modern? This chapter is a modest attempt to contribute to the search for answers to these questions. Obviously, this is not an easy task because this chapter seeks to focus on a theme that, I feel, has never been studied before.

In order to achieve its goals, the essay is broken into four components. The first introduces the salient cultural values and attitudes of traditional Somali society, as featured in its stories, plays, poems, and oral traditions. The second section explores the predominant cultural trends during the two and a half decades spanning the early 1940s to late 1960s, a landmark period in the development of Somali culture. The third part traces the present catastrophe to practices of social and cultural deformation that took place during the past twenty years. The major argument in this section is that a systematic social, cultural, and moral destruction has preceded and paved the way for political and economic collapse, precipitating the present insanity. A whole body of new and destructive political culture has set in, replacing the positive cultural values of the nation.

The concluding section attributes the present agony to the legacy of the ill-intended political excesses of the military regime under Siyaad Barre, its outrageous manipulations of the traditional kin system, and armed and clanist factions on the scene today. Finally, I suggest that a serious effort at cultural reconstruction and a rehabilitation of the Somali mentality are prerequisites for a political or economic reconstruction.

Culture and Society: The Precolonial Era

The definition of the term *culture* is still a matter of debate, and it is not the intention here to delve into this complex dialogue. Suffice to say that culture will be referred to, in this paper, as a people's mode of perceiving the world and reacting to it through various forms of creativity. At all times, culture is closely associated with the environmental, social, and political conditions of a society; at the same time, it plays a considerable role in the regeneration of these conditions.

Given the fact that the remote history of Somalia is shrouded in mystery, as well as the recent destruction of the locations of whatever reference material existed in Somalia, oral culture remains, in my view, the most reliable and effective resource to a better understanding of this society. I believe that study of Somali national culture can provide important insights into the modes of life and thinking of the Somalis throughout history. Such study can therefore be helpful for any serious attempt to deal with the current peculiar situation in Somalia.

The abundance of Somali oral expression and the exceptionally important role it plays in Somali life has repeatedly been confirmed by early testimonies of outside observers and scholarly works by contemporary researchers of different origins. As elsewhere, Somali society contains most contradictions: good and evil, right and wrong, constructive and destructive. The divisive character of kin ideology is evidence for the existence of some negative aspects in Somali traditional attitudes. This will be discussed later in this chapter. On the other hand, it must be emphasized from the outset that it has been the constructive virtues that have given the Somali national culture its salient features. The bulk of Somali oral culture provides ample evidence that a strong belief in (unwritten) law and reason and an unmistakable sense of respect for social institutions have been the prominent traits of Somalis. Poets and parents consciously and constantly used narratives and other forms of cultural heritage as educational tools to imprint in the minds of their children the ideals of tolerance, mutual aid, condemnation of violence, and commitment to the common good. In the pages that follow, I shall substantiate these statements through various illustrations of Somali verbal art. First, however, I shall consider the negative aspect mentioned above.

Anthropologists and political scientists believe that the sociopolitical organization of precolonial Somalia rested on a clan family system based on descent. In the absence of a centralized national state, the traditional clan system was a necessity. In contrast to the hypocritical clanism in the contemporary urbanized circles, the traditional clan family system established a high degree of mutuality among people who lived under harsh environmental conditions. However, there are many negative elements to a clan-based world

outlook, wherever it exists. Among Somalis, such attitudes and behaviors represented potential threats to national unity and the very
essence of a modern state. For example, consider the following Somali saying:

> Haba kuu darraadee dad waa ina adeerkaa.
> (However unhelpful to you, your cousin remains the best
> of people.)

According to the above saying, one has to judge people on
the basis of blood ties and not on their merits. This saying is derived from the widely held concepts of *sokeeye* and *shisheeye*, according to which people are divided into kin, for whom support
is compulsory, and strangers, who are often perceived as potential foes.

> Shisheeye shiilo duxa ma leh.
> (Expect no mercy from outsiders.)

Clan-based principles can potentially become dangerous. For example, if a man wants to commit a murder, he may be encouraged by
the feeling that he will be protected by his kin; likewise, the ag-
grieved party may seek to take vengeance not just on the murderer
but on his kin individually and collectively. As a result of this irra-
tional outlook, innocent people may be harmed, and culprits need
not be held accountable for their deeds.

The most disastrous application of this ideology is manifested
in the political life of present-day Somalia. A ruthless tyrant, Siyaad
Barre, and such similar culprits as the present warlords and war
criminals have succeeded in manipulating the kin mentality, protected—even encouraged—by the majority of their immediate kins-
people despite the fact that, unlike traditional clan members, these
"leaders" clearly do not represent the interests of the group. On the
contrary, their acts are potential threats to the very existence of their
own particular clans.

It must be noted here that in traditional Somali society, the
harmful consequences of this sort of clan "insurance" for wrong-
doers was avoided by the existence of a more powerful cultural
force operating within the kin group. The righteous majority of the
kin group, vested in the elders and wise men, were always able to
control violent actions and other evil practices that were likely to be
committed by extremists. Everyone had to abide by the *heer* (the

customary law) and the collective will of the community, i.e., the
clan family.

> Talo walaal diide, tagoog buu ka jabaa.
> (He who rejects brotherly advice, breaks his thighbone.)

> Nin qaldan qabashadi, nin qumman quweynti iyo nin
> qatan wax-siintii buu tol ku dhaqmaa.
> (It is in restraining those who are at fault, supporting those
> who are upright, and coming to the aid of those who are
> hungry that kinship is properly exercised.)[1]

In spite of a profound sense of dignity and pride, "the Somali is
willing to bow before reason as long as he is proven wrong." However, it must still be said that the above negative aspects in kin relations can be described as dark shadows in the generally bright
scene of Somali culture.

A mature knowledge of Somali custom disproves recent arguments widely propagated by the Western media that violence and
anarchy constitute the cornerstone of Somali culture, or that in Somali society political tolerance is anathema. This assessment by the
media accurately describes Siyaad Barre's regime, as well as those
who compete to replace him, but such anarchy was *not* always the
case. The following samples from Somali oral tradition illustrate the
extent to which people believed in reason and tolerance as supreme
cultural virtues.

The first is the well-known parable about a young man who, fed
up with his wife leaving him frequently, decided to cut her shins.
The man was charged and instructed that he could no longer divorce
his wife, that he could not marry a second wife, and that he had to
pay special attention and care for his wife for life because he disabled her. When the man's father heard the verdict some days later,
he asked if his son had accepted the sentence. Yes, was the answer.
The father replied with relief, "Then, I recognize him as my son."

The moral of this parable is clear. It is aimed at teaching the
coming generation to be tolerant, to side with justice and reason,
and to respect the majority rule, even if your immediate personal
interests are at stake. The popularity of this story and the way it has
been preserved in the collective memory of Somali oral traditions
signify the extent to which the story is a true expression of the collective consciousness. There are many proverbs and popular say-
ings that convey the same message, such as

Gar-diid waa Alle-diid.
(He who rejects a verdict rejects God.)

Somali oral tradition teems with hundreds of proverbs, poems, and prose narratives with explicit messages condemning violence and despotism. They preach the virtue of peace and the value of law and order. The following are but a few:

Dagaal waa ka-dare.
(War is worse.)

Xeer la'aan waa xukun iyo xoolo la'aan.
(Without moral and social codes, all is lawlessness and abject poverty.)

Gacmo wada jiraa galladi ka dhalataa.
(Joint hands bear success.)

Aan wadahadallo waa aan heshiinno.
(Let's talk means let's reconcile.)

Rag waxaad "walaal" uga weydey waran ugama heshid.
(What cannot be done by persuasion cannot be done by the spear.)

Nin talo ma yaqaane gun baa talo taqaan.
(A lone man knows no solution; a council knows it.)

In addition, oral narratives depict the characters of tyrannical rulers as villains. The stories of Arrawelo[2] and Geeddi Babow[3] may be cited as examples.

It is likely that self-governance of traditional Somali society was based on the rule of the majority. This is what I. M. Lewis calls *pastoral democracy* and Ali Musse Iye describes as *Go'aankii Geedka* (the decision under the tree);[4] all the mature men of the community would participate in collective decisionmaking under a tree (the lack of democracy in excluding women is another serious matter). These thorough discussions and verdicts demonstrate that there was a compulsory reference to tradition and customary law in the past. Each speaker was aware that the weight of the deliberations would be validated with the support of a whole range of literary background (such as proverbs, poems, quotations of wisdom, and historical events), just as the Islamic ulema would substantiate their preaching with verses from the *Quran* and *Hadith*. This form of decisionmaking is one of the practices that preserved and disseminated oral tradition.

It is worth emphasizing that the role of the intellect was traditionally very important in Somali culture. The kin community used to pay
its highest respect to cultural producers and intellectuals. Prominent
among the traditional intelligentsia were three groups: the poets; men
of erudition, experience, and competence; and the Muslim ulema. If a
member of these groups was present in any given circumstance that
required the resolution of a problem, he would be the one to be consulted. These intellectuals were members of *biri-ma-geydo* (those not
deserving a sword), a group of seven men who would not be killed in
the event of war. Complicated issues were referred to those esteemed
for their ability and experience. Their decisions were final and had to
be implemented because, as a traditional Somali saying goes, "a man
who is a year older than you is wiser than you."

The verses of poets had tremendous power. A vivid example of
this is that Ali Dhuh, a distinguished poet, put a whole kin group
into a disastrous war by reciting his well-known poem "Guba"
(That Which Burns).[5] On the other hand, Salan Arabey's declaration
"Waar tolow colka jooja" (Oh, my kin, please stop the hostility) dis-
armed the warring factions of the Ahmed Farah and Dahir Farah
subclans, who had reneged on all agreements and were ready that
day to annihilate each other.[6]

In a comparison of traditional Somali society with that of current times, it is self-evident that the former was far more thoughtful
and intelligent. Bullets and immorality dominate today, showing
the magnitude of intellectual and cultural bankruptcy. Undoubtedly, as with any other society, old Somali society had its own share
of negative values and vileness. But the positive elements usually
prevailed, thanks to the guidance of the traditional intelligentsia.
Today, however, it is the other way around.

Culture and Society:
The Era of Great Awakening, 1940s–1960s

The period of roughly two decades commencing around the end of
World War II and ending in the 1960s was significant in the history
of the development of Somali society and culture. The whole spectrum of Somali life was characterized by an overwhelming feeling
of rejuvenation or rebirth, a general sense of being on the threshold
of a new experience.

In this section, I endeavor to examine how this renaissance expressed itself in forms of cultural creation. I begin by looking briefly
at three salient aspects of this rebirth. The first was the transformation of people's consciousness from kin loyalty to a higher form of

national awareness based on *soomaalinimo* (Somalism). The second was the trend toward education, based on a general feeling that modern education was the only road to a better life. The third was the rise and flourishing of new works of art and oral expression. I shall pay particular attention to the last, through which the other two will be illustrated.

The richness and intensity of the experience of the time and the important social, political, and cultural changes that were under way inspired a whole body of new art and oral expression. This, in turn, greatly contributed to the regeneration of the changing social and cultural realities. The first half of the 1940s saw the rise of modern music; urban theater; and *heello*, which evolved into today's *hees* (songs), the most popular form of contemporary poetry.[7]

A review of the literary works of the time will provide important insights into the way in which the people of the predictatorial Somalia perceived themselves and the world around them. Here, I focus on how the poetry and theater of the 1950s and 1960s reflected the two principal sociopolitical concerns of the time: Somali nationalism and the search for enlightenment as a tool for progress.

Nationalism as a Major Theme of Oral Expression

Any examiner of the Somali verbal art of the past fifty years will note that soomaalinimo, or patriotism, is the major theme in almost all major works. The relation between Somali nationalism and oral expression is of paramount importance. First, a word of forewarning: what is routinely referred to as soomaalinimo need not be associated solely with the period of struggle for independence or even the days of Sayyid Mohamed Abdille Hassan. The concept of soomaalinimo as a communal identity has obviously existed since the time when the Somali entity was forged through culture, language, geographical location, and ethnicity. A camelboy would sardonically reply, "I'm Somali" to an inquiry about his clan. Similarly, a nomadic woman whose husband was not around used to say, "We're Somalis" in reply to strangers' questions about who her family was; it was a sign that the wife was not prepared to host guests. The travelers would in turn say, "We're all Somalis, but which clan?" The camelboy and nomadic woman were aware that their own lineage ultimately led to their Somalihood. This knowledge made Somalia unique among other sub-Saharan countries, where people do not identify themselves with the national name that their country assumed after independence.

Nationalism is not a mere political concern, as many have incorrectly believed. In fact, Somali nationalism existed long before the modern concept was given its political interpretation. In recent times, Somalis collaborated in an organized manner to achieve Somalism through a new structure: a modern and independent state shared by all Somalis. This became an ideology that superseded the kin consciousness for many people. Others, however, stuck to their old affinities or straddled the two worldviews, creating in their wake a jumble of contradictions. Contemporary poets and playwrights deal with this subject, voicing the new and criticizing the old. Although a detailed explanation of this phenomenon is beyond the scope of this chapter, I will present one reasonably elaborate depiction that stretches across three or four different periods of modern Somali history: the image of a symbolic she-camel called Maandeeq, a well-known character frequently used in most genres of Somali oral expression during the past forty years or so.

The imagination of Somali poets and playwrights created Maandeeq as a symbol of the country, the state, and sovereignty. The reason for choosing a she-camel to embody the most valued ideals lies in the nomadic cultural background of most of the authors. In this context, the she-camel is the most valued of all property. The man whose she-camel is stolen does not rest, and the one whose she-camel has just given birth misses no prosperity but has to protect it from the beasts. To understand the evolution of Maandeeq's image in oral narratives is to read the history of the modern Somali state.

In particular, changes in Maandeeq's image symbolize the history of Somalia over the past half a century, which can be divided into four different periods. The first was the preindependence period. The following stanza by Yusuf Hagi Adan is an example of the oral expression of this age:

Hadhuub nin sitoo hashiisa irmaan
"Ha maalin" la leeyahaan ahay
Dagaal nimuu haysto meel halisoo
Hubkiisu hangool yahaan ahay

(I'm a man with a milking vessel and a dairy camel
But told not to milk it for himself
I'm a man dangerously encompassed by war
Whose only weapon is a wooden hook)

The year 1960 marked the second period. An independent Somali Republic was born at last. The streets of Mogadishu, Hargeisa, and everywhere else were filled by jubilant people dancing in celebration:

> Maantay curatoo
> Caanaha badisee
> An maallo hasheenna Maandeeq

> (Today is its first delivery
> Her production increases
> Let's milk our she-camel, Maandeeq)

The months of June and July 1960 saw a gush of hundreds of songs composed in celebration of the joyous occasion of the independence,[8] but the feeling would soon change. What happened? Abdillahi Qarshi answers:

> Hashaan toban sano u heesaayey
> Hadhuubkiyo heeryadiiba cuntee
> Lixdankaan haybin jirey maxaa helay?

> (The she-camel I've been singing about for ten years
> Has eaten both the milking vessel and the saddle
> What happened to the [year of] sixty I so much longed for?)

The poet angrily depicts the people's concern by questioning the misallocation of the supposedly increased spring milk of the suckling Maandeeq. A Somali audience would easily decipher the message. The poet shows that independence was beginning to fail the people who struggled for it.

A later reference to Maandeeq was made by the significant composer Hussein Aw Farah. In a song that begins with "Markii ay gabeenee" (When they failed her [Maandeeq]), Farah portrays a she-camel flagrantly neglected by her herders—tortured by thirst, hunger, and blood-sucking ticks—that is finally rescued by good men who move her to rich pastures and protect her from the effects of chronic diseases. A great Somali artist customarily expresses the feelings of the majority of the people at any given time. In this example, Farah, in anticipation of badly needed reform, depicts the jubilation with which the majority welcomed the military coup in 1969.

Shortly thereafter, however, poets who used to complain about misallocation of the she-camel's milk and a drought during which she grossly suffered portrayed the slaughter of Maandeeq. Silence descended on the whole country as militaristic regimentation became the order of the times. "Abdulkadir Hirsi" (Listen to the Truth) captures the beginning of the suffocation of creativity:

Dhabanada ayaan labada suul dhaygag hayaaye
Dhibaatay runtii noqotay oo la isku dhaadhiciye
Sallax buu ku dhegayaa afkii laga dhawaajaaye[9]

(With my two thumbs pressed against the cheeks, staring
It's truly a difficulty to face imprisonment
The mouth that dares to shout sticks to a stony floor)

Finally, let us consider a portrait of Maandeeq being mutilated, found in a play called *Aqoon iyo Afgarad* (Knowledge and Understanding), jointly authored in 1972 by Mohamed Ibrahim Warsame "Hadrawi," Saeed Salah Ahmed, Mohamed Hashi Dhama' "Gariye," and Musse Abdi Elmi. In this play, Maandeeq is represented by a character named Dahson (Invisible), a girl from a poor family. Dahson is tormented and becomes blind. She visits a doctor, who cannot help her but prescribes medication anyway. The doctor's real advice to Dahson is to look for the one man with the power to cure her, an army officer named Dahir. Following the instructions of the doctor, Dahson takes the prescription note to Dahir. He supplies her with medication that makes her condition worse. Furthermore, Dahir seeks to use Dahson as bait for her sister, Dulmar, with whom he would like to have an extramarital affair. The play painfully depicts the anguish and distress of Dahson:

Cirrolihii dhulku aaway?
Yaa caruurtii halleeyey?
Caanihii dhashu aaway?
Hashii yaa candho gooyey?
Cindiid yaa na wadaajey?
Isna sii cayilaaya?
Camalkiinnu xumaa!
Bal ayaan u cawdaa?
Yaa codkayga kasaaya?
Dhaayahaygan caweermay
Yaa cruuqda dhayaaya?
Jinjimii cududaydiyo
Cambarkii surku aaway?
Mee hugaygi cusbaa?
Alla yaan cuskadaa?
Ciirsi yaan ka filaa?

(Where are the elders of the land?
Who has abused the children?
Where is the milk for the babies?
Who has cut the udder of the she-camel?
Who has made us share stupefying cocktail?
And is getting himself fatter?
How ridiculous are your deeds!
Whom should I complain to?
Who should understand my voice?
My blurred eyesight
Who should medicate the veins?
The bangles on my arms
Where is the amber on my neck?
Where is my new dress?
O Lord, whom should I turn to?
Whom should I expect to help?)

Even the dress and the fashionable jewelry of the defenseless and blind victim are stripped off her, one by one. With no guide, Dahson falls over a steep cliff, indicative of the times. In the end, a rescue operation must be mounted by the people to retrieve her.

This play *seems* to contain references about circumstances in the late 1960s. However, a careful analysis reveals that the play is a statement on what was happening in the 1970s. An example is the "infallible" officer, who has all the power yet no one dares to blame him for anything. The last scenes of the play seem to be a deliberate attempt to finish a sad story with an artificial happy ending. Such a practice was common during the military dictatorship. Moreover, this final act could be the result of last-minute censorship by the Ministry of Education, so that the play would meet the standards for study materials for secondary schools.

Education as a Major Theme of Oral Expression

One of the attributes of the great awakening of the period under discussion was a generalized realization of the importance of modern education. Earlier, the colonial administration was suspected of having covert designs to convert the Somalis to the Christian faith. By the 1950s, however, this attitude dramatically changed in favor of the campaign for modern education. Somali oral expression always reflects issues of public concern, so the idea that knowledge is the key to development and that the Somalis ought to take note of this was reiterated by many poets, including Ali Husein Hirsi,

Osman Yusuf Kenadid, Abdullahi Suldan "Tima-Adde," Mohamed Ismael "Balaya-Ass," Ali Elmi Afyare, and Areys Isse Karshe. All of these cultural notables are now dead, and their life histories wait to be written.

In regard to popular songs, Abdillahi Qarshi composed his most memorable piece in 1961:

Aqoon la'aani waa iftiin la'aane
Waa aqal iyo ilays la'aane
Ogaada ogaada dugsiyada ogaada
Oo gaada oo ogadaa
Walaalayaal oo adaa!

(Lack of knowledge is lack of enlightenment
Homelessness and no light
Be aware, be aware of schools, be aware
Be aware, be aware
Brother, be aware!)

John Johnson reminds us that this song was one of the most popular songs for several years, to the extent that it was chosen as the signature tune of Mogadishu Radio. It was later replaced by "Dhul-kayaga" (Our Land).

The immense popularity and memorization by the public of songs like this clearly reveal the eagerness with which most households and individuals received education in the 1960s. "Lack of education is lack of enlightenment" was a favorite expression. Plays, poetry, newspapers, and artist groups adapted names derived from the words and the intrinsic meaning of this song. One such derivative was given to the only literary journal of the time, *Iftiinka Aqoonta* (The Light of Education).[10] This was not merely a coincidence. Rather, the words *education* and *enlightenment* were often used in the dissemination of modern literature through the media. Plays were undoubtedly the major form of art advocating the quest for modern education. Ironically, the playwrights themselves, with the exception of a very few, had no chance for the formal education they were promoting.

In the 1950s and 1960s, plays depicted educated characters as positive protagonists. For instance, in Mohamed Ismael "Balaya-Ass"'s 1959 play *Inan Sabool* (A Poor Daughter), a pivotal character is a man named Elmi, a descriptive name meant to signify an educated man. The play is about a beautiful and worthy girl from a poor family (the girl symbolizes Somali sovereignty). She is vulnerable and needs care. Uneducated men try to seduce her and take advantage of her. They all fail to win her, but they keep pestering her until Elmi finally appears on the scene. The play has a simple plot, representative of the plays of the period. The underlying message, however, promotes nationalism and enlightenment, thereby expressing Mohamed Ismael's conviction that independence and true sovereignty can be achieved through education alone.

A later example is Hassan Sheikh Mumin's 1969 play *Gaaraa-Bidhaan* (Fireflies), in which the protagonist is a young man who goes abroad for higher education. The man returns after some years and is saddened by the state of backwardness in his country. He works hard to educate the people. The only sources of criticism Mumin has for this character concern the character's marriage to a European woman and the shaky relationship between his wife and his extended, tradition-abiding family. The play expresses disapproval of marriage to foreigners and what is seen as a serious deviation from cultural origins.

A pertinent question to ask is whether this image of the educated Somali in modern oral art forms (including plays) is typically accurate. Unfortunately, it is not. The artists were reflecting the feelings of those who had a profound understanding of the significance of education, but many of these artists became disappointed in the efforts of those who were given the opportunity, through the meager resources of the state, to become educated. The poems and songs of the last twenty years are replete with lamentations and condemnation, as the once-positive depiction of the educated is tarnished by images of surrender or cowardice. An example of this shift is found in a play called *Qaran iyo Qabiil* (State and Clanism), by Abdi Migane, staged in Djibouti in 1985. The protagonist is a character named Samadid, a young graduate in charge of a government agency. Instead of acting professionally, befitting his status, he plunges himself into clan politics. The agency becomes bankrupt, and he undermines his own future.

Although this period of great awakening came to an end around 1971 or 1972, its last thrusts delivered the creation of a Somali orthography, completed on 21 October 1972. Abdille Rage's poetry is representative of this moment:

Labaatan iyo laba aamustiyo shaqal irmaaneeya
Ebyaniyo haddaan magac-u-yaal ku arkay joornaalka
Mar haddii afkaygii la qoray aabbe iyo hooyo
Mar haddaan amaahsigi ka baxay lagu agoontoobey
Abaal waxa leh nimankii fartaa soo abaabulaye

Amiirnimo sin iyo garab jirtay nagu abuureene
Afafkaa qalaad iyo maxaa eregta ii dhiibtey
Anaa macallimoo raba dad loo furo iskuulaade

(Twenty-two consonants with vowels that make then
   sound
Having seen an article and a pronoun in the newspaper[11]
Having my mother and father's language written
Having relieved myself from the borrowing that made us
   orphans
Gratitude to the men who arranged the script
They created a mammoth pride in us all
Why should I accept foreign languages and borrowing
I too am a teacher who needs schools)

The cultural excitement and euphoria that greeted this important achievement, heady though it was, could not forestall the coming of despotism—a killer of human creativity.

Arrested Development:
The Extortion of a Culture

The popular characters that are often used in traditional Somali oral narratives include a small boy by the name of Higis and a beast called Afar-Bo'le (Four-Throats). This fictional beast, usually found in children's stories, is said to frighten youngsters out of their wits. Among the instructive and rich tales in which Higis and Afar-Bo'le appear is the following one:

> One day, Higis's mother left him at home. Afar-Bo'le, knowing that the little boy was alone, came to him. Afar-Bo'le is widely known for its cunning and tricks to deceive children when it is hunting them. The beast has the ability to disguise itself as someone familiar to the children. It dresses and wears a veil like Higis's old aunt, who usually brings milk to him. Afar-Bo'le knows that the boy is hungry and needs milk. From some distance, the beast mimics the voice of Higis's aunt. Higis cheerfully welcomes the imposter. When Afar-Bo'le enters the house, Higis joyfully comes close. Quickly, Afar-Bo'le takes off its disguise and grabs Higis, exposing its dreadful canine teeth with the aim of scaring the child to death.

Of course, Higis is not real, and nobody has ever seen Afar-Bo'le. Both are creations designed to deliver educative messages to each new generation. The emphasis is one of vigilance and alertness against the myriad deceits and sinister acts of evil forces.

The Somalis of the late 1960s and early 1970s apparently forgot the lessons that their ancestors stored in this tale. Like Higis, they fell into a deadly trap. Such is the fate of contemporary Somalia. The critical question is, why did Somalis, including some of the sagacious ones, embrace the military order that was introduced by the coup d'état of 1969? Obviously, the first reason is that most Somalis were sick of the incompetence and corruption of the civilian government of the day. Second, the army was regarded with a great deal of awe, verging on a romanticization of its role as the defender of the nation. Third, the Somalis are basically nonconformists; they like change. Fourth, Somalia was part of a pattern of military coups in Africa that year. The fifth reason is that events were moving at a fast pace and that the low level of public awareness made it impossible for Somalis to anticipate the true consequences of military rule.[12]

Culture and literature were among the areas most profoundly affected by the military regime. The cultural structures of the nation were undone and spiritual values distorted. As the traditional moral code of right and wrong became reversed, what was once seen as offensive assumed a degree of acceptance or was even perceived as salutary. For instance, theft, lying, hypocrisy, rape, and dishonesty began to be defined as indicators of *ragannimo* (manhood). *Xoogga Dalka* (the National Army), one of the most respected social institutions, turned into a much-feared tool of repression and killing.

The opposition groups that stepped forward were not much better than Siyaad Barre. They adopted the same policy of political intolerance, clanist rivalry, and blind violence, as though salvation lay in surpassing the regime in acts of killing and destruction. Two reasons, among others, can be suggested for this tragedy: The first is that the leadership of these groups consisted of former Siyaad Barre loyalists who fell out with him simply because they found their political ambitions threatened by Barre's perfidious manipulations. After all, many were military officers who had been involved in turning the National Army into a looting, raping, and intimidating concern. As the Somalis say, "Hal booli ahi nirig xalaal ah ma dhasho" (A stolen she-camel does not give birth to a rightful baby). The second factor for the spread of this grievous mischief is that the broad masses did not rise up in opposition, mainly because the new destructive political culture of "bowing before guns rather than reason" was already at an advanced stage.

Somalia has been ravaged by these kinds of people, who in turn are empowered by this perversion of traditional culture. The country is still hostage to them. Any attempt at rescue must start by defeating all those who dominated the country in recent times and depriving them of the weapons they have illegally inherited from the defunct National Army.

Conclusion

In this chapter, I have attempted to highlight the stark contradiction between traditional Somali thinking and that of the present. It is my contention that no neutral observer of Somali cultural production could fail to notice the astonishing distance between the dignity of the past and the current state of mindless degradation.

The corpus of oral expression and tradition examined in the first section of chapter has shown that precolonial Somali society was governed by a moral code of right and wrong based on reason, tolerance, rule of law, and a strong sense of obligation, on the part of the individual, to the general welfare. "People, know your leaders; leaders, know your limits" goes an ancient Somali saying. To be sure, negative attitudes and behaviors did exist, sometimes resulting in such events as kin or subkin fighting. It must be emphasized, however, that community elders, poets, and other wise individuals were always able to either preempt such conflicts or settle the issues quickly. Consequently, peace was maintained, and hatred was kept under control.

Much of the modern period, particularly the 1940s through the 1960s, represented a significant landmark in Somali history and cultural development. An entire body of art and oral expression emerged and blossomed, thereby playing a major role in the strengthening of political awareness—including the transformation from kin loyalties to a Pan-Somalist nationalism. This change was crucial to decolonization and the establishment of a modern state. Most took this period as the beginning of a better life, but such hope began to dry up by the end of the 1960s. Somalia's failure to bring about a system of competent leadership and governance capable of fulfilling Somali aspirations led to the current plight.

The bulk of material reviewed in this essay provides ample evidence that old Somali national culture had very little to do with the making of the ongoing bloody anarchy and political immorality. In fact, these are products of disrespect and are relentless violations of the deep cultural values and social norms of the Somali people.

But the voice of protest is not done, and poets continue to speak. The following are Abshir Nur Farah's words, reflective of the cry of the 1990s:

Mooryaan[13] hubaysani balaay, noo hor-kacayaane
Wixii hudurku nugu beeray bay, ku hamminaayaane
Haddaan laga hor-tagin wacad allaad, marin habowdeene
Helina wayde hadafkaan rabnaye, nugu habboonaaye.

(Armed Moryans would only lead us to disaster
They dream of the very thing that the sickness planted
   in us
If unchallenged, by Allah's word, you will lose your way
And you will not find that which we wish and deserve)

Finally, it is my firm belief that a systematic cultural renewal is as urgently needed as any plan for political and economic rebuilding. Preservation of what is left of the nation's cultural heritage is a monumental task, but such culture can do miracles in Somalia; it can restore sanity and hope, reintroduce democratic thinking, and help formulate a new vision of local community and national reconstruction. But to come to the aid of their country, poets, artists, and other traditional intellectuals must be helped to pick up the pieces of their own shattered lives and regroup.

Notes

The major references used in this chapter are unpublished works of oral expression collected by the author during the past fifteen years. These materials exist in the form of tape recordings and original manuscripts in the author's possession.

1. Translated in Andrzejewski, "Reflections," p. 77.
2. *Arrawelo* is a very popular oral narrative about a ruthless legendary queen. For details, see Xaange, *Sheeko Xariirooyin Soomaaliyed.*
3. According to the oral narrative, Geeddi Babow was a despotic ruler based in Bur Hakaba, in the area between the Shabelle and Juba rivers.
4. Iye, *Le Verdict.*
5. *Guba* has become the name of a famous series of poetic combats centered around a kin rivalry. It was initiated by Ali Adan Goroyo (Ali Dhuh) in the early 1930s. Other prominent poets who had combated with him included Qaman Bulhan and Salan Arabey.
6. See Andrzejewski and Lewis, *Somali Poetry.*

7. For more information about the emergence of the genre heello and its transformation into the present-day hees, see Johnson, *Heellooy*. For a detailed account of the history and nature of Somali theatre, see Afrax, *Fan Masraxeedka*.

8. Author's interview with two statesmen of modern Somali art, Abdillahi Qarshi and Hussein Aw Farah, Mogadishu, 1979.

9. The poet alludes to a Somali parable that ends with a well-known saying by a fictitious and irreverent pastoralist. The saying expresses the herdsman's protest against what he saw as the unfairness of muzzling him (sticking his mouth to a stony floor) in order to instruct him not to complain about the slaying of his goats by the order of Allah.

10. This journal was issued in Mogadishu during 1966 and 1967, and was edited by Shire Jama.

11. The poet refers to and uses the newly introduced terms of Somali grammar.

12. Despite the intimidating atmosphere, many literary creators attempted to portray the realities of military rule. Consider three examples from three major areas of creative writing: poetry, theatre, and fiction. The first example is Mohamed Warsame "Hadrawi"'s two 1973 poems, "Hal la qalay raqdeed" and "Wadnahaan far ku hayaa." Both were early warnings that led to the poet's exile to a remote village and his silence at gunpoint for several years. The second example is Abdi Mohomed Amin's play *Muufo*, which was performed as part of the official celebration of 1 May 1979 (Somali Workers' Day). It was staged at the Mogadishu National Theatre. Siyaad Barre himself attended the performance and immediately reacted with outrage. He attacked the playwright and everyone involved in a half-hour diatribe. The third example is my second novel, *Galti-macruuf*, which was serialized in the leading daily *Xiddigta Oktoobar* until it was suddenly discontinued. I was arrested and interrogated for several days by the National Security Service. The major events of the story take place in the offices of a parastatal (Wakaaladda Horumarinta Qudaarta), run by a middle-aged former military officer, Elmi Gurey, who is corrupt and sinister.

13. *Mooryaan* is a new Somali word invented to refer to the armed thugs who indulge in murder and extortion in Somalia.

Appendix

The Somali Challenge: Peace, Resources, and Reconstruction Conference Recommendations

Preamble

We, the participants of a conference entitled "The Somali Challenge: Peace, Resources, and Reconstruction," held in Geneva, Switzerland, 10–14 July 1992,

Having reviewed and examined the grave situation in Somalia, and having noted:

- the total destruction of the Somali state and the continuing debilitative effects of political stalemate, as a result of rivalries within and among factions
- the enormous human cost of the civil and political strife, which includes death, generalized destitution, and dispersion
- the collapse of the production and distribution systems of livelihood
- the erosion of cultural heritage and devastation of social institutions
- the precarious and deteriorating condition of the ecological base
- the enormous aggravation added to the Horn of Africa region, which is already reeling from relentless disorders of the past

Conclude

That the Somali people have *primary responsibility* for ending the pain of their people and reconstructing their country, and for their reentrance as viable members of the world community,

That violence and force are counterproductive and open dialogue is the *only* way to peace,

That full democratic participation of the Somali people is required in the determination of their future and the choice of institutions of governance,

That there is an urgent need to strengthen Islamic and cultural values conducive to a collective welfare and a common fate,

That the capacity to solve both immediate and long-term problems depends on the mobilization of human resources and the restorations of basic institutions,

That peace and stability in Somalia are prerequisite to a Somali contribution toward the socioeconomic development of the Horn of Africa.

Guidelines for Short/Long-term Actions

Governance and Security

1. An immediate cease-fire should be declared across the country, especially in zones of conflict, and followed by full disarmament.
2. International relief should be provided to all parts of the country, and such relief should be delivered primarily through local community organizations.
3. There should be immediate planning for and subsequent convening of a general and comprehensive conference.
4. A transitional process to democracy, the outcome of which will decide the future political order of Somali society, should be designed and accepted.
5. A United Nations mission should be established to monitor the implementation of agreements concerning the cease-fire and transitional processes to democracy.
6. A United Nations conference should be convened to express solidarity with the Somali people and to mobilize resources for the complex work of rehabilitation and reconstruction.

Ecology and Economy

Short-term measures.

1. The illegal exploitation of Somali marine resources by foreigners should be denounced, and all forms of foreign

environmental opportunism in the absence of a Somali state should be prevented.
2. The infrastructure and farm input needs to support the immediate production of grains and legumes should be estimated.
3. An inventory of shelter needs should be taken to anticipate construction requirements and needs for other building materials.
4. Domestic energy needs should be assessed.
5. An inventory of requirements for the restoration of livestock production and wildlife management should be taken.
6. Environmental health needs should be assessed to secure the lives of humans and animals located in zones that are marginal and unhealthy as a result of the war.
7. Urban sanitation should be reestablished.
8. Previous land use policies and land tenure laws should be reviewed.
9. Banking and credit institutions should be rehabilitated.

Long-term measures.

1. Plantations, irrigation systems, and basic industries should be rehabilitated.
2. Studies of the potential of geothermal, wind, biomass, and solar power sources as a basis of a sustainable energy policy should be conducted.
3. Studies of the potential of marine and freshwater fish as food sources and export earnings should be conducted.
4. Studies of the potential of mineral resources as a basis for domestic industry, employment opportunities, and export earnings should be conducted.
5. The concepts of security and sustainability should be adopted for water, food, energy, health, and employment as hallmarks of future Somali development policy.

Culture

1. A steering committee should be created to do the following:
   • survey and locate valuable cultural materials, individuals, groups, and institutions
   • establish a general forum for Somali creative expression
   • provide guidance and devise materials for international agencies providing temporary education in the refugee camps

- prepare cultural education and entertainment tailored in particular to the needs of the younger generation in the diaspora
- survey the immediate needs for the education of children and make proposals for the immediate establishment of schools
- rehabilitate the two radio services and other communications media
- survey and compile a list of skilled Somalis, in and outside of the country, who can be called upon to participate in the reconstruction of Somali society

2. A Somali Academy of Arts and Sciences, as well as other national literary and cultural institutions, should be reestablished.
3. A higher education and training system should be reestablished.

Regional Imperatives

Short-term Measures

1. Somali groups that are fighting must be made to realize the great damage their actions are causing neighboring countries and their peoples.
2. Leaders, as well as nongovernmental organizations of neighboring countries, must provide welcome and succor to constructive ideas and proposals by Somalis seeking peaceful resolution of the conflict.

Long-term Measures

1. Free movement of people, goods, and services in the region must be facilitated.
2. Popular forums and institutions for an exchange of local and national experiences in political, economic, and cultural fields must be established.

Bibliography

Abdillahi, A. "Tribalism, Nationalism, and Islam: The Crisis of Political Loyalty in Somalia." (Masters thesis) McGill University, Montreal, Canada, 1992.

Acharya, A. "Regionalism and Regime Security in the Third World: Comparing the Origins of the ASEAN and the GCC." In *The Insecurity Dilemma: National Security of Third World States*. Edited by B. Job. (Boulder: Lynne Rienner Publishers, 1992).

Adam, H. "Somalia: Militarism, Warlordism or Democracy?" *Review of African Political Economy* 54 (July 1992):11–26.

———. "Rethinking Somali Politics." *Proceedings of the Sixth Michigan State University Conference on North East Africa*. East Lansing: Michigan State University, 23–25 April 1992.

Adams, W. *Green Development: Environment and Sustainability in the Third World*. (London: Routledge & Kegan Paul, 1990).

Addis Ababa Agreement of the First Session of the Conference on National Reconciliation in Somalia. Addis Ababa, Ethiopia, 27 March 1993.

Addis Ababa Voice of Ethiopia Network. "Horn of Africa Humanitarian Summit Opens 8 April." In *Foreign Broadcast Information Service, Daily Report: Sub-Saharan Africa* (Washington, D.C.: U.S. Government, 10 April 1992):1.

"Address by the Deputy Assistant Secretary of State for African Affairs at the St. Paul Social Studies Institute," *American Foreign Policy, 1963*, Doc. VIII-1, 615–617.

"Address by the Secretary of State Before the Annual Convention of the National Association of Colored People (NAACP), St. Louis, July 1, 1977." *American Foreign Policy 1977–1980*, Doc. 608 (Washington, D.C.: U.S. Government Printing Office, 1981).

Afrax, M. *Fan Masraxeedka Somaalida* (Djibouti: Centre National de Promotion Culturele, 1987).

———. "Adwa Ala Alharaka Athaqafiya Fi Asomal." *Athaqafah Aljadidah* 5 (September 1986):70–84.

————. "Al-Haraka Al-Masrahiyah Fi Asomal." *Alhikma* 126 (October 1985): 9–18.

————. *Maanafaay.* (Mogadishu: Wakalada Madbacaada Qaranka, 1981).

Africa Contemporary Record, 1979–80, 1980–81, 1981–82, 1982–83, 1983–84, 1987–88.

Ahmed, A. *The Invention of Somalia.* (Trenton, N.J.: Red Sea Press, forthcoming).

————. "Of Poets and Sheikhs: Somali Literature." In *The Faces of Islam in African Literature.* Edited by W. K. Harrow. (London: Heinemann, 1991).

————. "Tradition, Anomaly and the Wave for the Future." Ph.D. dissertation. Comparative Literature, University of California, Los Angeles, 1989.

Ake, C. "Explanatory Notes on the Political Economy of Africa." *Journal of Modern African Studies* 14, 1 (1976):1–23.

Alavi, H. "State and Class Under Peripheral Capitalism." In *Introduction to the Sociology of Developing Societies.* Edited by H. Alavi and T. Shanin. (New York: Monthly Review Press, 1982).

Ali Shireh, Sultan A. M. *Conference Communique.* (Hadaftimo, Somalia) 8 July 1993.

American Foreign Policy, Current Documents (Washington: U.S. Government Printing Office, 1961).

Amin, S. *Imperialism and Unequal Exchange.* (New York: Monthly Review Press, 1977).

————. *Unequal Development: An Essay on the Social Formation of Peripheral Capitalism.* (New York: Monthly Review Press, 1976).

————. *Accumulation on a World Scale.* 2 vols. (New York: Monthly Review Press, 1974).

————. "Accumulation and Development: A Theoretical Model." *Review of African Political Economy* 1 (1974):9–27.

Amnesty International. *Somalia: A Human Rights Disaster.* (London: Amnesty International, 1992).

————. *Somalia: The July 1989 Jezira Beach Massacre.* (London: Amnesty International, 1990).

Amoo, S. *The OAU and African Conflicts: Past Successes, Present Paralysis and Future Perspectives.* (Fairfax: George Mason University Institute of Conflict Analysis and Resolution, May 1992).

Amsden, A. *Asia's Next Giant: South Korea and Late Industrialization.* (New York: Oxford University Press, 1989).

Anderson, B. *Imagined Communities: Reflections on the Origin and Spread of Nationalism.* (London: Verso, 1991 and 1983).

Andrzejewski, B. W. "Somali Literature." In *Literatures in African Languages.* Edited by B. W. Andrezjewski et al. (Cambridge: Cambridge University Press, 1987).

————. "Reflections on the Nature and Social Function of Somali Proverbs." *African Language Review* 7 (1968): 74–85.

————, and Lewis, I. M. *Somali Poetry: An Introduction.* Oxford: Clarendon Press, 1964).

————, and Galal, H. M. "A Somali Poetic Combat." African Studies Center, Report of 1963, Michigan State University, East Lansing.

Antinucci, F., and Axmed, F. A. *Poesia Orale Somala: Storia di una Nazione.* (Roma: Ministero degli Affari Esteri, 1969).

Apple, R. W. "Clinton Sending Reinforcements After Heavy Losses in Somalia." *New York Times* (5 October 1993):1, 3.

Aqli, A. "Historical Development of Islamic Movements in the Horn of Africa." Paper presented at the First Conference of European Association of Somali Studies, 23–25 September 1993, London, England.

Arendt, H. *Between Past and Future.* (New York: Penguin Books, 1977).

Aron, R. *Memoires.* (Paris: Julliard, 1983).

Aronson, D. "Kinsmen and Comrades: Towards a Class Analysis of the Somali Pastoral Sector." *Nomadic Peoples* 7 (1982):14–24.

Assefa, H. and Khadiagala, G. (editors). *Conflict and Conflict Resolution in the Horn of Africa.* (Washington, D.C.: Brookings Institution, 1994).

Awogbade, M., and Hassan, U. "Settlement Scheme for the Nomadic Pastoral Fulani of Nigeria: Some Relevant Issues." In *Camels in Development: Sustainable Production in African Drylands.* Edited by A. Hjort af Ornäs. (Uppsala: Scandinavian Institute of African Studies, 1988).

Ayoade, J. "States Without Citizens." In *The Precarious Balance.* Edited by D. Rothchild and N. Chazan. (Boulder: Westview Press, 1988).

Baran, P. *The Political Economy of Growth.* (New York: Monthly Review Press, 1957).

Barker, R. *Political Legitimacy and the State.* (Oxford: Clarendon Press, 1990).

Barre, A. *Salient Aspects of Somalia's Foreign Policy: Selected Speeches.* (Mogadishu: Ministry of Foreign Affairs, 1978).

Barre, M. "Speech to the Nation on October 21, 1979." In *African Contemporary Record, 1980.* Edited by C. Legum. (London: African Publishing Company, 1980).

Bates, R. *Markets and States in Tropical Africa: The Political Basis of Agricultural Policies.* (Berkeley: University of California Press, 1981).

Bayaanka Muqdisho ee Koowaad. (Mogadishu: n.p., May 1990).

Bayart, J. *L'etat en Afrique.* (Paris: Fayard, 1989).

Beckman, B. "The Post-Colonial State: Crisis and Reconstruction." *IDS Bulletin* 19, 4 (1988):26–34.

Beinart, W. "Soil Erosion, Conservationism, and Ideas About Development." *Journal of Southern African Studies* 11, 1 (1984):52–83.

Benjamin, W. *Illuminations: Essays and Reflections.* Translated by H. Zohn. (New York: Schocken Books, 1968).

Bentham, J. *Fragments on Government.* Edited by W. Harrison. (Oxford: Basil Blackwell, 1960).

Berlin, I. *The Crooked Timber of Humanity: Chapters in the History of Ideas.* (New York: Alfred Knopf, 1990).

Berry, S. "Social Institutions, and Access to Resources in Africa." *Africa* 59, 1 (1989):41–55.

———. "The Food Crisis and Agrarian Change in Africa: A Review Essay." *African Studies Review* 27, 2 (1983):58–112.

Beyer, J. "Africa." In *World Systems of Traditional Resource Management.* Edited by G. Klee. (New York: Halsted, 1980).

Biles, P. "Starting from Scratch." *Africa Report* (May/June 1991):56.

Blaikie, P. *The Political Economy of Soil Erosion in Developing Countries.* (London: Longman, 1984).

———, and Brookfield, H. "The Degradation of Common Property Resources." In *Land Degradation and Society.* Edited by P. Blaikie and H. Brookfield. (London: Longman, 1987).

Bliss-Guest, P. "Environmental Stress in the East African Region." *Ambio* 12, 6 (1983):290–295.

Bobbio, N. *Democracy and Dictatorship: The Nature and Limits of State Power.* Translated by P. Kennealy (Minneapolis: University of Minnesota Press, 1989).

Bondestam, L. "People and Capitalism in the North Eastern Lowlands of Ethiopia." *Journal of Modern African Studies* 12, 3 (1974):423–439.

Bongarty, M. *The Civil War in Somalia, Its Genesis and Dynamics.* (Uppsala: Scandinavian Institute of African Studies, 1991).

Bornstein, S. "The Case of African Drylands and Balanced Camel Production: A Veterinary Point of View." In *Camels in Development: Sustainable Production in African Drylands.* Edited by A. Hjort af Ornäs. (Uppsala: Scandinavian Institute of African Studies, 1988).

Boutros-Ghali, B. *An Agenda for Peace.* (New York: United Nations, 1992).

Bredvold, L., and Ross, R., editors. *The Philosophy of Edmund Burke.* (Ann Arbor: University of Michigan Press, 1960).

Brock-Due, V. "From Herds to Fish. And from Fish to Food Aid." *NORAD Report* (Oslo: Norwegian Agency for International Development, 1986).

Brokensha, D., et al., editors. *Indigenous Knowledge for Development.* (Washington, D.C.: University Press of America, 1980).

Bull, H. *The Anarchical Society.* (New York: Columbia University Press, 1977).

Burale, A. *Xeerkii Somaalidii Hore.* (Mogadishu: Akadeemiyaha Dhaqanka, 1977).

Burton, R. *First Footsteps in East Africa.* Edited by G. Waterfield. (New York: Praeger, 1966).

Buzan, B. *People, States, and Fear: The National Security Problem in International Relations.* (Chapel Hill: University of North Carolina Press, 1983).

Cabral, A. *Return to the Source.* (New York: Monthly Review Press, 1973).

Cahill, K. *Somalia: A Perspective.* (Albany: State University of New York Press, 1980).

Callaghy, T. "The State and the Development of Capitalism." In *The Precarious Balance.* Edited by D. Rothchild and N. Chazan. (Boulder: Westview Press, 1988).

———, and Rosberg, C., editors. *Socialism in Sub-Saharan Africa: A New Assessment.* (Berkeley: Institute for International Studies, 1979).

Caponigri, A. R. *Time and Idea: The Theory of History in Giambattista Vico.* (London: Routledge & Kegan Paul, 1953).

Caporaso, J., editor. *The Elusive State: International and Comparative Perspectives.* (Newbury Park, Calif.: Sage Publications, 1989).

Carnoy, M. *The State and Political Theory.* (Princeton: Princeton University Press, 1984).

Carter, J. "Annual Message to Congress, January 21, 1980." In *Public Papers of the Presidents of the United States.* (Washington, D.C.: U.S. Government Printing Office, 1981):114–180.

Cassanelli, L. *The Shaping of Somali Society: Reconstruction of the History of a Pastoral People, 1600–1900.* (Philadelphia: University of Pennsylvania Press, 1982).

Castagno, A. "Somali Republic." In *Political Parties and National Integration in Tropical Africa.* Edited by J. Colman and C. Rosberg, Jr. (Berkeley: University of California Press, 1964).

Center for Investigative Reporting, and Moyers, Bill. *Global Dumping Ground: The International Traffic in Hazardous Waste.* (Washington, D.C.: Seven Locks, 1990).

Chambers, R. "Microenvironments Unobserved." Gatekeeper Series No. 22. (London: International Institute for Environment and Development, 1990).

———. *Rural Development: Putting the Last First.* (London: Longman, 1983).

———, Pacey, A., and Thrupp, L., editors. *Farmer First.* (London: Intermediate Technology Publications, 1989).

———, Saxena, N. C., and Shah, T. *To the Hands of the Poor: Water and Trees.* (Boulder: Westview Press, 1989).

Chanock, M. *Law, Custom and Social Order: The Colonial Experience in Malawi and Zambia.* (Cambridge: Cambridge University Press, 1985).

Charney, C. "Political Power and Social Class in the Neo-Colonial African State." *Review of African Political Economy* 38 (1987):48–65.

Chase-Dunn, C. *Global Formation: Structure of the World Economy.* (Oxford: Basil Blackwell, 1989).

Chazan, N. "Patterns of State-Society Incorporation and Disengagement in Africa." In *The Precarious Balance.* Edited by D. Rothchild and N. Chazan. (Boulder: Westview Press, 1988).

———. *An Anatomy of Ghanaian Politics: Managing Political Recession, 1989–1982.* (Boulder: Westview Press, 1983).

Cheru, F. *The Silent Revolution in Africa.* (London: Zed, 1989).

Chhachhi, A. "Forced Identities: The State, Communalism, Fundamentalism and Women in India." In *Women, Islam and the State.* Edited by D. Kandiyoti. (Philadelphia: Temple University Press, 1991).

Clapham, C. "The African State." In *Africa Thirty Years On.* Edited by D. Rimmer. (London: Heinemann, 1991).

———. *Transformation and Continuity in Revolutionary Ethiopia.* (Cambridge: Cambridge University Press, 1988).

Clark, J. *The U.S. Government, Humanitarian Assistance, and the New World Order: A Call for a New Approach.* (Washington, D.C.: U.S. Committee for Refugees Issue Brief, September 1991).

Cliffe, L. "The Conservation Issue in Zimbabwe." *Review of African Political Economy* 42 (1988):48–58.

———, and Moorsom, R. "Rural Class Formation and Ecological Collapse in Botswana." *Review of African Political Economy* 15/16 (1979):35–52.

Cohen, D., and Odhiambo, E. S. A. *Siaya: The Historical Anthropology of an African Landscape.* (London: James Currey, 1989).

Cohen, R. "The State in Africa." *Review of African Political Economy* 5 (1976): 1–3.

Colburn, F., editor. *Everyday Forms of Peasant Resistance.* (Armonk, N.Y.: Sharpe, 1989).

Colchester, M., and Lohmann, L. *The Tropical Forestry Action Plan: What Progress?* (Penang/Sturminster Newton: World Rainforest Movement/ The Ecologist, 1990).

Collingwood, R. G. *Essays in Political Philosophy.* Edited by D. Boucher. (Oxford: Oxford University Press, 1989).

Conway, G. R., and Barbier, E. B. *After the Green Revolution: Sustainable Agriculture for Development.* (London: Earthscan Publications, 1990).

Copans, J. "The Sahelian Drought: Social Services and the Political Economy of Underdevelopment." In *Interpretations of Calamity.* Edited by K. Hewitt. (Boston: Allen & Unwin, 1983).

Costanza, R., editor. *Ecological Economics.* (New York: Columbia University Press, 1991).

Cushman, J. "5 GI's Are Killed as Somalis Down 2 U.S. Helicopters." *New York Times* (4 October 1993):1.

Dagne, T. S. *Somalia: War and Famine.* (Washington, D.C.: Congressional Research Office, 1993).

Dahl, G., and Hjort af Ornäs, A. *Having Herds.* (Stockholm: University of Stockholm, 1976).

Damaska, M. *The Faces of Justice and State Authority.* (New Haven, Conn.: Yale University Press, 1986).

Damrosch, L. (editor). *Enforcing Restraint: Collective Intervention in Internal Conflicts.* (New York: Council on Foreign Relations, 1993).

Dastane, N. G. *Salinity and Other Production Problems and Their Solutions in Irrigated Bananas Grown in the Lower Shabelli Region of Somalia.* (Rome: Food and Agricultural Organization, Som/81/015, 1985).

Davidson, B. "Somalia in 1975: Some Notes and Impressions." *Issue* 5, 1 (1975):19–26.

deGroot, P., Field-Juma, A., and Hall, D. *Taking Root: Revegetation in Semi-Arid Kenya.* (Nairobi/Harare: ACTS Press/Biomass Users' Network, 1992).

de Janvry, A. *The Agrarian Question and Reformism in Latin America.* (Baltimore: Johns Hopkins University Press, 1981).

Del Boca, A. "Dalla guerra nell'Ogaden alla battaglia per Mogadiscio." *Studi Piacenti* (1991):35–96.

Deng, F., and Minear, L. *Filling the Moral Void: Emergency Humanitarian Intervention in Sudan, 1983–1991.* (Washington, D.C.: The Brookings Institution, 1992).

Deng, F., and Zartman, I. W., editors. *Conflict Resolution in Africa.* (Washington, D.C.: The Brookings Institution, 1991).

de Waal, A. *Famine That Kills.* (Oxford: Clarendon Press, 1989).

Dewey, John. *The Public and Its Problems: An Essay in Political Inquiry.* (Chicago: Gateway Books, 1946).

Dhanani, S. "Forestry and Range: A Sector Review." Country Report Series 88–1. (Mogadishu: Food and Agriculture Organization, 1988).

Diamond, L. "Swollen Bureaucracies." *Journal of Modern African Studies* 25, 3 (1987): 567–596.

Dinham, B., and Hines, C. *Agribusiness in Africa.* (London/Trenton, N.J.: Earth Resources/African World Press, 1982).

Dirie, M. F., Wallbanks, K. R., Aden, A., Bornstein, S., and Ibrahim, M. "Camel Trypanosomiasis and Its Vectors in Somalia." *Veterinary Parasitology* 32 (1989):285–291.

Dirie, M. F., Wallbanks, K. R., Molyneux, D. H., Bornstein, S., and Omer, H. A. "Haemorrhagic syndrome associated with T. vivax infections of cattle in Somalia." *Acta Tropica* 42 (1989):291–292.

Dirie, M. F., Wardhere, M., and Farah, M. "Sheep Trypanosomiasis in Somalia." *Tropical Animal Health Periodical* 20 (1988):45–46.

Dixon, J., et al. *Economic Analysis of the Environmental Impacts of Development Projects.* (London: Earthscan Publications, 1986).

Donham, D. "Old Abyssinia and the New Ethiopian Empire: Themes in Social History." In *The Southern Marches of Imperial Ethiopia: Essays in History and Social Anthropology.* Edited by D. Donham and W. James. (Cambridge: Cambridge University Press, 1986).

Dowden, R. "Skeletons Mark the Death of a Country." *The Independent* (25 May 1991):16.

Draper, H. *Karl Marx's Theory of Revolution: State and Bureaucracy,* vol. 1. (New York: Monthy Review Press, 1977).

Drechsel, P., and Zech, W. "Site Conditions and Nutrient Status of *Cordeauxia Edulis (Caesalpiniaceae)* in Its Natural Habitat in Central Somalia." *Economic Botany* 42, 2 (1988):242–249.

Drechsel, P., Zech, W., Kaupenjohann, M., Nurr, E. A., and Klein, O. "About the ecology of *Cordeauxia edulis (yeheb)*—an outstanding multipurpose tree at the Horn of Africa." Institute of Soil Science and Soil Geography, University of Bayreuth, 1987.

Drew, D., and Snow, D. *Making Strategy: An Introduction to National Security Processes and Problems.* (Maxwell Airforce Base, Ala.: Air University Press, 1988).

Drysdale, J. *Somaliland 1991: Report and Reference.* (Hove, England: Global-Stats, Ltd., 1991).

———. *The Somali Dispute.* (London: Pall Mall Press, 1964).

Duffy, C., and Feld, W. "Wither Regional Integration Theory?" In *Comparative Regional Systems: West and East Europe, North America, the Middle East, and Developing Countries.* Edited by W. Feld and G. Boyd. (New York: Pergamon Press, 1980).

Dunn, J. *Interpreting Political Responsibility.* (Cambridge: Polity Press, 1990).

Easton, D. *The Political System.* (New York: Alfred Knopf, 1953).

Economist Intelligence Unit. *Country Report: Uganda, Ethiopia, Somalia, Djibouti.* No. 4 (London: The Economist, 1988).

Ekins, P., and Max-Neef, M., editors. *Real-Life Economics: Understanding Wealth Creation.* (London: Routledge & Kegan Paul, 1992).

Engels, F. *The Origins of the Family, Private Property, and the State.* Edited with an introduction by E. B. Leacock. (New York: International Publishers, 1972).

Ergas, Z., editor. *The African State in Transition.* (New York: St. Martin's Press, 1987).

"Ethiopia: New Government, New Map." *Africa Confidential* 32, 22 (8 November 1991):7.

Evans, J. O., and Powys, J. G. "Camel Husbandry in Kenya: Increasing the Productivity of Ranch Lands." In *The Camelid—an All-Purpose Animal.* Vol. 1, Proceedings from the Khartoum Workshop on Camels. (Uppsala: Scandinavian Institute of African Studies, 1979).

Evans, P., Rueschemeyer, D., and Skoçpol, T., editors. *Bringing the State Back In.* (Cambridge: Cambridge University Press, 1985).

"Excerpts from UN Resolution on Getting Aid to Somalia." *The New York Times* (4 December 1992):A14.

Falenmark, M. "New Ecological Approach to the Water Cycle: Ticket to the Future." *Ambio* 13, 3 (1984).

———. *Close Sesame.* (London: Allison & Busby, 1983).

———. *Sardines.* (London: Allison & Busby, 1981).

Farah, N. *Sweet and Sour Milk.* (London: Allison & Busby, 1979).

Farzin, Y.H. "Food Aid: Positive or Negative Economic Effects in Somalia?" *The Journal of Developing Areas* 25 (1991):261–282.

Fenet, A. "Djibouti: Mini-State on the Horn of Africa." In *Horn of Africa: From "Scramble for Africa" to East-West Conflict.* (Bonn: Forschungsinstitut der Friedrich Ebert Stiftune, 1986):59–69.

Ferguson, A., and Leeuwenburg, J. "Local Mobility and the Spatial Dynamics of Measles in a Rural Area of Kenya." *Geojournal* 5 (1981):315–322.

Ferrari, J. "Oil on Troubled Waters." *Ambio* 12, 6 (1983):354–357.

Field, M., and Golubitsky, M. *Symmetry in Chaos: A Search for Patterns in Mathematics, Art and Nature.* (Oxford: Oxford University Press, 1991).

Finn, D. "Land Use and Abuse in the East African Region." *Ambio* 12, 6 (1983):296–301.

Fisk, M. *The State and Justice: An Essay in Political Theory.* (Cambridge: Cambridge University Press, 1989).

Foreign Broadcast Information Service. *Daily Reports: Sub-Saharan Africa* (Washington, D.C.: U.S. Government, various issues).

Franke, R., and Chasin, B. *Seeds of Famine.* (Montclair, N.J.: Allenheld, 1980).

Friedberg, A. *The Weary Titan.* (Princeton: Princeton University Press, 1988).

Furedi, F. *Mythical Past, Elusive Future: History and Society in an Anxious Age.* (London: Pluto Press, 1992).

Galaty, J. G., Aronson, D., and Salzman, P. C., editors. *The Future of Pastoral Peoples.* (Ottawa: International Development Research Center, 1980).

Gelb, L. "Shoot to Feed Somalia." *New York Times* (19 November 1992):A27.

Gerlach, J. "A U.N. Army for the New World Order?" *Orbis* (Spring 1993): 233–236.

Gerschenkron, A. *Economic Backwardness in Historical Perspective.* (Cambridge: Harvard University Press, 1962).

Gersony, R. *Why Somalis Flee: Synthesis of Accounts of Conflict Experience in Northern Somalia.* (Washington, D.C.: United States Department of State, August 1989).

Gerstin, J. "No Permanent Condition: The Rainforests of Africa." In *Lessons of the Rainforest.* Edited by S. Head and R. Heinzman. (San Francisco: Sierra Club, 1990).

Geshekter, C. "Anti-Colonialism and Class Formation: The Eastern Horn of Africa, 1920–1950." Paper presented at the Second International Congress of Somali Studies, Hamburg, August 1983.

———. "Entrepreneurs, Livestock and Politics: British Somaliland, 1920–1950." In *Entreprises et Entrepreneurs en Afrique: XIXe et XXe Siecle.* Edited by C. Coquery-Vidrovitch. (Paris: Editions L'Harmattan, 1983).

Goldman, A. "Stand-Off in Somaliland." BBC African Service Radio, 13 March 1992.

Gorman, R. *Political Conflict in the Horn of Africa.* (New York: Praeger, 1981).

Gottlieb, G. *States Against Nations: A New Approach to Ethnic Conflicts, the Decline of Sovereignty and the Dilemmas of Collective Security.* (New York: Council on Foreign Relations, 1993).

Government of Somalia. *Three-Year Development Plan, 1979–1981.* (Mogadishu: 1979).

Grainger, A. *The Threatening Desert: Controlling Desertification.* (London: Earthscan Publications, 1990).

Gray, C. *War, Peace, and Victory: Strategy and Statecraft for the Next Century.* (New York: Simon and Schuster, 1990).

Great Britain, Public Records Office, Colonial Records Office. Series 535, No. 5, Cordeaux (30 June 1906) and Notes on Military Transport.

———. *Annual Colonial Reports,* No. 1180, Somaliland 1937. (London, 1938).

———. Series 535, No. 52, Archer (25 February 1918).

————. Series 535, No. 51, "Notes on System of Relieving Destitutes in Berbera, February 1918." (February 1918).

————. Series 535, No. 46, L. M. Kent (30 January 1917).

————. Series 535, No. 40, A. S. Lawrence (20 June 1915).

————. Series 535, No. 35, Archer (28 October 1914).

————. Series 535, No. 33 (3 July 1913).

————. Series 535, No. 30 (27 June 1913).

————. Series 535, No. 9 (1907).

————. Series 535, No. 8 (1907).

Green, L. *The Authority of the State*. (New York: Clarendon Press, 1988).

Gurr, T. "Tensions in the Horn of Africa." In *World Politics and Tension Areas*. Edited by F. Gross. (New York: New York University Press, 1966).

Guyer, J., editor. *Feeding African Cities*. (Manchester: Manchester University Press, 1987).

Gyerye, K. *An Essay on African Philosophical Thought*. (Cambridge: Cambridge University Press, 1987).

Hadjor, K. *Africa in an Era of Crisis*. (Trenton, N.J.: Africa World Press, 1990).

Hadrawi, M. *Hal la Qalay Ragdeed*. (Mogadishu: n.p., 1973).

————. *Wadnahaan Far Ku Hayaa*. (Mogadishu: n.p., 1973).

Hadrawi, M., et al. *Aqoon iyo Afgarad*. (Mogadishu: Wasaaradda Waxbarashada iyo Barbaarinta, 1972).

Hamlin, A., and Peffit, P., editors. *The Good Polity: Normative Analysis of the State*. (Oxford: Basil Blackwell, 1989).

Hanley, G. *Warriors and Strangers*. (London: Hamish Hamilton, 1971).

Harbeson, J. "The International Politics of Identity in the Horn of Africa." In *Africa in World Politics*. Edited by J. Harbeson and D. Rothchild. (Boulder: Westview Press, 1991).

Hardoy, J., and Satterthwaite, D. *Squatter Citizen: Life in the Urban Third World*. (London: Earthscan Publications, 1989).

Hardoy, J., Cairncross, S., and Satterthwaite, D., editors. *The Poor Die Young: Housing and Health in the Third World*. (London: Earthscan Publications, 1990).

Harrison, P. *The Greening of Africa*. (London: Penguin Books, 1987).

Harsch, R. "Somalia: Restoring Hope." *Africa Recovery*, Briefing Paper. (New York: United Nations, January 1993).

Harsch, R. "Strengthened Somalia Effort Threatened by Continued Fighting." *Africa Recovery* (New York: United Nations, 1993).

————. "Strengthened Somalia Relief Effort Threatened by Continued Fighting." *Africa Recovery*, Briefing Paper. (New York: United Nations, 1991).

Harvey, D. *The Urbanization of Capital: Studies in the History and Theory of Capitalism*. (Baltimore: John Hopkins University Press, 1985).

————. *The Limits to Capital*. (Chicago: University of Chicago Press, 1982).

Hedlund, H. "Contradictions in the Peripheralization of a Pastoral Society." *Review of African Political Economy* 15/16 (1979):15–34.

Hegel, *Lectures on the Philosophy of World History*. (Cambridge: Cambridge University, 1975).

Hegel, *The Philosophy of Right*. Translated with notes by T. M. Knox. (Oxford: Oxford University Press, 1967).

Held, D. *Political Theory and the Modern State: Essays on State, Power, and Democracy*. (Stanford: Stanford University Press, 1989).

————. *Models of Democracy*. (Stanford: Stanford University Press, 1987).

Helland, J. "Some Issues in the Study of Pastoralists and the Development of Pastoralism." Working Document 14. (Nairobi: International Livestock Center for Africa, 1980).

Henze, P. *The Horn of Africa: From War to Peace*. (New York: St. Martin's Press, 1991).

Hess, R. *Italian Colonialism in Somalia*. (Chicago: University of Chicago Press, 1966).

Hill, S., and Rothchild, D. "The Contagion of Political Conflict in Africa and the World." *Journal of Conflict Resolution* 30, 4 (September 1987):716–735.

Hintze, O. *The Historical Essays of Otto Hintze*. Edited by F. Gilbert. (Oxford: Oxford University Press, 1975).

Hitchcock, R. K., and Hussein, H. "Agricultural and Non-Agricultural Settlements for the Drought-Afflicted Pastoralists in Somalia." *Disasters* 11 (1987):30–39.

Hjort af Ornäs, A., editor. *Camels in Development: Sustainable Production in African Drylands*. (Uppsala: Scandinavian Institute of African Studies, 1987).

Hobbes, T. *The Leviathan*. (Harmondsworth, U.K.: Penguin Books, 1968).

Hodgkin, T. "The African Middle Class," *Corona* (March 1956):88.

Hopf, T. "Managing Soviet Disintegration: A Demand for Behavioral Regimes." *International Security* 17, 1 (Summer 1992):44–75.

Horowitz, M., and Little, P. "African Pastoralism and Poverty: Some Implications for Drought and Famine." In *Drought and Hunger in Africa*. Edited by M. Glantz. (Cambridge: Cambridge University Press, 1987).

Horowitz, M., and Salem-Murdock, M. "The Political Economy of Desertification in White Nile Province, Sudan." In *Lands at Risk*. Edited by M. Horowitz and P. Little. (Boulder: Westview Press, 1987).

Huizinga, J. *Men and Ideas: History, the Middle Ages, the Renaissance*. (Princeton: Princeton University Press, 1959).

Hunter, F. *Grammar of the Somali Language Together with a Short Historical Notice*. (Bombay: n.p.,1880).

Huntington, S. *The Third Wave: Democratization in the Late Twentieth Century*. (Tulsa: University of Oklahoma Press, 1991).

Hussein, A. "The Political Economy of Famine in Ethiopia." In *Rehab: Drought and Famine in Ethiopia*. Edited by A. Hussein. (London: International African Institute, 1976).

Hussein, M. A., and Hjort af Ornäs, A. "Camel Herd Dynamics in Southern Somalia: Long Term Development and Milk Production Implications." In *Camels in Development*. Edited by A. Hjort af Ornäs. (Uppsala: Scandinavian Institute of African Studies, 1989).

Hyden, G. *Beyond Ujaama in Tanzania: Underdevelopment and an Uncaptured Peasantry*. (Berkeley: University of California Press, 1980).

Ignatieff, M. *The Needs of Strangers: An Essay on Privacy, Solidarity, and the Politics of Being Human*. (Harmondsworth, U.K.: Penguin Books, 1984).

Independent Commission on International Humanitarian Issues. *The Encroaching Desert: The Consequences of Human Failure*. (London: Zed Books, 1986).

International Fund for Science (IFS). *Trees for Development in Sub-Saharan Africa*. Proceedings of a regional seminar held by the IFS. (Stockholm: IFS, 1989).

International Institute for Environment and Development/Overseas Development Institute. "Rethinking Range Ecology." Issues Paper. Drylands

Programme. (London: International Institute for Environment and Development, 1992).

International Labour Office. *Economic Transformation in a Socialist Framework.* (Addis Ababa: Jobs and Skills Programme for Africa, 1977).

International Monetary Fund. *Somalia—Recent Economic Developments.* (Washington, D.C.: IMF, 1983, 1985, 1987, 1988, 1989).

————. *Supplement to the Staff Report for 1988.* Article IV, Consultation (Washington, D.C.: IMF, 3 June 1988).

Iye, A. *Le Verdict de L'Arbre (Go'aankii Geedka): Le Xeer Issa Etude d'une Democratic Pastorale.* (Djibouti: n.p. 1990).

Jackson, R. *Quasi-States: Sovereignty, International Relations and the Third World.* (New York: Cambridge University Press, 1990).

————, and Rosberg, C. "Why Weak African States Persist." In *The State and Development in the Third World.* Edited by A. Kohli. (Princeton: Princeton University Press, 1986).

Jamal, V. "Somalia: Survival in a 'Doomed' Economy." *International Labour Review* 127, 6 (1988):783–812.

————. "Nomads and Farmers: Incomes and Rural Poverty in Somalia." In *Agrarian Policies and Rural Poverty in Africa.* Edited by D. Ghai and S. Radwan. (Geneva: International Labour Office, 1983).

James, F. L. *The Unknown Horn of Africa: An Exploration from Berbera to the Leopard River.* (London: George Philip, 1888).

Jerve, A. M. "Livestock Trypanosomiasis and the Pastoral Crisis in Semi-arid Africa: An Approach to Future Land-Use with Examples from Southern Somalia Cattle, Sheep, Goats, Pest Control, Land Use Planning." DERAP Working Papers No. A 256. (Bergen, Norway: Chr. Michelsens Institute, 1982).

Job, B., editor. *The Insecurity Dilemma: National Security of Third World States.* (Boulder: Lynne Rienner Publishers, 1992).

Jodha, N. "Rural Common Property Resources: A Growing Crisis." Gatekeeper Series, No. 24. (London: International Institute for Environment and Development, 1991).

Johnson, J. *Heellooy Heellooy: The Development of the Genre Heello in Modern Somali Poetry.* (Bloomington: Indiana University Press, 1974).

Johnston, B., and Kilby, P. *Agricultural Transformation: Economic Strategies in Late-Developing Countries.* (New York: Oxford University Press, 1975).

Jordan, B. *The State: Authority and Autonomy.* (Oxford: Basil Blackwell, 1985).

Jowitt, K. "Scientific Socialism in Africa." In *Socialism in Sub-Saharan Africa: A New Assessment.* Edited by C. Rosberg and T. Callaghy. (Berkeley: Institute for International Studies, 1979).

Juma, C. *The Gene Hunters.* (London and Princeton: Zed Books and Princeton University Press, 1989).

Kabjits, G. L. *Maahmaahyada Somaalida ee ku qoran afka Somaaliga iyo afka Ruushka oo ay weheliyaan maahmaahyada Ruushka ee ay isu dhigmaan.* (Moscow: Izdatel'stovo Nauka, 1983).

Kalyalya, D., Mhlanga, K., Semboja, J., and Seidman, A. *Aid and Development in Southern Africa: A Participatory Learning Process.* (Trenton, N.J.: Africa World Press, 1988).

The Kampala Document: Towards a Conference on Security, Stability, Development and Cooperation in Africa. (Kampala, Uganda, 19–22 May 1991).

Kaplan, I. "The Society and Its Environment." In *Somalia: A Country Study*. Edited by H. Nelson. (Washington, D.C.: U.S. Government Printing Office, 1982).

Kaplan, I., et al. *Area Handbook for Somalia*. (Washington, D.C.: U.S. Government Printing Office, 1987).

Kaplan, R. "Tales from the Bazaar." *The Atlantic* 270, 2 (August 1992):59.

Kapteijns, L. *Women and the Somali Pastoral Tradition: Corporate Kinship and Capitalist Transformation in Northern Somalia*. Working Paper No. 153. (Boston: Boston University African Studies Center, 1991).

————, and Spaulding, J. "Counsels of Despair: Social Vignettes of 19th-Century Colonial Aden." Forthcoming.

————. "Class Formation and Gender in Precolonial Somali Society: A Research Agenda." *Northeast African Studies* 11, 1 (1989):19–38.

Kazancigil, A., editor. *The State in Global Perspectives*. (Brookfield, Vt.: Gower, 1986).

Kendie, D. "Which Way the Horn of Africa: Disintegration or Confederation?" Paper presented at the Sixth Michigan State University Conference on Northeast Africa, East Lansing, 23–25 April 1992.

Kennedy, J. F. "Remarks by President Kennedy at a Reception Marking African Independence." In *American Foreign Policy, Current Documents* (Washington, D.C.: U.S. Government Printing Office, 1961).

"Kenya: Forcible Return of Somali Refugees and Government Repression of Kenyan Somalis," *Africa Watch* (17 November 1989).

Khadiagala, G. "Security in Southern Africa: Cross-national Learning." *Jerusalem Journal of International Relations* 14, 3 (1992):82–97.

Khaldun, I. *The Muqaddimah: An Introduction to History*. Translated by F. Rosenthal. (Princeton: Princeton University Press, 1967).

Kirki, J. W. *A Grammar of the Somali Language*. (Cambridge: Cambridge University Press, 1936).

Kitching, G. *Development and Underdevelopment in Historical Perspective: Populism, Nationalism and Industrialization*. (London: Methuen, 1982).

Kloos, H. "Development, Drought, and Famine in the Awash Valley of Ethiopia." *African Studies Review* 25, 4 (1982):21–48.

Kohli, A., editor. *The State and Development in the Third World*. (Princeton: Princeton University Press, 1986).

Kramer, R. "Suffering Rises as Civil Strife Persists." *African News* (20 July–2 August 1992):1.

Kundaeli, J. "Making Conservation and Development Compatible." *Ambio* 12, 6 (1983):326–331.

Laitin, D. "The Political Crisis in Somalia." *Horn of Africa* 5, 2 (1982):60–64.

————, and Samatar, S. *Somalia: Nation in Search of a State*. (Boulder: Westview Press, 1987).

————. "Somalia's Military Government and Scientific Socialism." In *Socialism in Sub-Saharan Africa: A New Assessment*. Edited by C. Rosberg and T. Callaghy. (Berkeley: Institute for International Studies, 1979).

Lan, D. *Guns and Rain: Guerrillas and Spirit Mediums in Zimbabwe*. (Berkeley/London: University of California/James Currey, 1985).

Lancaster, C. "The Horn of Africa." In *After the Wars: Reconstruction in Afghanistan, Indochina, Central America, Southern Africa, and the Horn of Africa*. Edited by A. Lake. (Washington, D.C.: Overseas Development Council, 1990).

Lange, K. "Horn of Misery." *Africa News* (11–24 May 1992):9.

Laurance, M. *A Tree for Poverty.* (Nairobi: Eagle Press, 1954).

Lefebvre, J. *Arms for the Horn: U.S. Security Policy in Ethiopia and Somalia, 1953–1991.* (Pittsburgh: University of Pittsburgh Press, 1991).

Lefort, R. *Ethiopia: An Heretical Revolution?* (London: Zed Books, 1983).

Legum, C. "Somali Liberation Songs." *Journal of Modern African Studies* 1, 4 (October 1987): 503–519.

Lewis, H., and Wisner, B. "Refugee Rehabilitation in Somalia: Report of a Mission." Regional Planning and Area Development Project Consulting Report No. 5. (Madison: University of Wisconsin, 1981).

Lewis, I. M. *A Modern History of Somalia.* (Boulder: Westview Press, 1988).

————. "In the Land of the Living Dead." *The Sunday Times* (London, 30 August 1992):8–9.

————. *A Pastoral Democracy: A Study of Pastoralism and Politics Among the Northern Somali of the Horn of Africa.* (London: Oxford University Press, 1981).

————. "Lineage Continuity and Modern Commerce in Northern Somaliland." In *Markets in Africa.* Edited by P. Bohannan and G. Dalton. (Evanston: Northwestern University Press, 1962).

Lewis, P. "Disaster Relief Proposal Worries Third World." *New York Times* (13 November 1991):A9.

Li, R., and Thompson, W. "The 'Coup Contagion' Hypothesis." *Journal of Conflict Resolution* 19, 1 (March 1975):63–87.

Lindijer, K. "Mayhem in Northern Somalia." *Daily Nation* (29 March 1991):11.

Little, P., and Horowitz, M., editors. *Lands at Risk in the Third World: Local-Level Perspectives.* (Boulder: Westview Press, 1987).

Livingstone, I. *Poverty in Africa.* (New York: Oxford University Press, 1988).

Locke, J. *Two Treatises of Government.* (Cambridge: Cambridge University Press, 1963).

Lonsdale, J. "States and Social Process in Africa: A Historical Survey," *African Studies Review* 24, 2/3 (1981):139–226.

Loughran, K. S., Loughran, J. L., Johnson, J. W., and Samatar, S. S., editors. *Somalia in Word and Image.* (Washington, D.C./Bloomington: Foundation for Cross Cultural Understanding/Indiana University Press, 1986).

Lutz, J. "The Diffusion of Political Phenomena in Sub-Saharan Africa." *Journal of Political and Military Sociology* 17, 1 (Spring 1989):93–114.

Lyons, T. "The Horn of Africa Regional Politics: A Hobbesian World." In *The Dynamics of Regional Politics.* Edited by H. Wiggins. (New York: Columbia University Press, 1992).

MacGaffey, J. *Entrepreneurs and Parasites: The Struggle for Indigenous Capitalism in Zaire.* (New York: Cambridge University Press, 1987).

————. "Women and Class Formation in a Dependent Economy." In *Women and Class in Africa.* Edited by C. Robertson and I. Berger. (New York: Holmes and Meyer, 1986).

Machiavelli, N. "Lo Stato." In *The Prince.* (Harmondsworth, U.K.: Penguin Books, 1975).

————. *The Discourses.* (London: Routledge & Kegan Paul, 1950).

Macpherson, C. P. *The Life and Times of Liberal Democracy.* (Oxford: Oxford University Press, 1977).

Maino, M. *La Lingua Somalia—Strumento d'insegnemento Professionale.* (Alessandria, Italy: Ferrari, Occella & Co., 1953).

Makdisi, J. *Beirut Fragments: A War Memoir*. (New York: Persea Books, 1990).
Malinowski, B. *Argonauts of the Western Pacific*. (London: Routledge & Kegan Paul, 1961 and 1921), 9.
Mandeeq. "An Togobelney." (Song.) Hargeisa, 1964–1965.
Marglin, F. A., and Marglin, S. A., editors. *Dominating Knowledge*. (Oxford: Clarendon Press, 1990).
Mariam, A. G. "Pastoral Systems at Loggerheads." In *Camels in Development*. Edited by A. Hjort af Ornäs. (Uppsala: Scandinavian Institute of African Studies, 1988).
Markakis, J. *National and Class Conflict in the Horn of Africa*. (London: Zed Books, 1990).
———. "The Ishaq-Ogaden Dispute." In *Ecology and Politics: Environmental Stress and Security in Africa*. Edited by A. Hjort af Ornas and M. Salih. (Stockholm: Scandinavian Institute of African Studies, 1989).
Markovitz, I. L. *Power and Class in Africa*. (Englewood Cliffs, N.J.: Prentice-Hall, 1977).
Marx, K. *The Critique of Hegel's Philosophy of Right*. Edited and Introduced by J. O'Malley. (Cambridge: Cambridge University Press, 1970).
———. *The German Ideology*. (London: Lawrence & Wishart, 1965).
———. *The Eighteenth Brumaire of Louis Bonaparte*. (New York: International Publishers, 1963).
———, and Engels, F. *The Communist Manifesto*. (Harmondsworth, U.K.: Penguin Books, 1987).
Mbitiru, C. "Fighting Breaks Out in Northern Somalia." Associated Press, 30 December 1991.
McCarthy, J.W. "A Soil and Water Conservation Project in Two Sites: Seventeen Years Later." *AID Project Impact Evaluation Report*, No. 62. (Washington, D.C.: U.S. Agency for International Development, 1985).
Meillassoux, C. *Qui se nourrit de la famine en Afrique?* (Paris: Maspero, 1973).
Melander, G. *Refugees in Somalia*. Research Report No. 56. (Uppsala: Scandinavian Institute of African Studies, 1980).
Michelsen, A., and Rosendahl, S. "Mycorrhizal symbiosis in *Acacia-Commiphora* bushland in Somalia and the significance of VA-mycorrhizal fungi for re-vegetation of degraded semi-arid areas." *Mitteilungen aus dem Institut fur Allgemeine Botanik Hamburg* 23a (1990):387–394.
Migdal, J. *Strong Societies and Weak States*. (Princeton: Princeton University Press, 1988).
Miliband, R. *Marxism and Politics*. (Oxford: Oxford University Press, 1922).
Mill, J. *An Essay on Government*. (Cambridge: Cambridge University Press, 1937).
Mitchell, A. "Fifth Horseman of Somalia: Stealing." *New York Times* (24 January 1993):7, 16.
Mogadishu Radio. "Aidid Decries Kenya's Treatment of Refugees." In *Foreign Broadcast Information Service, Daily Report: Sub-Saharan Africa* (19 August 1992):5.
Mogadishu Radio. "SLA Condemns Kenyan Aid to Barre 'Remnants.'" *Foreign Broadcast Information Service, Daily Report: Sub-Saharan Africa* (27 July 1992):6.
Mohamed, M. A. "Etude Géologique et Hydrologique du Bassin Central Somalien." Thèse de Docorat. Université de Besançon, France, 1983.

Mohamed, O. "Calanyaho." (Song.) Hargeisa, 1962–1963.

Mohamoud, O. "Somalia: Crisis and Decay in an Authoritarian Regime." *Horn of Africa* 4, 3 (1981):7–11.

Molutsi, P. "Environment and Peasant Consciousness in Botswana." *Review of African Political Economy* 42 (1988):40–47.

Monod, T., editor. *Pastoralism in Tropical Africa*. (London: Oxford University Press, 1975).

Mooney, M. *Vico and the Tradition of Rhetoric*. (Princeton: Princeton University Press, 1991).

Moris, J. *Extension Alternatives for Africa*. Agricultural Administration Unit Occasional Paper No. 7. (London: Overseas Development Institute, 1991).

Morrow, L. "Africa: The Scramble for Existence." *Time* (7 September 1992): 40–46.

Mortimore, M. *Adapting to Drought*. (Cambridge: Cambridge University Press, 1989).

Mudimbe, V. Y. *The Invention of Africa: Gnosis, Philosophy, and the Order of Knowledge*. (Bloomington: University of Indiana Press, 1988).

Mumford, L. *The Conduct of Life*. (New York: Harcourt Brace Jovanovich, 1951).

————. *The Condition of Man*. (New York: Harcourt Brace Jovanovich, 1944).

Mumin, H. *Leopard Among the Women: Shabeelnaagood, A Somali Play*. Translated with an introduction by B. W. Andrzejewski. (London: Oxford University Press, 1974).

Munslow, B., O'Keefe, P., Pankhurst, D., and Philips, P. "Energy and Development on the African East Coast: Somalia, Kenya, Tanzania and Mozambique." *Ambio* 12, 6 (1983):332–337.

Mustafa, I. E. "An Appeal for a Modified Camel Productivity." In *Camels in Development: Sustainable Production in African Drylands*. Edited by A. Hjort af Ornäs. (Uppsala: Scandinavian Institute of African Studies, 1988).

Nairobi KTN Television. "USC Forces Raid Kenya, Search for Siad." *Foreign Broadcast Information Service, Daily Report: Sub-Sahara Africa* (28 April 1992):7.

Naji, A. "Dalkaygow." (Song.) Geneva (13 June 1992).

————. "Qomamo." (Song.) Geneva (13 June 1992).

National Academy of Sciences. *Scientists and Human Rights in Somalia*. (Washington, D.C.: National Academy Press, 1988).

National Research Council. *Food Production Systems and Environmental Rehabilitation in Somalia*. (Washington, D.C.: U.S Agency for International Development, Bureau for Science and Technology, Somali Research Group, 1981).

Nelan, B. "A Very Private War." *Time* (14 January 1991):25.

Nemeth, M. "City of Slaughter." *McLean's* (14 January 1991):28.

Niamir, M. "Traditional woodland management techniques of African pastoralists." *Unasylva* 41, 160 (1990):49–58.

"Not a Nice Way to Come Home." *The Economist* (9 July 1988):48–49.

Nozick, R. *Anarchy, State and Utopia*. (New York: Basic Books, 1974).

Nyong'o, P. "The Implications of Crises and Conflicts in the Upper Nile Valley." In *Conflict Resolution in Africa*. Edited by F. Deng and I. W. Zartman. (Washington, D.C.: The Brookings Institution, 1991).

Oakeshott, M. "Political Education." In *Philosophy, Politics, and Society*. Edited by P. Laslatt. (Oxford: Basil Blackwell, 1956).

O'Connor, J. *The Meaning of Crisis*. (Oxford: Basil Blackwell, 1987).

O'Keefe, P. "Toxic Terrorism." *Review of African Political Economy* 42 (1988):84–90.

Omaar, R. and de Waal, A. *Somalia, Operation Restore Hope: A Preliminary Assessment.* (London: Africa Rights, 1993).

Ostrom, E. *Governing the Commons*. (Cambridge: Cambridge University Press, 1990).

Ottaway, M. "Nationalism Unbound: The Horn of Africa Revisited." *SAIS Review* 12, 2 (Summer-Fall 1992):111–128.

Pacey, A. *The Culture of Technology*. (Cambridge: MIT Press, 1983).

Pacey, A., with Cullis, A. *Rainwater Harvesting: The Collection of Rainfall and Runoff in Rural Areas*. (London: Intermediate Technology Publications, 1986).

Packard, R. "Industrial Production, Health and Disease in Sub-Saharan Africa." *Social Science and Medicine* 28, 5 (1989):475–496.

Pankhurst, R. "The Trade of the Gulf of Aden Ports of Africa in the Nineteenth and Early Twentieth Centuries." *Journal of Ethiopian Studies* 3, 1 (1965):36–82.

Parkipuny, M. "Some Crucial Aspects of the Maasai Predicament." In *African Socialism in Practice: The Tanzanian Experience*. Edited by A. Coulson. (London: Spokesman, 1979).

Parson, J. "Class, Cattle and the State in Botswana." *Journal of Southern African Studies* 7, 2 (1981):236–255.

Patman, R. *The Soviet Union in the Horn of Africa: The Diplomacy of Intervention and Disengagement*. (Cambridge: Cambridge University Press, 1990).

Pearce, D., Barbier, E., and Markandya, A. *Sustainable Development: Economics and Environment in the Third World*. (London: Earthscan Publications, 1990).

Pearce, D., and Turner, R. K. *Economics of Natural Resources and the Environment*. (Baltimore: Johns Hopkins University Press, 1990).

Perlez, J. "How One Family, Some of It, Survives." *New York Times* (16 November 1992):A1, A6.

———. "A Somali Place That Even the Alms Givers Fear." *New York Times* (9 November 1992):A3.

———. "U.N. Let the Somali Famine Get Out of Hand, Aide Says." *New York Times* (16 August 1992):A12.

———. "Factional Fighting in Somalia Terrorizes and Ruins Capital." *New York Times* (8 December 1991):1.

Physicians for Human Rights. "Somalia: No Mercy in Mogadishu." (Washington, D.C.: Africa Watch, 26 March 1992).

Plato. *The Republic*. (Harmondsworth, U.K.: Penguin Books, 1974).

———. *Laws*. (Harmondsworth, U.K.: Penguin Books, 1970).

Post, K., and Wright, P. *Socialism and Underdevelopment*. (New York: Routledge, 1989).

Pradervand, P. *Listening to Africa*. (New York: Praeger, 1989).

Prendergast, J. "Somalia's Silent Slaughter," *America* (24 March 1990).

Prothero, R. M. *Migrants and Malaria*. (London: Longman, 1965).

Prothero, R. M., editor. *People and Land in Africa South of the Sahara*. (New York: Oxford, 1972).

Rabeh, O. "Somalia: Psychology of the Nomad." Paper presented at the Congress of the International Somali Studies Association, Hamburg, Germany, 1–6 August 1983.

Radcliffe-Brown, A. R. "Preface." In *African Political Systems*. Edited by M. Fortes and E. E. Evan-Pritchard. (Oxford: Oxford University Press, 1970 and 1940).

Rafferty, F. W., editor. *The Works of Edmund Burke VI*. (Oxford: Oxford University Press, 1928).

Raikes, P. *Modernizing Hunger: Famine, Food and Farm Policy in the EEC and Africa*. (London: James Currey, 1988).

Ranger, T. *Peasant Consciousness and Guerrilla War in Zimbabwe*. (London/Berkeley: James Currey/University of California Press, 1985).

Rau, B. *From Feast to Famine*. (London: Zed Books, 1981).

Ravenhill, J. "The Theory and Practice of Regional Integration in East Africa." In *Integration and Disintegration in East Africa*. Edited by C. Potholm and R. Fredland. (Washington, D.C.: University Press of America, 1980).

Reij, C. "Indigenous Soil and Water Conservation in Africa." Gatekeeper Series, No. 27. (London: International Institute for Environment and Development, 1990).

Republic of Kenya. *Kenya-Somalia Relations: Narrative of Four Years of Inspired Aggression and Direct Subversion Mounted by the Somali Republic Against the Government and People of the Republic of Kenya*. (Nairobi: Government Printer, 1967).

Republic of Somalia. *French Somaliland: A Classic Colonial Case*. (Mogadishu: n.p., 1965).

———. *Somalia: A Divided Nation Seeking Reunification*. (Mogadishu: Ministry of Information, 1965).

———, Planning and Coordinating Commission for Economic and Social Development, *First Five-Year Plan, 1963–1967*. (Mogadishu: n.p., July 1963).

Resnick, P. *The Masks of Proteus*. (Montreal: McGill-Queens's University Press, 1990).

Reusse, E. "Somalia's Nomadic Livestock Economy: Its Response to a Profitable Export Opportunity." *World Animal Review* 43 (1982):2–11.

Richards, R. *Indigenous Agricultural Revolution: Ecology and Food Production in West Africa*. (London: Hutchinson, 1985).

———. "'Alternative' Strategies for the African Environment: 'Folk Ecology' as a Basis for Community Oriented Agricultural Development." In *African Environment: Problems and Perspectives*. Edited by R. Richards. African Environmental Report 1. (London: International African Institute, 1975).

Ridgeway, J. *Who Owns the Earth*. (New York: Collier, 1980).

Rigby, P. *Persistent Pastoralists: Nomadic Societies in Transition*. (London: Zed Books, 1985).

Riker, W. *Liberalism Against Populism*. (San Francisco: W. H. Freeman, 1982).

Rinehart, R. "Historical Setting." In *Somalia: A Country Study*. Edited by H. Nelson. (Washington, D.C.: U.S. Government Printing Office, 1982).

Rirash, M. A. "Camel Herding and Its Effect on Somali Literature." In *Camels in Development: Sustainable Production in African Drylands*. Edited by A. Hjort af Ornäs. (Uppsala: Scandinavian Institute of African Studies, 1988).

Rocheleau, D., Weber, F., and Field-Juma, A. *Agroforestry in Dryland Africa.* (Nairobi: International Council for Research on Agroforestry, 1988).

Rodney, V. S., "Coral Reefs of the Western Indian Ocean: A Threatened Heritage." *Ambio* 12, 6 (1983):349–353.

Rogers, B. *The Domestication of Woman.* (London: Tavistock, 1980).

Rothchild, D., and Chazan, N., editors. *The Precarious Balance.* (Boulder: Westview Press, 1988).

Roundy, R. W. "Altitudinal Mobility and Disease Hazards for Ethiopian Populations." *Economic Geography* 52 (1976):103–115.

Rousseau, J. J. *The Social Contract.* Translated by M. Cranston. (London: Penguin Books, 1968).

———. *The First and Second Discourses.* Edited by R. D. Masters. (New York: St. Martin's Press, 1964).

Ruiz, H. *Beyond the Headlines: Refugees in the Horn.* (Washington, D.C.: U.S. Committee for Refugees, 1988).

Rutagwenda, R. "The State of Knowledge on Camel Diseases in Northern Kenya." In *Camel Pastoralism Seminar in Marsabit.* (1984).

Sachs, W., editor. *The Development Dictionary: A Guide to Knowledge as Power.* (London: Zed Books, 1992).

Samatar, A. "Structural Adjustment, Private Foreign Investment and Development: Bananas, Boom and Poverty in Somalia." *Economic Geography*, forthcoming.

———. "Destruction of State and Society: Beyond the Tribal Convention." *Journal of Modern African Studies* 30, 4 (1992): 625–641.

———. "Social Classes and Economic Restructuring in Pastoral Africa: The Somali Experience." *African Studies Review* 35, 1 (1992):101–128.

———. *The State and Rural Transformation in Northern Somalia 1884–1986.* (Madison: University of Wisconsin Press, 1989).

———, Salisbury, L., and Bascom, J. "The Political Economy of Livestock Marketing in Somalia." *African Economic History* 17 (1988):81–97.

———. "Merchant Capital, International Livestock Trade, and Pastoral Development in Somalia." *Canadian Journal of African Studies* 21, 3 (1987):355–374.

Samatar, A., and Samatar, A. I. "The Material Roots of the Suspended African State: Arguments from Somalia." *Journal of Modern African Studies* 25, 4 (1987):669–690.

Samatar, A. I. "In Search of the Somali Wazi: From Feral Politics to Covenantal Order." Forthcoming.

———. "Under Siege: Blood, Power, and the Somali State." In Assefa, H., and Khadiagala, G. (editors). *Conflict and Conflict Resolution in the Horn of Africa.* (Washington, D.C.: The Brookings Institution, forthcoming).

———. "Somali Studies: Towards an Alternative Epistemology." *Northeast African Studies* 11, 1 (1989):3–17.

———. *Socialist Somalia: Rhetoric and Reality.* (London: Zed Books, 1988).

———. "Somalia's Impasse: State Power and Dissent Politics." *Third World Quarterly* 9, 3 (July 1987):871–890.

———. (editor). "Somalia: Crises of State and Society." Special issue, *Africa Today* 32, 3 (1985):5–70.

Samatar, S. *Somalia: A Nation in Turmoil.* A Minority Rights Report. (London: The Minority Rights Group, 1991).

————. "The Somali Dilemma: Nation in Search of a State." In *Partitioned Africans: Ethnic Relations Across Africa's International Boundaries, 1884–1984*. Edited by A. Asiwaju. (New York: St. Martin's Press, 1985).

————. *Oral Poetry and Somali Nationalism*. (Cambridge: Cambridge University Press, 1982).

Schaar, J. *Legitimacy and the Modern State*. (New Brunswick, Canada: Transaction Books, 1981).

Scheffer, D. "Toward a Modern Doctrine of Humanitarian Intervention." *University of Toledo Law Review* 23, 2 (Winter 1992):253–293.

Schifter, Assistant Secretary. Letter to *New York Times*, 18 August 1989.

Schmitt, C. *Political Theology*. Translated by G. Schwab. (Cambridge: The MIT Press, 1985).

Schraeder, P. "Ethnic Politics in Djibouti: From 'Eye of the Hurricane' to 'Boiling Cauldron.'" *African Affairs* 92, 367 (April 1993):203–221.

Scott, J. C. *Domination and the Arts of Resistance: Hidden Transcripts*. (New Haven, Conn.: Yale University Press, 1990).

————. *The Weapons of the Weak*. (New Haven, Conn.: Yale University Press, 1985).

"Seeking Refuge, Finding Terror: The Widespread Rape of Somali Women Refugees in North Western Africa." *Africa Watch, Women's Rights Project* 5, 13 (4 October 1993):1–24.

Selznick, P. *The Moral Commonwealth: Social Theory and the Promise of Community*. (Berkeley: University of California Press, 1992).

Sen, G., and Grown, C. *Development, Crises, and Alternative Visions: Third World Women's Perspectives*. (New York: Monthly Review Press, 1987).

Sheikh, M. *Arrivederci a Mogadiscio*. (Roma: Edizioni Associate, 1991).

Shepherd, G. "The Communal Management of Forests in Semi-arid and Sub-humid Regions of Africa: Past Practice and Prospects for the Future." *Development Policy Review* 9, 2 (1990):151–176.

Shields, T. "Red Cross Establishes Beachhead Deliveries for Desperate Somalis." *Washington Post* (1 May 1992):A16.

"Shirweynaha Dib-U-Heshiisiinta Shacbiga Soomaaliyeed Oo Ay Ka Soo Qaybgaleen Jabhadaha SSDF, SPM, USC, SDM, SDA, USE-Jabuuti 15–21 Juulyo, 1991." (Document resulting from the Reconciliation Meeting in Djibouti, 15–21 July 1991.)

Simpson, J. R., and Evangelon, P., editors. *Livestock Development in Sub-Saharan Africa: Constraints, Prospects and Policy*. (Boulder: Westview Press, 1984).

Skinner, Q. *The Foundations of Modern Political Thought*. Vol. 1. (Cambridge: Cambridge University Press, 1978).

Sklar, R. "Developmental Democracy." *Comparative Studies in Society and History* 29, 4 (October 1987): 686–714.

Skoçpol, T. *States and Social Revolution: A Comparative Analysis of France, Russia, and China*. (Cambridge: Cambridge University Press, 1979).

Smith, Anthony. "National Identity and the Idea of European Unity." *International Affairs* 68, 1 (1992):55–76.

Smith, Adam. *The Wealth of Nations*. (New York: Modern Library, 1937).

Smith, S. "Mogadishu Diary." *London Review of Books* (23 July 1992):21.

Somalfruit. *Statistical Reports*. (Mogadishu: National Printing Agency, 1989).

Somali Democratic Republic. *National Development Strategy and Programme, 1989–91*. (Mogadishu: Ministry of National Planning, 1989).

———. *National Development Strategy and Programme, 1987–1989.* (Mogadishu: Ministry of National Planning, 1987).

———. *National Development Strategy and Programme, 1985.* (Mogadishu: Ministry of National Planning, 1985).

———. *Go From My Country.* (Mogadishu: Ministry of Foreign Affairs, 1978).

———. *Food Early Warning System Tables.* (Mogadishu: Ministry of Agriculture, 1988).

———. *Agriculture in the Service of the Nation: More Production with More Effort.* (Mogadishu: Ministry of Agriculture, 1974).

Somali National Movement. "Shir ay Yeesheen guddiga nabadgelyada ee ururka dhaqdhaqaaqa wadaniga Soomaaliyeed (SNM)." 14 August 1991. (Unreferenced record of a secret meeting held by the SNM's Committee for Public Safety of Somaliland.)

"Somali PM in Threat to Bomb Capital." *The Nation* (Nairobi) (4 January 1991):1.

Somali Republic. *The Somali Peninsula: A New Light on Imperial Motives.* (London: Ministry of Foreign Affairs, 1962).

"Somalia: Death by Looting." *The Economist* (18 July 1992):41.

"Somalia: Nasty, Brutish, Split." *The Economist* (7 September 1991):42.

"Somalia: One State or Two?" *Africa Confidential* 32, 12 (14 June 1991):5–6.

Sörbö, G. *Tenants and Nomads in Eastern Sudan: A Study of Economic Adaptation in the New Halfa Scheme.* (Uppsala: Scandinavian Institute of African Studies, 1985).

Southall, A., editor. *Small Urban Centres in Rural Development in Africa.* (Madison: African Studies Program, University of Wisconsin, 1979).

Spaulding, J. "The Recruitment of the Khatmiyya Leaders on Echo Island, 1860–1900." Unpublished manuscript, 1992.

Starr, M. A. "Risk, Environmental Variability and Drought-Induced Impoverishment: The Pastoral Economy of Central Niger." *Africa* 57, 2 (1987):29–49.

"Statement of Lannon Walker, Acting Assistant Secretary of State for African Affairs Before the Subcommittee on Africa, Committee on Foreign Affairs, House of Representatives, 2 April 1981." In *Foreign Assistance Legislation for Fiscal Year 1982, The Horn: The Prospects for Regional Conflict and Global Confrontation.* (Washington: U.S. Government Printing Office, 1981):345–359.

"Statement Made in the Security Council by Francis O. Wilcox, Assistant Secretary of State for International Affairs, on 5 July 1960." *Department of State Bulletin,* XLIII, 1100 (25 July 1960):151.

Stedman, S. "Conflict and Conflict Resolution in Africa: A Conceptual Framework." In *Conflict Resolution in Africa.* Edited by F. Deng and I. W. Zartman. (Washington, D.C.: The Brookings Institution, 1991).

Stingle, A. "Eyewitness to Horror." *Africa News* (3–16 August 1992):2.

Stock, R. "Environmental Sanitation in Nigeria." *Review of African Political Economy* 42 (1988):19–31.

———. *Cholera in Africa.* (London: International African Institute, 1976).

Storäs, F. "Does 'Development' Always Imply Progress?" In *Camels in Development: Sustainable Production in African Drylands.* Edited by A. Hjort af Ornäs. (Uppsala: Scandinavian Institute of African Studies, 1988).

Suliman, M. "Wa Mahaad Allah Madaxeen Banaan." (Song.) Hargeisa, 1963–1964.

Swayne, Captain H. G. C. *Seventeen Trips Through Somaliland: A Record of Exploration and Big Game Shooting, 1885 to 1893.* (London: Rowland Ward and Co., 1895).

Swift, J. "Why Are Rural People Vulnerable to Famine?" *IDS Bulletin* 20, 2 (1989):8–15.

———. "The Development of Livestock Trading in a Pastoral Economy: The Somali Case." In *Pastoral Production and Society: Proceedings of the International Meeting on Nomadic Pastoralism.* (Cambridge: Cambridge University Press, 1979).

———. "Pastoral Development in Somalia: Herding Cooperatives as a Strategy Against Desertification and Famine." In *Desertification: Environmental Degradation In and Around Arid Lands.* Edited by M. Glantz. (Boulder: Westview Press, 1977).

Taylor, C. *Multiculturalism and the Politics of Recognition.* (Princeton: Princeton University Press, 1992).

———. *Philosophy and the Human Sciences.* (Cambridge: Cambridge University Press, 1985).

Thompson, V., and Adloff, R. *Djibouti and the Horn of Africa.* (Stanford: Stanford University Press, 1978).

Thucydides. *History of the Peloponnesian War.* (New York: Modern Library, 1951).

Thurow, T. L., and Hussein, A. J. "Observations on Vegetation Responses to Improved Grazing Systems in Somalia." *Journal of Range Management* 42, 1 (1989):16–19.

Tilly, C. *Coercion, Capital, and European States, A.D. 990–1990.* (Oxford: Basil Blackwell, 1990).

———. "War Making and State Making as Organized Crime." In *Bringing the State Back In.* Edited by P. Evans, D. Rueschemeyer, and T. Skoçpol. (Cambridge: Cambridge University Press, 1985).

———. "Reflections of the History of European State-Making." In *The Formation of National States in Western Europe.* Edited by C. Tilly. (Princeton: Princeton University Press, 1975).

Timberlake, L. *Africa in Crisis.* (London: Earthscan Publications, 1985).

Tolba, M. K. "Disposal of Hazardous Wastes in Somalia." United Nations Environmental Program (UNEP) News Release, Statement by UNEP executive director, Nairobi, 9 September 1992.

Toulmin, C. "Economic Behaviour Among Livestock-Keeping Peoples: A Review of the Literature on the Economics of Pastoral Production in the Semi-Arid Zone of Africa." Development Studies Occasional Paper No. 25. (Norwich: School of Development Studies, University of East Anglia, 1983).

Touval, S. *Boundary Politics of Independent Africa.* (Cambridge: Harvard University Press, 1972).

Trenchard, E. "Rural Women's Work in Sub-Saharan Africa and the Implications for Nutrition." In *Geography of Gender.* Edited by J. Momsen and J. Townsend. (Albany/London: State University of New York Press/Hutchinson, 1987).

"UN Demands Arrest in Ambush." *The Globe and Mail* (Toronto) (7 June 1993):1.

United Nations, "Somalia Progresses Towards Recovery." *Africa Recovery* 7, 2 (October 1993):4.

United Nations, Food and Agriculture Organization (FAO). *Joint Meeting of the FAO Panels on Technical, Ecological and Development Aspects of the*

Programme for the Control of African Animal Trypanosomiasis and Related Developments. Report FAO-AGA-TRYP/EDA/88/22. (Rome: FAO, 1988).

United Somali Party. *Crisis in Somalia: A Call for Peace and Stability—A United Somali Party (USP) Perspective.* (N.p.: United Somali Party, March 1992).

———. "The Truth About SNM's Declared Secession of Northern Somalia." Press Release by United Somali Party, Djibouti, 17 July 1991.

United States, Agency for International Development. *Congressional Presentation for Somalia, FY68.* (Washington, D.C.: U.S. Government Printing Office, 1968).

———, Agency for International Development–Somalia. *Country Development Strategy Statement-ECPR,* 9 June 1989.

———, Committee for Refugees, *World Refugee Survey, 1991.* (Washington, D.C.: U.S. Committee for Refugees, 1991).

———, Department of State. "Address by Chester A. Crocker, Assistant Secretary for African Affairs, Before the Baltimore Council on Foreign Relations." *Current Policy* 431, 4 (28 October 1982).

———, Department of State. *Congressional Presentation on Security Assistance.* 1980–1989. (Washington D.C.: U.S. Government Printing Office, 1991).

———, Embassy in Somalia. Letter from Ambassador Crigler to President Siyaad Barre, 24 May 1987. (Mogadishu: American Embassy, 1987).

———, Embassy in Somalia. Remarks by Ambassador Crigler. (Mogadishu: American Embassy, October 1988).

———, Embassy in Somalia. Remarks by Ambassador Crigler. (Mogadishu, American Embassy, August 1988).

———, General Accounting Office. *Somalia: Observations Regarding the Northern Conflict and Resulting Conditions, 4 May 1989.* (Washington, D.C.: U.S. Government Printing Office, 1990).

———, General Accounting Office. *Somalia: U.S. Strategic Interests and Assistance.* (Washington, D.C.: U.S. Government Printing Office, 16 February 1990).

Unruh, J. D. "Nomadic Pastoralism and Irrigated Agriculture in Somalia: Utilization of Existing Land Use Patterns in Designs for Multiple Access of 'High Potential' Areas of Semi-arid Africa." *Geojournal* 25, 1 (1991):91–108.

———. "Integration of Transhumant Pastoralism and Irrigated Agriculture in Semi-arid East Africa." *Human Ecology* 18, 3 (1990):223–246.

Vahcic, A. "Jowhar Sugar Factory." In *A Casebook of Public Enterprise Studies.* Edited by P. Fernandes and A. Kreacic. (Ljubljana, Yugoslavia: International Center for Public Enterprises, 1982).

Vail, L., editor. *The Creation of Tribalism in Southern Africa.* (Berkeley: University of California Press, 1989).

Van Onselen, C., and Phimister, I. "The Political Economy of Tribal Animosity: A Case of 1929 Bulawayo Location 'Faction Fight'." *Journal of Southern African Studies* 6, 1 (October 1979):1–43.

Verhelst, T. G. *No Life Without Roots: Culture and Development.* (London: Zed Books, 1990).

Vico, G. *The New Science of Giambattista Vico.* Translated by T. Bergin and M. Fisch. (Ithaca: Cornell University Press, 1984).

Vincent, A. *Theories of the State.* (Oxford: Basil Blackwell, 1987).

von Clausewitz, C. *On War.* Edited by A. Rapaport. (London: Penguin Books, 1968).

Wade, R. *Governing the Market: Economic Theory and the Role of Government in East Asian Industrialization.* (Princeton: Princeton University Press, 1990).

Wallace, B. "Somali War Draws Scribes, Hustlers." *Africa News* (26 October–8 November 1992):2.

Wallerstein, I. *The Capitalist World Economy.* (Cambridge: Cambridge University Press, 1979).

———. "Three Stages of African Involvement in the World Economy." In *Political Economy of Contemporary Africa.* Edited by P. Gutkind and I. Wallerstein. (Los Angeles: Sage Publications, 1976).

Wasaaradda Waxbarashada iyo Barbaarinta. *Sugaan: Dugsiga Sare Fasalka Koowaad.* (Mogadishu: Wakaaladda Madbacadda Qaranka, 1976).

Watts, M. "The Agrarian Crisis in Africa: Debating the Crisis." *Progress in Human Geography* 13, 1 (1989):1–41.

———. "Drought, Environment and Food Security: Some Reflections on Peasants, Pastoralists and Commoditization in Dryland West Africa." In *Drought and Hunger in Africa.* Edited by M. Glantz. (Cambridge: Cambridge University Press, 1987).

———, editor. *State, Oil and Agriculture in Nigeria.* (Berkeley: University of California Press, 1987).

———. *Silent Violence.* (Berkeley: University of California Press, 1983).

Weldon, Fay. *The Cloning of Joanna May.* (New York: Viking Press, 1990).

Weller, M. "The International Response to the Dissolution of the Socialist Federal Republic of Yugoslavia." *American Journal of International Law* 86, 3 (July 1992):569–607.

Whitaker, D. P. "The Economy." In *Somalia: A Country Study.* Edited by H. Nelson. (Washington, D.C.: U.S. Government Printing Office, 1982).

Wieland, R. G. "Native Legumes in Southwestern Somalia of Potential Economic Value." *Nitrogen Fixing Tree Research Reports* 3 (1985):39–41.

Wilson, R. T. *The Camel.* (Harlow, England: Longman, 1984).

Wisner, B. "Teaching African Science: Notes on 'Common Sense', 'Tribal War', and the 'End of History'." In *African Studies and the Undergraduate Curriculum.* Edited by P. Alden, D. Lloyd, and A. I. Samatar. (Boulder: Lynne Rienner Publishers, forthcoming).

———. "Development as Destruction." Paper presented at the annual meeting of the Association of American Geographers, San Diego, April 1992.

———. *Power and Need in Africa: Basic Human Needs and Development Policies.* (London/Trenton, N.J.: Earthscan Publications/Africa World Press, 1988/89).

———. "Nutritional Consequences of the Articulation of Capitalist and Non-capitalist Modes of Production in Eastern Kenya." *Rural Africana* 8/9 (1980/81):99–132.

———. *The Human Ecology of Drought in Eastern Kenya.* Ph.D. dissertation, Graduate School of Geography, Clark University, Worcester, Mass., 1978.

———. "An Example of Drought-Induced Settlement in Northern Kenya." In *Abaar: The Somali Drought.* Edited by I. M. Lewis. (London: International African Institute, 1975).

———, and Mbithi, P. "Drought in Eastern Kenya: Nutritional Status and Farmer Activity." In *Natural Hazards.* Edited by G. White. (New York: Oxford University Press, 1974).

Wolfe, A. *Whose Keeper? Social Science and Moral Obligation.* (Berkeley: University of California Press, 1989).

Woodward, D. J., and Stockton, G. *A Study of the Profitability of Somali Exports*. (Mogadishu: U.S. Agency for International Development, 1989).

World Bank. *Somalia: Crisis in Public Expenditure Management*. (Washington, D.C.: World Bank, 8 March 1991).

―――. *Sub-Saharan Africa: From Crisis to Sustainable Growth*. (Washington, D.C.: World Bank, 1989).

―――. *World Development Report*. (Washington, D.C.: World Bank, 1988).

―――. *Somalia: Agricultural Sector Survey, Main Report and Strategy*. No. 6131–So. (Washington D.C.: World Bank, 1987).

―――. *Proposed Credit to the Somali Democratic Republic in Support of an Agricultural Sector Adjustment Program*. (Washington, D.C.: World Bank, 27 May 1986).

―――. *Somalia: Policy Measures for Rehabilitation and Growth*. (Washington, D.C.: World Bank, 6 May 1983).

―――. *Accelerating Development in Sub-Saharan Africa*. (Washington, D.C.: World Bank, 1981).

―――. *Somalia: Agricultural Extension and Farm Management Training Project*. Staff appraisal report, Implementation volume. (Washington, D.C.: World Bank, 12 April 1979).

―――. Somalia: Appraisal of the Northern Rangelands Development. Annex 2. (Washington, D.C.: World Bank, 1975).

World Commission on Environment and Development. *Food 2000*. (London: Zed Books, 1987).

Xaange, A., editor. *Sheeko Xariirooyin Somaaliyeed, Somali Folktales*. (Uppsala: Scandinavian Institute of African Studies, 1988).

Yachir, F. *Mining in Africa Today*. (Tokyo/London: United Nations University/Zed Books, 1988).

Yasin, A. A., and Holt, R. "Increasing fodder production in arid and semi arid central Somalia: preliminary results and observation." *Rivista di Agricoltura Subtropicale e Tropicale* 81, 3–4 (1987):379–382.

Young, C. "Patterns of Social Conflict: State, Class, and Ethnicity." *Daedalus* (Spring 1992):72.

Zartman, I. W. *Ripe for Resolution*. (Oxford: Oxford University Press, 1990).

―――, and Thompson, W. "The Development of Norms in the African System." In *The Organization of African Unity After Ten Years*. Edited by Y. El-Ayouty. (New York: Praeger, 1975).

Zimmerman, E. W. *World Resources and Industries*. (New York: Harper & Brothers, 1951).

Zohar, Y., and Lovenstein, H. "Food, Fodder and Firewood: Cultivation Under Water-Harvesting Systems in the Arid Regions of Israel." *Second International Conference on Desert Development*, Cairo, Egypt, 1987.

Index

About the Contributors

Maxamed D. Afrax is a doctoral candidate in African theater and literature at the School of African and Oriental Studies, University of London (England). He is the editor of *Hal-Abuur: Journal of Somali Literature and Culture.*

Lidwien Kapteijns has her doctorate from the University of London, and is an Associate Professor of History at Wellesley College, Massachusetts.

Hassan A. Mirreh holds a doctorate from Princeton University and was a former Director General of the Somali Institute of Public Administration and ex–Minister of Education in Somalia. He is currently residing in Nairobi, Kenya.

Terrence Lyons has a Ph.D. from Johns Hopkins University and is a Senior Research Analyst at The Brookings Institution, Washington, D.C.

David Rawson has a doctorate from American University and is a Foreign Service Officer with the U.S. Department of State. He served as Deputy Chief of Mission in the U.S. Embassy in Mogadishu between 1986–1988, and undertook the study in this volume while a Senior Fellow at the Center for the Study of Foreign Affairs, Foreign Service Institute, Washington, D.C., USA.

Abdi I. Samatar has a Ph.D. from the University of California–Berkeley and is Associate Professor of Geography at the University of Iowa, Iowa City, Iowa, USA.

Ahmed I. Samatar holds a doctorate from the University of Denver and is Dean of International Studies at Macalester College, St. Paul, Minnesota.

Ben Wisner holds a Ph.D. from Clark University and is Henry Luce Professor of Food, Resources, and International Policy at Hampshire College, Amherst, Massachusetts.

About the Book

A multifaceted inquiry into the circumstances surrounding the implosion and consequent breakdown of the state and society in Somalia, this book attempts to make sense out of what Somalis now describe as *burbur*, or catastrophe.

The book focuses on four questions: What is the morphology of the Somali crisis? How did it occur? What options, if any exist or can be created to reverse the situation? And what lessons can be learned from the Somali experience? In addressing these questions, the authors dynamically link explorations of a range of issues—economic, environmental, cultural, political, and international—to provide new insights regarding the essence and confounding mutations of Somali reality today, as well as the search for solutions.